Philip Warner, well known as a military historian and lecturer, joined the Army after graduating from Cambridge in 1939, and served throughout the war, mainly in the Far East. Among his works are *Panzer, Alamein, The D-Day Landings* and *Auchinleck**. Until recently he was a Senior Lecturer at the Royal Military Academy, Sandhurst.

*Also available in Sphere Books

*Also by Philip Warner in Sphere Books:*

AUCHINLECK: THE LONELY SOLDIER

# The Special Air Service

**PHILIP WARNER**

SPHERE BOOKS LIMITED
30/32 Gray's Inn Road, London WC1X 8JL

First published in Great Britain by
William Kimber 1971
Copyright © Philip Warner 1971
Additional material copyright © Philip Warner 1982
Published by Sphere Books Ltd 1983

This is the first complete official history of
the Special Air Service Regiment 1941–1971.
New additional material bringing the history
up-to-date is not taken from official sources.

Set in Plantin

Printed and bound in Great Britain by
Cox & Wyman Ltd, Reading

# Foreword

by David Stirling


Many books have been written on the different facets of the Special Air Service Regiment during its thirty years of existence and from many different standpoints. Some of these books are excellent but none of them, individually or even collectively, provides a comprehensive and coherent account of the SAS story. This lack was evident to all who served at different times in the Regiment, but it was Colonel Brian Franks who took action and asked Philip Warner to tackle the task.

The straightforward, unpompous yet well researched and discerning way in which Philip Warner unfolds his survey and analysis of the wide-ranging activities of the Regiment, together with the carefully balanced allocation of space to each phase of the Regiment's development, precisely achieves what was intended for the official Regimental history.

My purpose in writing this foreword is to thank, on behalf of all members, past and present, of the Regiment, Colonel Brian Franks and Philip Warner for their respective roles in bringing about the writing and publishing of this book.

# Contents

**Appendices**

**Maps and Diagrams**

# Author's note

The story which follows is not of course a complete account of all the deeds of this remarkable regiment. If such a record could be compiled it would require several volumes and, even then, there would be gaps because some of those who took part in the early raids are dead or untraceable, and many of the later activities are unavailable for security reasons. Even where written records are full and available it has been necessary to make a selection for the sake of balance, but as far as possible each phase contains enough information to enable the reader to obtain a fair grasp of what was going on.

The author was not and is not a member of the SAS and, therefore, where praise or blame is recorded it is done quite impartially. It is indeed typical of the SAS that they should choose to have their history written by someone who is not a member of the regiment, and while giving every possible assistance over obtaining facts should never make the slightest attempt to influence the presentation or approach. And of course they are absolutely right. Regiments which fuss over every detail being recorded, and every incident being given its right weight, usually finish up with a history which is unreadable by even the most devout member, and quite incomprehensible to a person without military experience in the times and theatres concerned. The SAS view is in complete contrast. They believe that, if you appoint someone with a reasonably detached view to write up your regimental history, the facts will speak for themselves.

# Acknowledgements

The author gratefully acknowledges permission to quote from the following: *Long Range Desert Group*, W.B. Kennedy-Shaw, OBE (Collins); *G Patrol*, M. Crichton Stuart, MC (Kimber); *Born of the Desert*, M. James, MC (Collins); *Winged Dagger*, R. Farran, DSO, MC (Collins); *Operation Tombola*, R. Farran, DSO, MC (Collins); *The Desert My Dwelling Place*, D.L. Lloyd-Owen, DSO, MC (Collins); *The Filibusters*, J. Lodwick, MC (Methuen); *Eastern Approaches*, Sir Fitzroy Maclean, CBE (Cape); *Anders Lassen, VC*, Suzanne Lassen (Muller); *Parachute Padre*, J. Fraser McLuskey, MC (S.C.M. Press); *World War 1939-1945*, Peter Young, DSO, MC (Arthur Barker); *These Men are Dangerous*, D.I. Harrison (Cassell); *Anything but a Soldier*, J.H. Hislop (M. Joseph); *Going to the Wars*, J. Verney, MC (Collins); *Moussey*, C. Sykes (*Mars and Minerva*); and *The Gazala Raid*, Charles West.

Unless otherwise stated, all the photographs were provided by the SAS to whom I would like to express my gratitude.

# Guideline

*As the history of the SAS may at times appear rather complicated readers may find the following summary useful.*

The SAS began in July 1941 as 'L' Detachment, SAS Brigade. There was at that time no SAS Brigade.

Its first action was 16/17th November 1941. The 'birthday' date is 17th November. The term 'L' Detachment was soon dropped and the regiment became known as the SAS.

Lieutenant Colonel A.D. Stirling, founder of the regiment, was taken prisoner in January 1943 but by this time the SAS had developed a considerable water-borne element, known as the Special Boat Section, and a 2nd SAS regiment had been created by the founder's brother, Lieutenant Colonel W.S. Stirling. The later unit was with 1st Army.

At the conclusion of the African campaign 1 SAS was renamed SRS (Special Raiding Squadron) and put under the command of Lieutenant Colonel R.B. Mayne. The Special Boat Section became the SBS (Special Boat Service) and was under the command of Lieutenant Colonel the Earl Jellicoe. The SBS stayed in the Aegean and Adriatic; SRS was used in Commando-type raids in Sicily and Italy; 2 SAS fought in Italy.

In January 1944 SAS units, less SBS, were formed into SAS Brigade, under the command of Brigadier R.W. McLeod. It comprised:

1 SAS (Lt. Col. R.B. Mayne), the former SAS and SRS.
2 SAS (Lt. Col. B.M.F. Franks).
3 SAS (French) Lt. Col. J. Conan.

4 SAS (French) Lt. Col. P. Bourgoin.
5 SAS (Belgian) Lt. Col. E. Blondeel.
'F' Squadron from Phantom (GHQ Reconnaissance Regiment).

In 1945, 1 and 2 SAS were disbanded; and 3 and 4 went to the French Army; 5 SAS went to the Belgian Army.


November 1945. Regimental Association formed.
1947   21 SAS (Artists) TA formed under command of Lieutenant Colonel B.M.F. Franks.
1950   Malayan Scouts formed under the command of Lieutenant Colonel J.M. Calvert. Joined by volunteers from 21 SAS (Artists) TA.
1952   22 SAS formed in Malaya from Malayan Scouts. Subsequently joined by squadrons from Rhodesia, New Zealand, and Parachute Regiment.
1957   Australian SAS unit formed.
1959   SAS leaves Malaya. Settled temporarily in Malvern but then transferred to permanent camp at Hereford (1960).
1959   23 SAS (TA) formed in London. Transferred to Birmingham.
1962   Regimental Headquarters transferred from Duke's Road, Euston to Centre Block, Duke of York's Headquarters, Chelsea, London S.W.3.

# CHAPTER I

# Definitions

Although the Special Air Service regiment has been in existence for nearly forty years, and has fought with distinction in Africa, Europe, the Middle East and the Far East, very few members of the general public have heard of it, and fewer still understand how and why it functions. This is not, perhaps, surprising because the SAS has had the wide variety of tasks which come to people to whom no military task is unacceptable, and the nature of its work meant that onlookers were seldom present. Unfortunately, though perhaps inevitably, what is known about the SAS is often distorted, and it is sometimes thought to be a collection of ruthless, expendable thugs, mainly engaged on death or glory missions. In these pages we shall give the bare and sober facts about the SAS, and endeavour to correct misunderstandings about the rôle and characteristics of this regiment; fortunately the whole story is so crammed with adventure, personality and extraordinary incidents that the truth is more exciting than the fiction.

'Special' forces are often the subject of envy, dislike and misunderstanding, because they are usually selected for secret missions, trained on a wider variety of weapons than other soldiers may use, and are issued with equipment which is often more lavish than that provided to their parent units. Often they wear a distinctive marking, a badge or specially coloured beret, and this, whether they like it or not, gives them a certain glamour. Furthermore, they have a more exciting and varied life than the comrades they have left behind them. Some will envy them, some will curse them and others will say with considerable conviction: 'Better you than me, chum'. If a man is returned to his unit after having failed the training course he is scarcely likely to understress its hardships, which for him, without success to cheer him on, were much greater than for those who passed. The losing boat race crew is always more exhausted than the winners.

But there are, of course, plenty of first-class soldiers who would qualify for the SAS but who prefer to stay with their regiments. They are happiest, and at their best, going into battle with platoon, company or battalion.

Sometimes men who would be far more useful in other units volunteer for the SAS. Very often they are accepted; sometimes they fail. If the latter, no one thinks the worse of them; only that their best use is elsewhere. Nobody in the SAS looks down on any other unit of the army as being less important; no regiment in the entire army is so well aware of the essential attributes of what are often dismissed contemptuously as 'administrative' troops. The SAS knows by experience that a few men may do more damage to the enemy by destroying a railway line, a rear HQ, or even a cookhouse, than may be accomplished by an attack at battalion strength on the front line. The battalion might never reach the critical objective, its approach would be obvious and the key centre would have moved. Yet the destruction of that key centre, manned perhaps by unsoldierly administrative soldiers, might ultimately be worth more than the elimination of an entire division. The SAS man, the fighting soldier par excellence, suffers from no delusions about his own importance. He knows his rôle is vital but he knows that a cipher clerk, or a cartographer, or even the skill of the opposing general's cook, may in fact be more important to the success of the campaign than quite a number of daring soldiers. However, attitudes towards Special Forces can easily become critical and bitter, often through misunderstanding. Naturally enough, a regiment which is already below strength will resent losing some of its best officers, NCOs and soldiers, to a Special Force. Feelings will not be soothed if a man returns from a tour with the Special Force having learnt many new skills he can no longer use, but has

2

forgotten much of the knowledge he requires in his normal regimental employment. The situation will not be improved if he is now obviously bored with the everyday routine of his own unit. Nevertheless, the majority of people who do tours of duty in Special Forces settle quickly in their own units, which often benefit from the enthusiasm and experience which have been acquired on the tour of duty.

Rather more serious is the sense of injustice which may be felt by other units when Special Forces are given tasks which seem to belong more properly to orthodox rather than special forces. Commanding officers are likely to ask, with some vigour, why Commandos, Paras, or SAS had to be used for this or that operation when their own units are trained, ready and longing for such an opportunity. This was mistakenly felt in 1958/1959 when the SAS went from Malaya to the Oman. The fact that the operation was brilliantly successful did not really mollify other units who considered that the task should have been theirs. It was said that this was scarcely the rôle for which the SAS was selected and trained. On the other hand, there was a good case for using the SAS, whose rôle is to function anywhere in the world at short notice; it was an excellent test of the regiment's adaptability, in the event no other unit could be available as quickly, and the lessons learnt were more likely to be disseminated to the rest of the Army through the SAS than through a unit which was not composed of personnel on temporary attachment.

There were other powerful reasons for using the SAS in the Oman; one was the fact that two infantry regiments had already tried unsuccessfully to scale the Jebel, and the other was the fact that the Parachute Regiment, who had been chosen to drop on the top, were banned by the Prime Minister; he felt that to commit a world-famous regiment in such a spectacular operation over-emphasised the importance of the situation. Consequently, one squadron of the SAS was sent as the nucleus of a small, highly-trained strike-force, and was subsequently joined by another squadron when the time had come for finalising matters.

To the general public the name of the regiment is

misleading, though there are excellent reasons for it. The word 'service' gives the impression that the SAS has some humble but useful rôle far removed from the fighting line. It is indeed often far from the front line but instead of being behind it is usually many miles ahead of it. Inevitably, also, the word 'air' gives the impression that the regiment must be in some way a part of the Royal Air Force. The connection with the RAF is certainly very close, and members of the SAS know very well how often the courage and skill of the RAF has made success possible, but, nevertheless, the SAS is part of the Army and not of the Royal Air Force. The abbreviation SAS also appears on aircraft of the Scandinavian Air Services, who are as much entitled to it as the regiment are, but here again, needless to say, there is no connection. The word 'Air' figures in the nomenclature of the regiment for traditional reasons, much as we still have fusiliers and dragoons although their weapons and methods of employment have changed considerably since their formation. The SAS acquired its name in 1941 when an attempt was being made to persuade the Germans that we had a parachute brigade in the Middle East. The Germans may or may not have been deceived but there is no doubt that a little later if given the option they would have preferred to deal with a parachute brigade rather than the tantalizing yet devastating activities of the SAS. The SAS is not an airborne unit, although every operational member must be a parachutist, and its methods and function are quite distinct from those of the Parachute Brigade. The SAS regard the parachute as but one of the many means at their disposal for reaching the target area. Other means are boat, submarine, glider, helicopter, truck, train, canoe, skis, coracle or legs; and, from the very earliest days, the value of legs in getting a person to his objective has been strongly emphasised. There are very few parts of the world where a pair of legs is not the best and quietest, though not perhaps the quickest or easiest, means of reaching an objective.

The most damaging misconception about the SAS is that it is a 'cloak and dagger' unit, partly composed of spies. On the

4

contrary, the SAS is a regular army unit which always fights in uniform (although this fact has not prevented its members being executed by the Gestapo and others in the past). It co-operated very closely with underground units like the Maquis, Greek Resistance, and Italian partisans, but is not itself such a unit.

At this point, having spent some time on discussing what the SAS is not, and does not do, it is appropriate to consider what, in fact, it is and does do.

It has always been a small unit and will probably always be so. A basic point of SAS philosophy is that a small group is more likely to reach its objective than a large one is. Small units do not require much in the way of supplies, they can move unobtrusively, and rarely cause the alarm which a larger formation would arouse. There is of course no room for mistakes in a very small unit; there is no one to cover up and every man is vital. This brings one to an essential point in SAS philosophy; the only test of men and materials in the SAS is whether they can do the job better in the circumstances than anyone or anything else. Tradition and convention do not matter. A method is tried, and if it succeeds is retained; if it fails it is discarded or drastically modified. Initially it was thought that parachuting was the quickest and best way to an objective; experience proved otherwise, but parachuting is now used in a variety of ways which were not envisaged in the early days. The SAS function is strategic, not tactical (although it has sometimes been used tactically very successfully) and therefore the regiment has had to train its members to adapt themselves to a wide variety of different conditions. (Their ability to do this was proved in 1959 when they switched from Malaya to the Oman.) But there is no such thing as a specialist fighter in the SAS. He must be prepared to fight in desert or jungle, on sea or land, on mountain or plain, in freezing cold or burning heat; if it is rough for him it will be rough for the opposition and therefore his extra training should see him through.

Except on formal occasions the SAS do not wear rank badges. To wear a badge of rank when confronting an enemy is of course a sure way of selecting yourself as an early target so if you are not going to wear a rank badge in action it is just as well for men to recognize you before you get there; otherwise they will tend to look at arms and shoulders rather than faces, and a vital order might not be obeyed promptly in a crisis. This, of course, also underlines the point that a man in command should appear worthy of his position without any exterior trappings; it is not always quite as easy as that – it is hard to tell a surgeon from his appearance – but the principle broadly remains true. However, absence of apparent rank does not mean absence of discipline or general smartness. As a unit which in its earlier days had been recruited from Guards Commandos, which since 1947 has had close links with the Greenjackets, and whose members have been drawn from the most distinguished regiments in the British (and other) armies, the SAS has always been well aware that the best regiments are always among the smartest, if required. Parades are a very rare requirement in the SAS, but the SAS, in common with any other unit of highly trained intelligent men, can match more practised performers in both drill and turnout.

Discipline in the SAS is self-discipline. Every man knows what is required of him. A man who disobeys an order – or even waits for an order once he has been briefed – is not for the SAS, and goes. Officers, NCOs and soldiers are interdependent. Overall there is the discipline of being able to meet the requirement, and this applies to everyone. The officer knows that if the soldier is not up to the job he must go; the soldier knows that if the officer does not match his responsibilities he will not last long. It is essentially a fair system but like all 'fair' systems at times seems unduly severe.

One interesting aspect of this is that if an SAS man is commissioned he stays with the SAS. Most units are reluctant to have an officer who has served in the ranks, and he is usually posted elsewhere after commissioning. But if the man was really worth commissioning his merit should have been obvious and his own unit should be all the stronger for his return. However, policies are usually based on experience, good or bad. The SAS find that their selection, training, and operations, enable them to benefit from retaining men commissioned from the ranks.

The SAS is always on the look-out for officers, whether from internal or external sources. It is frequently assumed that the SAS is short of officers because of very high physical standards; in fact the SAS finds that the physical standard is the least of its problems and that the intelligence requirement is the major headache; officers and men need to be acutely mentally alert, adaptable, good linguists and capable of constantly improving their own knowledge without much external aid.

With this background it is not surprising that the regiment has no time for 'canteen cowboys'. Although, naturally enough, there have occasionally been lapses, the SAS man is required to reserve all his toughness for training and operations. Fighting and toughness in bars or dance halls is regarded with a very cold eye, and has rarely occurred. Yet one of the problems of the SAS is to throw off a reputation of general toughness, scruffiness and ill-discipline which was rightly earned by other units – often good fighting units – but which has always been completely contrary to SAS principles and philosophy.

Nevertheless, the SAS has had times which no one recalls with enthusiasm. When the regular regiment was re-formed in 1952 there were a number of 'canteen cowboys' in its ranks. Later they were weeded-out, but for a time the SAS – which was not having much success in the jungle – had a disastrous period of bigger talk than deeds. The phase passed but the reputation lingered.

Nowadays, if a man gets stupidly drunk and misbehaves he is returned to his original unit. It may be a first offence, and the man may have an excellent record in operations, but it makes no difference. Everyone knows the penalty and its fairness is recognised. There is no punishment; but the man goes.

Establishing this code of self-discipline has taken nearly thirty years. In a unit which has expanded and contracted, included many nationalities and a variety of types in its ranks, this was inevitable.

The scope of this book is to show why, how and where the SAS began, and the philosophy and attitudes which originated at that time, and are still preserved. This part of the story is relatively uncomplicated. Before the end of the African campaign however there were many other developments. From a unit practising guerilla warfare in the desert, and moving around in jeeps, it took on a much more complicated and diverse rôle. Some of its members (in the Special Boat Service) harassed the German garrisons in the Aegean, Adriatic and Balkans, others spearheaded the landings in Sicily and Italy, some were parachuted into France, and worked with the Maquis, others fought side by side with the Italian partisans in Italy, and eventually the SAS was functioning in Belgium, Holland, Germany and Norway. At one point it seemed likely that the SAS would operate in the Far East against Japanese forces, but the Pacific War came to an end and in 1945 the SAS was disbanded. By that time it contained two British, two French and one Belgian regiment, plus supporting units.

But the SAS did not stay disbanded for long. It came back to life as 21 SAS (Artists) TA, having been recreated in conjunction with the Artists Rifles which had fought in the South African War and First World War but had been used as an Officer Cadet Training Unit in the Second. 21 SAS continued to flourish and in 1952 established the extraordinary precedent of giving birth to a regular army unit – 22 SAS. This latter fought in Malaya from 1952 to 1959 and subsequently in Borneo, the Oman and Aden.

In 1959 23 SAS came into being. It had already had a precarious existence for eighteen months as the Reserve Reconnaissance Unit but was now given a wider rôle and a larger establishment. It inherited the rôle of MI9 in World War II.[*]

Today there are one regular and two TA regiments in

* See *Saturday at MI9*, Airey Neave, London 1969.

England, plus two Royal Signals supporting squadrons. Belgium has an SAS regiment, the very active ESR. There are SAS regiments in France and in Australia, and in New Zealand there is a squadron. Zimbabwe has an SAS squadron. The Greeks have the 'Heros Lokos', the Sacred Regiment whose forebears died at Thermopylae, and this wears the SAS badge. Other countries have units which do similar training and perform parallel functions to the SAS but the essential difference is that they lack SAS philosophy.

The SAS has had a curious history and may well have an even more peculiar future. It was created to play havoc with German communications and airfields, and soon adapted itself to a wider rôle. The basic concept of the very small, highly trained, mobile, aggressive unit still remains. It was extraordinary that it ever came into being at all for its creator was a mere Ensign (2nd Lieutenant) in an infantry regiment, and Second Lieutenants' views on army organisation are never sought and, if voiced, are either ignored or received with displeasure. Almost as astonishing is the fact that the regiment survived after the capture of its creator, but perhaps the most surprising feature of all is that it has become the prototype of the army unit of the nuclear age. The days of massed divisions, D Day landings are over; the future lies with a very different type of organisation and function.

A study of the history and experience of the SAS can therefore be a useful guide to what such units can or cannot accomplish. It will not necessarily provide the complete answer, for times and circumstances differ but it can provide the basic principles. The original SAS units were fortunate in being able to draw on the best soldiers in the huge wartime armies; present SAS members are of no less quality but there are fewer of them and recruiting is considerably more restricted. Therefore it might be difficult to increase the number of SAS regiments without lowering the quality. However, that is a problem which can be met if and when it arises.

The last point in this introduction to the SAS is perhaps the most important. The incidents described in the following

9

pages are often full of acts of outstanding physical courage. What may be overlooked is that a primary SAS requirement was moral courage. Moral courage is a peculiar quality which is not widespread and by no means always accompanies physical courage. A man will sometimes take his men into physical danger although he knows that at that particular moment he should wait, but he is afraid of being thought 'windy' and will therefore make a bad decision. A man without much moral courage will be more afraid of unpopularity than physical pain and, if left to his own, will perform much less efficiently than when surrounded by others. Survival may depend more on moral courage than physical endurance. SAS men, by virtue of their isolation and danger, are particularly liable to capture, and 'interrogations', with all that the latter word can entail in these days of mind-bending. When a man has been kept in solitary confinement, with nothing in prospect but torture and death, courage may enable him to bear pain with dignity but it is moral courage which will preserve him intact to the end. And it will not have been in vain. SAS troops captured and murdered by the Gestapo did not die in vain. Even when kept in solitary confinement, prisoners often know what is happening and the behaviour of doomed SAS troops helped to sustain the resolve of others. Furthermore, the man who meets his own cold-blooded execution with dignity has a disturbing effect on enemy morale.

In less extreme situations it is the combination of moral and physical courage that makes the leader. He will, of course, have other attributes and accomplishments. But the factor which makes him trusted in all circumstances is that combination of moral and physical courage. Instinctively his men know that he will never ask them to do anything he would not prefer to do himself and, whatever the circumstances, will never let them down. This was the secret of Mayne, Lewes, Lassen, and many others including men who are alive today but who would be embarrassed at being described in this way. The best men are usually modest; it is only the minor performers who like to act the part in everyday life.

However, even though brave, tough, modest and self-sacrificing, an SAS man may well not be popular. Just as he is trained to be physically tough – which is not too difficult – so he is also conditioned to be mentally tough, in which process he may learn to be indifferent to the opinions of others. He is trained not to accept at face value what he sees or hears. He may well seem too alert and unrelaxed to be much of a companion. He probably always had a tendency to be a 'loner' and the fact that he is thought to be unsociable will not worry him. Like a cat, he will walk alone.

This may be so, but is by no means inevitable or usual. Most people who have contact with the SAS know only too well the extremes to which their sociability can go. As someone recovering from SAS hospitality once pointed out: 'If they are as deadly to their enemies as they are to their friends they must be a menace indeed.'

## CHAPTER II

# Origins in the Desert

In the summer of 1941 Britain was very much on the defensive against a powerful and all-conquering Germany. We had been swept out of France and failed to stop Germany's triumphal career through Europe from Scandinavia in the north to Greece in the south. Even our early successes in the western desert against the Italians had been nullified when Rommel arrived on the scene. Judging by what had already happened it would need a stupendous optimist to predict a British victory. But fortunately there was a supply of stupendous optimists, and the worse the situation became the more they exercised their ingenuity.

Among them was a subaltern in the Scots Guards. There was nothing in particular about this young man to mark him out from his contemporaries, apart from the fact that he was unusually tall, being 6 feet 5 inches. His career at school, at Ampleforth, or at Trinity College, Cambridge, had not produced any clues to special distinction. Subsequently he had gone out to North America and had various adventures, mostly connected with climbing; his ambition was to climb Mount Everest.

This was David Stirling. When war was declared in September 1939 he was in the Rocky Mountains. He came home and joined the Scots Guards, which was the family regiment. In 1940 he transferred to No.8 Commando, the brainchild of another ingenious and determined young officer, Captain Robert Laycock. Towards the end of 1940 Laycock's Commando, with two others, set sail for the Middle East with the object of capturing Rhodes, and denying it to the Germans. Laycock was given the command of all three units – a total of some two thousand men, which thereafter became known as 'Layforce'. Unfortunately for Layforce the plan was overtaken by events. Rommel appeared in Africa and drove us out of territory recently captured from the Italians; German troops swept through Yugoslavia and Greece before capturing Crete in a brilliant parachute operation. Long before this programme was complete Brigadier Robert Laycock's force had been dismembered; he himself commanded a rearguard action in Crete, a part was holding a sector in Tobruk, and the remainder had made a landing in Syria. Layforce was still in existence on paper but the problem was how to employ it in a permanent useful capacity.

The best plan that could be devised was to use it for raiding along the North African coast, a normal enough commando operation, but the only difficulty was that it depended entirely on the Navy for delivery at the objective, and the Navy had its hands far too full elsewhere to risk scarce shipping resources. Three expeditions were, in fact, launched, but only one landing was made. It was all too obvious that we had not the shipping to spare, the Germans were alert to, and prepared for, this type of operation, and that Layforce was making insufficient use of trained men who were badly needed as replacements in their own original units – or others. The recent fighting had not lasted long but some units had had heavy casualties.

A decision was made; Layforce must be disbanded. It was a perfectly reasonable decision in the circumstances. However, like many other perfectly reasonable decisions it was made by people without the experience or imagination to make a few changes, and thus make the impossible possible. The situation cried out for a raiding unit on the lines of Layforce, although perhaps not so large. The German army had a line of communication that was so long that it was intensely vulnerable. So far it had been threatened from the sea only, and even then, because shipping was scarce, the full possibilities of this method had not been fully tested. Furthermore, there had recently been a demonstration in

Crete of what could be achieved by parachute. As well as the sea and air there was the overland approach which was being used very successfully by the Long Range Desert Group, of which more later. Eventually all three elements were used by the SAS, and still are.

In Layforce there were a number of extremely efficient and enterprising officers and soldiers. Among them were many formidable characters of whom we shall hear more later – Brian Franks, Randolph Churchill, Roger Courtney, Lord Jellicoe, David Sutherland, Ian Collins, Tom Langton, Gavin Astor and Jock Lewes. There were, of course, many others, officers, NCOs and soldiers, but their achievements lie mainly outside the scope of this book.

J.S. 'Jock' Lewes, an officer in the Welsh Guards who had come out to the Middle East with No.8 Commando, probably had more influence on the formation of the SAS than anyone except David Stirling, and it would probably be true to say that without his practical enterprise the unit might never have been formed at all. Lewes' two greatest contributions were his acquisition of parachutes, and the development of a suitable time-bomb.

The acquisition of the parachutes seems to be enshrouded by a little of the mystery which sometimes accompanies unorthodox enterprise. There were no plans for parachute training in the Middle East, nor were there any instructors, nor parachutes. There were, however, plans for parachuting in India and a consignment of fifty parachutes destined for that country were unloaded by mistake in Alexandria. Here they found their way into the custody of Lewes, who decided to find out how to use them, and was encouraged in this by his CO, Brigadier Laycock. As parachuting is now such a highly organised activity it may seem to many today improbable that anyone would ever wish to experiment with a parachute. However, in 1941 parachuting was very much in its infancy. If you went up in an RAF plane you sat on your parachute and in the event of disaster were expected to leap out of the aircraft, count five, and then pull the ripcord. If you pulled it too soon you would tangle with the plane; if you pulled it too late it might not open in time. Your thoughts – if any – were that you would hope to clear the plane and would not land in a gorse bush. It was not therefore quite so wild an enterprise as might be thought for Lewes to assume that if he and his friends had a few practice jumps they might become reasonably efficient at the art of dropping somewhere near the target area. After all, there is a lot of desert and, even if they landed a mile or two off the required spot, it would not matter much. But it should not be assumed from this that Lewes and Stirling were naive in their attitude. All they required a parachute to do was to land them secretly behind the enemy lines. They knew enough about parachuting to appreciate the use of static lines, though not, unfortunately, all the attendant snags. They were not concerned with the methods being developed by British, German, Russian or Italian airborne units. These were for larger and different operations.

However, there were soon various setbacks which would have discouraged any but the most dedicated. The only aircraft that Lewes was able to acquire was an old Valentia. How suitable this was may be judged from the fact that it had never been used for parachuting, the static lines had to be fixed to the legs of the aircraft seats, and owing to the construction of the fuselage there was a very good chance of the parachute snagging itself on the tail. This latter was precisely what happened to Stirling. He landed on rocky ground and injured his back severely. Of the four who made the first jump he was the only one hurt, but both his legs were paralysed temporarily and he had to spend two months in hospital. This disaster might well have caused a less determined person to abandon the enterprise. However, Stirling viewed these things differently and considered it 'an ideal opportunity to evaluate the factors which would justify the creating of a special service unit to carry on the Commando rôle, and amass a case to present to the C-in-C in favour of such a unit'.

The original memorandum has now disappeared but Stirling subsequently reproduced the gist of it as follows:

(a) The enemy was exceedingly vulnerable to attack along the line of his coastal communications and on his various transport parks,

15

aerodromes and other targets strung out along the coast, and that the rôle of No.8 Commando which had attempted raids on these targets was a most valuable one.

(b) The scale on which the Commando raids had been planned, that is the number of bodies employed on the one hand and the scale of equipment and facilities on the other, prejudiced surprise beyond all possible compensatory advantage in respect of the defensive and aggressive striking power; and that moreover the facilities that the Navy had to provide to lift the Force resulted in the risking of Naval units valuable out of all proportion to the maximum possible success of the raid.

(c) There were considerable possibilities in establishing a unit which would combine minimum manpower demands with maximum possibilities of surprise. Five men could cover a target previously requiring four troops of a Commando – about 200 men. I sought to prove that, if an aerodrome or transport park was the objective of an operation, then the destruction of 50 aircraft or units of transport was more easily accomplished by a sub-unit of five than by a force of 200. 200 properly selected, trained and equipped men, organised into sub-units of five, should be able to attack at least thirty different objectives on the same night as compared to only one objective using the Commando technique; and that only 25 per cent success in the former was the equivalent to many times the maximum possible result in the latter.

A unit operating on these principles would have to be so trained as to be capable of arriving on the scene of operation by every practical method, by land, sea or air. If in any particular operation a sub-unit was to be dropped by parachute, training must be such as to enable it to be dropped from any type of aircraft conveniently available without any modifications; if by sea, then the sub-unit must be transported either by submarine or caiques and trained in the use of folboats; if by land the unit must be trained either to infiltrate on foot or be carried by the Long Range Desert Group.

(d) The unit must be responsible for its own training and operational planning and that therefore the Commander of the unit must come directly under the C-in-C.

(e) The initial operation was to drop by parachute five parties immediately before the approaching offensive (November 1941), two to attack the five main forward fighter and bomber enemy landing grounds at Tmimi and Gazala. The Dropping Zones of these units would be some twelve miles south into the desert from their objective. They would then move into position and observe the target. Each party would carry a total of 60 incendiary cum explosive bombs equipped with two-hour, half-hour and ten-minute time pencils and a twelve-second time fuse. In the early stages of the raid a two-hour fuse would be used followed later by the hour and half-hour. Thus they would all explode at approximately the same time.

(This operation took place on the night of 17/18th November 1941 which is now accepted as the official date of the formation of the unit. However, July 1941 could well have been chosen instead.)

Even at this early stage Stirling was bursting with ideas for the organisation and use of the unit. Very soon he reduced the ideal number of raiders from five to four, and he felt that for the best possible results it should be composed of mixed nationalities.

The fact which made his plans possible was the extremely long and dispersed line of communication. For about one hundred miles behind each side's front line there would be airfields, huts, headquarters, camps or workshops. An airfield was little more than a flat patch of desert surrounded by a few huts, tents and workshops. Wandering about in this area would be British, Australians, Americans, French and Polish, but one nationality was scarcely distinguishable from another as all wore the same dress – if it may be called such – of shorts and a hat. Nobody displayed much interest in anyone passing through the area. Stirling guessed that the Germans and Italians had much the same casual atmosphere. Yet each side had a long unguarded sea flank on the north, and a long unguarded desert flank on the south.

But it was one thing to have an idea, and another to get it implemented. Stirling knew very well that if he applied through what are called 'the usual channels' they would prove not to be channels at all but dead ends. He had no intention of seeing his brilliant idea settling under the weight of papers in some obscure bureaucratic in-tray. There was only one person to go to and that person was the Commander-in-Chief.

However, it is not usual for Commanders-in-Chief to be called on by Second-Lieutenants. Stirling knew very well that he would never obtain an interview if he applied formally for one; he therefore decided to crash the barriers. But to get into Headquarters Middle East Command a pass was necessary and he had no pass. Still on crutches, he tried to bluff the sentry into letting him in without one but when this device failed he nipped smartly behind him when the man's attention was distracted by the arrival of a staff car. But his ruse did not pass unnoticed. The sentry soon realised he had been tricked and Stirling had to get under cover as soon as possible; to be wandering about the corridors would be courting instant discovery and ejection. His only hope was to find some high-ranking officer, interest him in his scheme, and obtain an assurance that the C-in-C would hear of it.

Unfortunately the first door he opened contained a Major who remembered Stirling from his early days with the Scots Guards: the reason he remembered him was that Stirling had constantly fallen asleep during the Major's lectures. The ensuing conversation was brisk and unhelpful. Stirling did not try to persuade the infuriated Major, but listened meekly to his homily, saluted and departed. But before leaving the building he took one more chance. He walked through a door marked DCGS and found himself face to face with the Deputy Commander Middle East, one General Ritchie. Stirling apologised for his unannounced arrival, gave a brief explanation for his visit and handed over an outline plan for the General to study. Ritchie took a brief look at it, thought for a moment, then announced that he would discuss the plan with the C-in-C and summon Stirling for a conference if necessary. This interview is held by many to be Stirling's greatest achievement, it being one thing to defeat the Germans, but another thing entirely to brush bureaucracy to one side. Perhaps the episode does even more credit to General Ritchie.

The Commander-in-Chief was General Auchinleck. He had succeeded General Wavell the previous July, at the point when our entire Middle Eastern army was on the defensive.

Resources were scarce, but if gains could be made Auchinleck would certainly see that they were. In consequence he saw Stirling and gave him permission to recruit a force of sixty-six from Layforce – or what was left of it. The sixty-six would include seven officers and many NCOs. The basic unit was a four-man section. Permission was granted to set up a training camp in the Canal Zone; the first objective would be the German airfields the night before Auchlinleck's major offensive in November and not least of the concessions was the fact that the unit would be under the direct authority of the C-in-C. This was an independent command beyond Stirling's wildest dreams; it would be called 'L' detachment of the Special Air Service Brigade. The Special Air Service Brigade did not of course exist, but HQ Middle East were anxious that the Germans should think that it did. Nevertheless official blessing did not mean that everything in the garden was rosy. There was considerable resentment and jealousy about the favour being granted to this jumped up young subaltern – now to be a captain. Accordingly the supply situation was full of insurmountable difficulties; the best they could be allocated was two tents; 'There were other and greater priorities.' Stirling shrugged his shoulders. Supplies were the least of his problems. He had permission and he had the men; supplies could, and doubtless would, follow.

Clearly the first officer to recruit must be Jock Lewes. Lewes was an Australian who had joined the Welsh Guards at the start of the war. Before that he had been at Oxford, at Christ Church, where he had read Modern Greats (Philosophy, Politics and Economics). But Lewes had done much more at Oxford than obtain a degree. He had won a 'blue' for rowing, and what is more, as President of the Oxford University Boat Club he had brought Oxford their first win after successive Cambridge victories. Lewes was not a man to be deterred by difficulties and, as the episode with the parachutes had shown, he was quick to take advantage of an opportunity. At the time Stirling saw him he was on night patrol work in Tobruk with his commando detachment. He hesitated a little before abandoning such useful and interesting work (at which he was brilliant), but he agreed to join as soon as possible. From Tobruk Stirling went to Geneifa where he held a recruiting meeting. From this came such valuable recruits as Cooper, Seekings, Rose, Lilley and Bennet, of whom we shall hear much more later. Four more officers were McGonigal, Bonnington, Thomas and Fraser. Later the SAS would only take five per cent of those who volunteered, but at this stage they were lucky enough to have volunteers who would have been accepted whatever the competition. The remaining officer was destined to become the most famous of all. He already had a reputation of no common sort. This was R.B. (Paddy) Mayne, an Irish Rugby football international. Mayne was not at the meeting because he had had an unfortunate disagreement with his CO a short time before and was under close arrest for knocking him out. Mayne was already a legendary figure in Rugby football and was an excellent boxer. Normally very placid, he had a quick temper and was liable to impulsive behaviour. One of these impulses had landed him in the situation in which Stirling interviewed him. Mayne was slightly dubious about the feasibility of the enterprise but, realising that it offered great chances of really getting at the Germans, he volunteered. 'L' Detachment of the first Special Air Service had recruited the men who were to be its backbone in future months. Stirling had won the first round.

Training began at Kabrit. This was a small village on the edge of the Great Bitter Lake, about one hundred miles from Cairo. It was a typical desert scene, hot, barren, but infested with flies. The number of tents had now been increased to three, but this and a three-ton truck represented the sum total of their equipment.

Toughness, Stirling told them, would be shown against the enemy only; it would not be apparent in bars or in conversation. Training included all the normal activities such as map-reading (which had to be excellent) but also stripping every known make of gun, including all those of the enemy. Long marches into the desert were so gruelling that even men

20

with a background of commando training found them exacting. But the value of this type of endurance test was to be proved over and over again later when men walked quite incredible distances. Dedication and self-discipline were also essential. On one of these early training sessions Private Keith marched 40 miles over the desert in bare feet carrying a load of 75 pounds. His boots had fallen to pieces so he removed them and carried on. This was the sort of spirit which Stirling infused into his men, and which the men were capable of generating.

The parachute training, although an advance on the earlier adventures in this field, was still somewhat crude. The original intention was that forward and backward rolls should be practised by jumping off wooden platforms set on trolleys. However, there was no material for this equipment when training began and trucks had to be used instead. Jumping off trucks moving at 30 mph worked fairly well for forward rolls, but was somewhat disastrous backwards.

At this time British parachute training was done at Ringway airfield, near Manchester. Ringway also had its problems, for with insufficient resources, instructors or experience, it was expected to produce an impossibly high number of trained parachutists – about 4,000 more than they could possibly manage. Stirling wrote repeatedly for advice, but it was very slow in coming – understandably in the circumstances – although ultimately the adviser who was sent proved very useful and stayed on to join the SAS.

At Kabrit the SAS had the use of a Bombay aircraft, which was considerably more suitable than the Valentia. However, training began with a disaster which might well have destroyed the unit's morale but in the event only strengthened it. Stirling jumped with the first two trial runs, which went perfectly. For the third he stayed on the ground to see whether the landing skills were satisfactory. To his horror he saw two men jump from the plane and land in front of him with unopened parachutes. A third had narrowly missed following, but was held back by the despatcher just in time. Stirling promptly cancelled training for the day, but announced it would be resumed at dawn. Meanwhile he set to work to find out what had gone wrong. It was found to be a fault in the clip attaching the static line to the rail. If the line twisted from the effects of the slipstream that particular type of clip could detach itself. A similar accident had happened at Ringway, but they did not know this till much later. A different clip was substituted and next day they jumped again. Stirling was the first to jump. Having seen two men killed in front of him he had to make the decision to trust his life to an untried clip. All went well. But, as RSM Bennet says: 'It was the worst 24 hours any of us had ever spent in our lives. We sat in our tents and smoked one cigarette after another and tried not to think about it. But we did'.

From then on training went ahead smoothly but there were plenty of other problems to be solved. Foremost among them was the type of bomb which could be taken by a raiding party which would be small enough to be carried but big enough to do the job. Ideally they should be both explosive and incendiary but this apparently was an impossible combination. The answer eventually came from Lewes, who experimented in a rough-and-ready workshop. For a long time one bomb after another failed, and then one day he hit on a formula of oil, plastic and thermite that did all that was required of it. This became known, most appropriately, as the Lewes bomb.

Although General Ritchie regarded the progress of the SAS with a benevolent eye there were others who tended to be more sceptical. One of them was an RAF Group-Captain who regarded the whole enterprise as being quite unrealistic. Somewhat nettled Stirling informed him that the SAS could raid our own airfields and would do so, using labels instead of bombs. He chose Heliopolis, the main Cairo airfield, for the experiment. Four groups of ten men marched across the desert, moving by night and resting, camouflaged, by day; the distance was ninety miles. Each man had two bottles of water and a pound of dates.

It took them three days, and they arrived unobserved. The RAF had sent out recce planes to observe any movement in the desert, although they did not really expect the raid, if it came at all, to come from that quarter. There were many grim faces in the RAF when their planes were found to be plastered with labels one morning. But it was not the fact of scoring off the Group-Captain that gave Stirling the satisfaction – it was the knowledge that his ideas and his plan worked, and his men could carry out all that was asked of them.

As mentioned, the first raid against the Germans was planned for the 17th November 1941. Auchinleck's attack to relieve Tobruk was planned to open on the morning of the 18th. The SAS plan was to parachute down on the night of the 16th, get into position, and observe targets, then raid the five airfields in the Gazala-Tmimi area. By this it was hoped to cripple most of Rommel's forward fighters.

In the event the raid was a disastrous failure, but the lessons learnt from it were of great value to the future of the SAS. The weather reports on the 16th were conflicting; some predicted good conditions but others sounded slightly ominous. Stirling was advised to postpone or cancel the enterprise, but when he asked his officers their opinion they agreed with him that it justified the risk. So they went. In the event the wind raised a sandstorm, landmarks were blotted out, and the planes had to take evasive action against anti-aircraft fire. Even worse was the fact that when the drop was made the parachutes were blown miles (literally) out into the desert. The wind speed averaged 45 with 90 mph gusts. Most of the supply parachutes had been lost and some men had disappeared altogether.

The fact that the fuses of the Lewes bombs were with the missing supply parachutes seemed at the time more of a disaster than it turned out to be. They were miles from any point they could raid, but they realised, for future reference, that it was vital to keep essential components in the same compartments. The gale was followed by rainstorms. Eventually the survivors arrived at their rendezvous with the Long Range Desert Group. All in all it was a tale of disaster. Sixty men, including three officers, had set out with the raid, twenty-two survived.

The story of the raid, and explanation of the disaster, comes best from the pilot of one of the aircraft, Charles West. His account of the journey follows.

On the night of 16th November, 1941, five Bristol Bombay aircraft of 216 Squadron took off from Fuka Satellite, an aerodrome in Cyrenaica, laden with fifty-five parachutists of the SAS – ex-commandos who had trained for months in the Canal Zone under the command of Captain David Stirling in conditions of extreme secrecy.

For months the scanty Desert Air Force had been fighting a gallant battle against the ever-increasing might of the Luftwaffe. A few overworked Hurricanes – even ancient out-classed Gloster Gauntlet bi-planes – had been flung into battle against the sleek, powerful Messerschmitt 109s. Now, at a time when General Auchinleck was on the verge of mounting his offensive, the Luftwaffe had received powerful reinforcements of the latest type Me 109F, equipped for the first time with cannon. To this the RAF had no answer, so a simple and daring plan was conceived by David Stirling to destroy the Me 109Fs on the ground.

Parachutists were to be dropped in two groups ten miles inland from the two aerodromes of Maleme and Tmimi, where the Me 109Fs were, two nights before General Auchinleck's offensive, due to be launched on 18th November. They would march that night and find hiding places around the perimeter of the airfields, and from there all the next day they would observe the dispositions of the aircraft, guards, etc. The following night they would move in and plant their bombs on the aircraft; then they would start the long trek back inland to their rendezvous with the Long Range Desert Group.

The five plane-loads of parachutists took-off. The pilots were all on course; the night was clear and fine, and practically no wind was blowing at the height at which the planes were flying. In fact, the meteorological report could not have been more favourable for the operation. But as the planes droned on, so the wisps of cloud drifting lazily across the sky thickened and deepened. Soon nothing existed in the world but cloud, rain and flashes of lightning. The smooth passage of the planes became a mad, bucketing switchback through the sky, and the pilots needed all their strength and skill to hold the course and airspeed. All the carefully checked navigational calculations were useless. It was impossible to even guess the force and direction of the wind which was driving the planes off course, and even less possible to sight the sea over which they were flying.

24

One plane bound for Tmimi, piloted by Warrant Officer Charles West, with Lieutenant Bonnington as officer in command of the parachutists, managed in the last few despairing moments of visibility to get a sea marker flare down and snatch a quick, rough calculation on wind strength and direction.

A hasty check showed that if the parachutists were dropped at the originally calculated time they would overshoot the target by forty or fifty miles, so the only thing left to do was to try to break cloud about twenty minutes earlier, attempt to pick up a landmark, and proceed from there. So the pilot throttled gently back and the plane nosed downwards; the altimeter dropping quickly to 5,000 feet – 4,000 – 3,000 – 2,000 – 1,000, and still solid cloud. Slower now the rate of descent – 800 feet – 600 – 400, and at 200 just clear of cloud at last, the instrument panel disintegrated in one shocked impact as the aircraft reared like a frightened horse under the concentrated anti-aircraft fire. Instinctively, the pilot heaved back on the control column, and the Bombay shuddered back into cloud cover. The port engine had been hit and was losing power, and the instrument panel, vital for cloud flying, was completely useless. Also the petrol was rapidly streaming out of the wing tanks. The pilot, flying in and out of the cloud fringe, attempted desperately to locate his position, but nothing stood out in the black sea of sand below to identify. So, setting his only undamaged instrument, the magnetic compass, to due east he swung the aircraft on to the course for base, and on and on the Bombay lumbered with the petrol getting lower every minute. Finally, after about fifty minutes the gauges flickered back to zero. A few gallons probably remained washing around the bottom of the tanks, but there was nothing for it but to land before the engines cut out. So, land they did! A bumpy, bouncing, slithering landing on a black, moonless night in the midst of torrential rain and high wind; a wind of such strength that it carried the 13-ton Bombay, when on the ground, backwards against the full brakes, until the tommy-gun boxes were chipped from their stowage on the ice-laden bomb racks and jammed behind the wheels. Towards dawn the wind slackened, and Charles Bonnington took out his patrol in an attempt to ascertain the exact position, leaving the crew of the aircraft checking on the damage sustained. Despite the damaged starboard engine and shrapnel-riddled wings and fuselage, it appeared that if petrol could be found there might be a reasonable chance of flying the aircraft off again.

As the first true light of day appeared, the relieved crew, secure in the knowledge that at least they were in Allied territory, realised that

25

about a mile away on the desert road which ran parallel with the coast, columns of vehicles and troops were moving including, thank goodness, petrol tankers. Almost at the same time Lieutenant Bonnington and the patrol appeared, and with their appearance the situation changed abruptly, for with them was the most frightened little Italian soldier that was ever snatched from his sentry post in Cyrenaica. Now it was only too clear that the aircraft and its occupants were well and truly behind enemy lines. Hastily the pilot checked his magnetic compass, re-checked again and found a piece of shrapnel lodged right underneath the compass pivot. Fifty minutes in the air after they had been hit had been spent flying round in a gigantic circle all the time guided by a jammed compass that pointed misleadingly east.

Now they had to try to get the aircraft airborne again. Already it was daylight and it could only be a matter of minutes before the German troops moving along the road realised that this was a British plane – and came to investigate. Feverishly the aircrew primed the engines; the port burst into life with a sudden roar, and the starboard more slowly with peculiar noises as the air whistled through the holed cylinders. Hurriedly, the parachutists clambered aboard, dragging the unwilling Italian with them and installing him with scant ceremony astride the empty long-range petrol tank inside the fuselage. Gently the pilot opened the throttles and in a swerving, lolloping run, dodging sand dunes and slit-trenches, the aircraft staggered off the ground neatly removing a section of telegraph wires as it barely cleared the desert road. Circling right the Bombay turned its nose hopefully to Tobruk where at least were British forces; but it was not long before the waving of the German troops gave way to the dull rattle of their machine guns and even rifles, as they identified the plane that flew just over their heads. Keeping as low as possible, in an effort to avoid AA fire, the pilot skidded the aircraft round the coastline. Still the engines ran! Would the petrol tank hold out to Tobruk? Suddenly the aircraft gave a mighty shudder, and then another! Above the noise of the engines, the pilot heard the AA shells exploding in the fuselage as the guns found the range. Laconically the second pilot reported: 'Long range petrol tank's blown up and is on fire. The Eyetie's got a scorched backside, and half the skin's blown off the fuselage.' But now the tail-heaviness of the aircraft – due to the empty petrol tanks and AA damage – rendered it almost impossible to control. Both the pilot and co-pilot exerted all their strength to keep the nose down, but gradually the aircraft climbed to six or seven hundred feet and now only a miracle could help! Ahead lay Tobruk, but astern now lay a Me 109F. Red tracer lines converged ahead of the battered, old Bombay. With shocking suddenness the pilot felt the control column go lifeless in his hands, and at the same time the nose of the aircraft dropped almost vertically. Instinctively trying to control the plunging plane, although all the controls had been shot away, he snapped the throttles shut and ordered the second pilot to put the flaps fully down in an attempt to reduce the speed of impact.

Twelve days later in a German field dressing station the pilot opened his eyes. From one of the parachutists, Sergeant Bond, lying in the next bed, he learned that his second pilot and the wireless operator had been killed in the crash, and one of the parachutists had later died from his wounds, but the others had escaped with injuries. The force of the impact had broken the already weakened fuselage in which they were travelling clear of the rest of the aircraft, and it had slid along the surface of the sand like a toboggan on the snow. The Italian sentry, although physically all right, lost his voice through shock and was only saved from being shot as a traitor by the Germans by the explanations of the parachutists.

West had a fractured skull, broken shoulder, broken ribs, internal injuries and a ruptured diaphragm. By some miracle, his injuries healed themselves, although part of his 'treatment' consisted of lying on a concrete floor for three weeks without even a blanket. Subsequently he escaped from an Italian prison camp and fought as a guerrilla with Italian partisans in the mountains of northern Italy.

After the raid the Germans circulated an ingenious propaganda story that one of the planes had been 'talked down' by an English-speaking German ground control man who had persuaded him that he was over his own territory. It was, of course, pure fabrication but because West had disappeared it was assumed that the story must be true. As may be imagined, West was justifiably angry to have this slander attached to him.

The Gazala raid was a turning point in SAS thought. Three main points emerged from it; one was that parachutists could not take chances with the weather, the second was (as mentioned above) the need to keep supplies in self-contained units, the third was that the objective might be more easily reached by co-operation with the Long Range Desert Group. This was the force which had collected them and taken them back to safety after the Gazala raid. Why, thought Stirling, should not it, or something like it, be used to transport them to their objective?

The Long Range Desert Group had been in existence for considerably longer than the SAS and drew on a fund of experience stretching back to 1915. In that year the Senussi, who were desert Arabs, had joined the Turks against the Italians. The Italians, it will be remembered, had recently broken their alliance with Germany and come in on the Allied side. By the end of 1915 the Senussi, with German and Turkish officers and money, had approached Mersah Matruh and become a threat to Egypt. On the coastal areas they were tackled by British Yeomanry units, as mobile as the horses they rode, which in that area was not very considerable. Further south, patrolling was carried out by Light Car Patrols using T Model Fords. These hardy pioneers penetrated into the desert well beyond the range of the camel caravans and safeguarded vital oases. In the course of their unsung but immensely valuable experiences they invented the sun-compass,* and also made water condensers for radiators. These two inventions made the later work of the LRDG possible. The sun-compass solved the problem of navigation in the vast desert, which was not featureless, but whose landmarks were constantly changing. An ordinary compass would not be accurate enough for desert navigation, but the sun-compass enabled bearings to be checked in minute detail. The water condenser was an ingenious but simple device. As the water boiled in the radiator it was funnelled into a can at the side. As it cooled it was sucked back into the radiator by the vacuum thus created. By this means vital water was conserved and what might have boiled away within a few miles now lasted for hundreds.

The desert in which SAS, LRDG, and many thousands of others fought was not all of one type. It is approximately the

* See appendix 1.

same size as India – 1,200 by 1,000 miles. It is enclosed by the Nile on the east, the Mediterranean on the north, the Tibesti mountains on the south and Libya proper on the west. The northern half is mainly limestone, the southern half roughly sandstone. Within this area are huge sand seas, one of them about the size of Ireland. The northern coastal strip – at an average ten miles wide – has regular rain and is fertile. And there are oases. But the population of both is approximately one person per square mile; in the remainder of the 100,000 square miles – no one. The temperature ranges from 120° Fahrenheit in the shade in June, to 0° Fahrenheit in the winter. The nights too can be bitterly cold. In the north the country abounds with dust and flies. Dust was in food, hair, engines and guns; flies were a perpetual torment which settled on food as it was being eaten and created endless problems of disease and discomfort. In the south the desert was clear of flies and essentially clean: this and a stark beauty seem to have been its fascination.

Strategically, at a time when the British had their backs to the wall and looked like having their vital lifelines cut, the desert was extremely important. If the Germans could capture Cairo and Alexandria there would be little point in Britain trying to make any further use of the Mediterranean. The nearest route to India would be denied and the Germans would be able to link up with their troops in the Balkans. Whatever the final outcome between Germany, Russia and America, Britain would have lost any real influence in the war.

But the pioneering of the Light Car Patrols would not, in itself, have been sufficient to have made all the work of the LRDG possible. From the early thirties there had been a series of excursions into the desert led by the then Major R.A. Bagnold. They pushed deeply into the unknown – some five or six thousand miles at a time – at their own expense. They were purely a private enterprise, and they cost the enthusiasts who went on them an average of £100 a head per trip. Only about thirty men and women took part but the influence they had went far beyond their numbers. They improved on the

29

sun-compass, they developed ways of extracting trucks stuck in the sand and they learnt how to penetrate deeply into 'impassable' sand seas.

The LRDG itself did not come into being until September 1940 but from then on it was all action. Initially their patrols were made up of two officers, thirty men, eleven trucks, eleven machine guns, four Boys anti-tank rifles, one 37-mm Bofors gun, and a wide selection of side arms. Later the numbers were halved and the weapons became lighter and more powerful. They used 30-cwt trucks which could go for 1,100 miles without refuelling. Every man on every patrol was an indispensable specialist but the least dispensable of all were the signallers. The primary role of the LRDG was reconnaissance and in this first-class, reliable signalling was essential.

Perhaps the least known, yet most important of the pre-war discoveries was the 'steel channel'. These dated back to a trip Bagnold had made across the Sinai desert in 1926. To cross soft sand he had used corrugated iron troughs which had originally been designed for roofing. They proved so effective that in the Second World War most of the Army vehicles carried and used them.

By 1941 the LRDG had firmly established its own role and it was by no means certain that it would agree with Stirling's ideas. Fortunately for him it did; and his plans in this field were considerably assisted by the fact that General Ritchie had, in the course of the Eighth Army offensive, taken over command of it. Ritchie had a warm attitude to Stirling's enterprise. Stirling by now realised that he could not make the SAS fully effective without full and regular backing from one of the regular units; this was vital for supply, apart from any other considerations. Ritchie was sympathetic and Stirling was attached to the LRDG. We have already given an outline picture of this enterprising unit but to obtain a fuller grasp of its potential and activities the reader is advised to turn to Appendix 1 where he will find accounts of the LRDG by various officers who served in it. Extracts are taken from books by David Lloyd-Owen, DSO, OBE, MC, W.B.

Kennedy-Shaw, OBE, and Michael Crichton-Stuart, MC. As will be seen, SAS and LRDG activities often overlapped but the primary aims of each unit were different. As the SAS readily recognised, for the LRDG to put themselves and their 'know-how' completely at the disposal of a new and relatively unestablished unit with a more active and adventurous role was an act of great generosity.* The first phase of SAS operations based on LRDG co-operation was launched from Jalo oasis. The objective was the destruction of the German airfields near Benghazi which was to be taken by the British army towards the end of December. Sirte airfield, on the coast well to the west of Benghazi, was to be the objective of Stirling and Mayne. The airfield was 350 miles from Jalo, and the raid was planned for the night of the 14th December 1941. At the same time Lewes would raid Agheila. On the 21st Fraser would raid Agedabia which was much closer to Benghazi.

Stirling set off with eleven men, including Mayne, and was escorted by S Patrol, LRDG. The seven 30-cwt trucks were camouflaged in dull pink which, although conspicuous on the ground, makes excellent camouflage from the air. The journey was uneventful for nearly three hundred miles – punctures and mechanical breakdowns were so commonplace as not to call for comment; they were soon mended or repaired. On the third day the going was rocky and rough, and they were spotted by an Italian reconnaissance plane at midday. There was an exchange of fire and the plane flew off. Inevitably it was soon followed by three bombers who strafed the area where the patrol was thought to have taken cover. Fortunately there was no damage and there were no casualties. They pressed on to within four miles of their destination but on the way were again spotted by an Italian reconnaissance aircraft – again a Gibli. (They were very light on firepower, and slow, but were highly manoeuvrable.) It was clear that by this time the Italians would have a fairly

* Particularly as the activities of the SAS provoked enemy reaction which made the reconnaissance work of the LRDG more difficult.

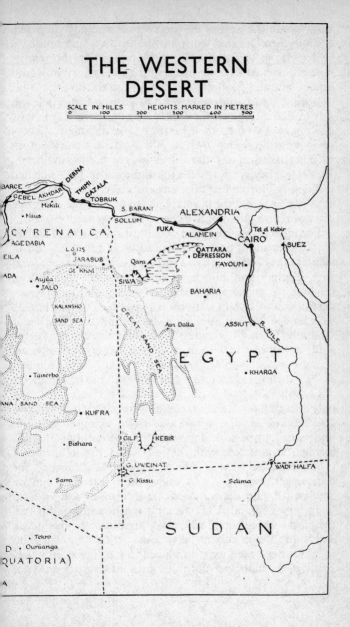

# THE WESTERN
# DESERT

SCALE IN MILES    HEIGHTS MARKED IN METRES
0    100    200    300    400    500

BARCE

DERNA

GEBEL AKHDAR

TMIMI

GAZALA

TOBRUK

Mekili

Nisus

S. BARANI

SOLLUM

FUKA

ALAMEIN

ALEXANDRIA

Tel el Kebir

CAIRO

SUEZ

CYRENAICA

AGEDABIA

L.G.125

JARABUB

EILA

St' Khod

Qara

QATTARA
DEPRESSION

FAYOUM

ADA

Aujila

JALO

SIWA

BAHARIA

KALANSHO

SAND SEA

Ain Dalla

GREAT SAND SEA

ASSIUT

R. NILE

E G Y P T

Taiserbo

KHARGA

ANA SAND SEA

KUFRA

GILF   KEBIR

Bishara

G. UWEINAT

WADI HALFA

Sarra

G. Kissu

Selima

S U D A N

Tekro

Ounianga

QUATORIA)

clear idea of the aims of the exercise and would be prepared. Stirling therefore decided to divide his party and sent half, under Mayne, to Tamit, which was a new airfield thirty miles west of Sirte. At the conclusion of the enterprise they would rendezvous at a point eighty miles out in the desert.

Stirling's party moved forward to Sirte on foot. Their aim was to find a ridge on the far side, lie up to it the next day, observe, and then do their best the following night. Everything went according to plan, although they stumbled on to the airfield in the dark, and gave a premature alarm. However, they went undetected and took up their planned position. Unfortunately, the Italians had chosen that day to evacuate Sirte and the planes which took off in the afternoon did not return. By nightfall the airfield was empty.

Fortunately Mayne's raid had been successful. Twenty-four planes and a petrol dump had been destroyed and in addition they had burst into a party in the Mess and sprayed it with Tommy gun bullets. Raiding the field took fifteen minutes. A memorable feature of this raid was Mayne's destruction of a plane with his bare hands. The panel lights were on and Mayne, thinking it was occupied, approached it stealthily. It was empty, so he pulled out the instrument panel – for a souvenir as he put it. Mayne's enormous physical strength was well known both on and off the Rugby football field, but this was more than anyone could have expected.

Lewes's raid on Agheila was unfruitful; the airfield was only a staging point and no planes were left there overnight. He therefore decided to raid a nearby roadhouse, which he understood to be a conference point for enemy VIPs. He planned to get close with the help of an Italian Lancia, a vehicle singularly unsuited for desert travel but excellent for deceiving the enemy. As soon as the first enemy convoy approached, the Lancia joined it, and the British vehicles followed on behind. Unfortunately the British markings on the trucks were spotted when they arrived at the roadhouse and before Lewes and his party could get near enough to do much damage they were enveloped in a hail of enemy fire. Frustrated but not cast-down, Lewes split his party into two,

34

left one firing at the roadhouse and with the other planted thirty bombs in the nearby transport park. Lewes's bag on this occasion included no aircraft but numbered a healthy collection of transport.*

Fraser was the most successful of all. He had reached Agedabia and destroyed a total of thirty-seven aircraft. This was a notable achievement for the airfield was well wired and guarded. It was midnight before they penetrated, but once inside they made an excellent job of it. As in other raids, once the bombs started to explode the confusion on the airfield was so great that getting away was no problem. Fraser's party consisted of himself and three men.

No time was lost before setting out on the next raid. The debrief from the different raids brought certain conclusions and immediate decisions. From now on surprise would be the top priority. There would be no more previous reconnaissance; nor would there be any shooting before bombs were placed. Disguise, by such means as the Lancia, would be abandoned; it was felt that if the enemy was taken unawares all that was needed could be done before the reactions took effect. As part of the surprise they decided to raid Sirte and Tamit again. Rommel was now retreating and would need all available aircraft to cover his retreat. It was the SAS task to reduce that number.

Stirling took one party, Mayne the other. Stirling met an unexpected obstacle in the presence of a German armoured division which for some four hours occupied the road on which he hoped to travel. Apart from this, most of the latter part of the route was full of enemy transport settled down for the night. By the time Stirling reached the airfield perimeter it was 4.30 am and he had arranged to rendezvous with the LRDG before 5 am. Reluctantly he abandoned the attempt on the airfield, but was so preoccupied on his return to the LRDG that he forgot to give the password; the sentry fired,

* Lewes was not only brilliant on operations, he was exceptionally able at training. Stirling considers that Lewes's training was the key to success.

35

but fortunately the round was a dud. It was Stirling's luckiest escape.

Meanwhile, Mayne had visited Tamit with five men. There he blew up aircraft which had just arrived as replacements.

So much for success; the tragedy of this raid was the death of Lewes. On the way back from Nufilia where they had only managed to destroy one plane they had been caught in an aerial attack. The aircraft came low and were not driven off by counter-fire. Lewes was badly wounded and died within minutes. The attack continued and though it destroyed all but one of the trucks did not succeed in killing any more men.

Fraser and his men were in little better shape. He had found his objective – the Marble Arch airfield* – deserted and had returned to the rendezvous. Unfortunately there had been confusion over this and the patrol waited six days – till their water supply was nearly finished. At that point they decided to walk home – two hundred miles – or more if they had to avoid enemy, with little food and half a pint of water only. Their battle against heat, thirst, hunger and fatigue was appalling, but fully justified Stirling's arduous training schedule. In eight days – in impossible conditions – they had covered two hundred miles.

As the raids went on and the enemy became more alert the SAS improved. The desert was so well patrolled that the trucks had to be expertly camouflaged and also do much of their movement at night. Navigating across the desert by day is difficult enough but is even more so after dark; they became good at it by experience. Much the same applied to camouflage. As Pleydell put it: 'There is no lesson which improves camouflage as well as a low level machine-gunning attack'.

These early raids, and some of the subsequent ones, are described in detail because they were usually very effective, were instrumental in causing the SAS to take the shape and follow the path it did, and are historically interesting. Nevertheless there are many omissions, sometimes of

* Mussolini had built a triumphal arch as a symbol of his African Empire.

complete raids which are not markedly different from others already described, and sometimes of incidents before, after, or during raids. The keynote of many of them is complete disregard for danger. Courage, like fear, is infectious.

In one raid on Benghazi Captain Cumper's jeep was knocked out and he leapt on to the one driven by Sergeant Bennet; his hold was not very secure and after a while he fell off. Bennet stopped the jeep and ran back. Cumper was lying in the middle of the road, head supported on arm, as if on a vicarage lawn. All around was an inferno of fire and explosion. As Bennet came up – to find Cumper unhurt – Cumper said: 'Now, look here, Bennet, if that's the way you treat your passengers, I'm going to stay here and have a nice quiet read until you've learnt to drive properly'.

Cumper was in his forties and heroics were absolute anathema to him. 'Blimey', he said on being introduced to Dr Malcolm Pleydell, 'a sawbones! If things are going to get rough, I'm going to get out of here. What do you take me for anyway?'

On hearing of an impending raid he would say: 'Not for me, mate; I'm too old. What time do we start?'

Once he arrived in a mess and sat down next to a newly-joined officer from a distinguished regiment. The newly-joined took one look at Cumper – with a detonator behind his ear, and a running fire of ribald conversation, shuddered, and buried himself in his magazine. The waiter came up. 'Bring me a cup of tea will you, chum, same as the officer', said Cumper. The newly-joined apologised and they became good friends.

Another remarkable character was Sergeant Phillips. On one occasion a detachment was stranded in the desert following a brisk engagement after which they had had to move out rapidly. Sergeant Phillips spotted a German truck. He pulled a blanket over his head and made a rough imitation of a desert Arab. Thus disguised he flagged down the truck. When it stopped he shot the two occupants dead and drove to safety in the truck.

From time to time retired members of the SAS find records

of former events. A few years ago there came to light notes dictated by Captain Mayne to Sergeant Thornton.

3rd Operation
Objective: Agedabia Aerodrome
Method: LRDG
Date: 18 December 1941

Operation: Party consisting of Capt Fraser, Sgt Tait, Sgt DuVivier and Ptes Phillips and Burns. Left Jalo about 10 Dec with LRDG S Patrol. Walked into drome and destroyed 37 planes without opposition. Spent one night in the middle of Germans who were digging in but were undiscovered. Attacked next night. 37 planes definitely destroyed but may have been more as planes were closely packed. On return journey met Brigadier Reid's force. Whilst having breakfast were attacked by two Blenheims, killing two LRDG men and wounding two more. Returned to Jalo.

[*An unfortunate consequence of being behind the enemy lines was that you were liable to be attacked by your own aircraft.*]

4th Operation
Objective: Sirte Aerodrome
Method: LRDG Patrol

Operation: Party consisted of Capt Stirling, Sgt Brough, Ptes Cooper, Cattoll and Seekings. Left Jalo about 23 December 1941. Travelled night and day to hit the road 14 kilos west of Sirte. Heavy concentration of enemy armour on road going towards the front. Had to wait 7 and 8 hours before able to get on road. Halted 3 miles from Sirte and parked trucks with drivers. Started to walk. After 2 kilos hit new perimeter. Sentries patrolling so tried to get through road block but were challenged from several points so went back to trucks. Pulled up on road and went back to strafing and blowing up trucks with bombs, destroying lines of communication. No answer to MG and Bofor fire. Left road at 5.30 am. Next morning nearly picked up by two 109Fs. Picked up Mayne's party from Tamit and returned to Jalo going south of Marada to avoid patrols. Losses – nil.

5th Operation
Objective: Tamit Aerodrome
Method: LRDG S Patrol
Date: 24 December 1941

Operation: Party consisting of Major Mayne, Sgt McDonald, Ptes Bennet, White, Chesworth and Hawkins. Left Jalo with Sirte party and broke off at Wadi Timet. Motored to within 3 miles of drome and then walked in. Destroyed 27 aircraft but were fired on by MGs etc. and had to run for it. Sergeant McDonald and Private White were cut off but were picked up later. Contacted patrol and returned to Jalo. Both parties celebrated Xmas on the way back. Plenty of beer, Xmas pudding, gazelle etc.

10th Operation
Objective: Derna Aerodrome
Method: LRDG
8 March 1942

Operation: Party consisting of Major Mayne, Bennet, Rose and Burns. Walked in to drome 30 miles and arrived at 0400 hours. Walked round drome and split up. Major Mayne and Pte Bennet destroyed 15 planes. Cpl Rose and Burns destroyed 15 torpedo bombs, petrol and equipment. On subsequent walk back Burns fell out. We met but failed to find rendezvous but were picked up next day. Searched for Burns but without success. Whole party returned to Siwa and subsequently to Kabrit.

Meanwhile Stirling was preparing for the next phase. It was clear that by now the SAS could deal effectively with airfields but there were other tasks which might be equally important. He decided that as the Germans could no longer use Benghazi they must rely on Bouerat – 350 miles to the west. His plan was to blow up as many ships and installations as he could and accordingly he went to General Auchinleck and obtained permission to recruit up to six more officers and forty more men. The General was so pleased with Stirling's achievements so far that he promoted him to Major and Mayne to a Captaincy. Recruitment was not easy, for men were needed in their own units, but this problem was resolved when he acquired some fifty Free French parachutists who had just arrived from Syria. They were trained in the use of explosives by that remarkable Royal Engineers Officer, Captain Bill Cumper.

For some time previously Stirling had been trying to obtain permission for the SAS to have its own badge and insignia.

Permission had been withheld on the grounds that the SAS was only a detachment and the men belonged to their original regiments whose badges they should wear. Nevertheless he went ahead and had the winged dagger made up as a cap badge,* with the motto *who dares wins*. At this point he was fortunate in obtaining approval for the badge from General Auchinleck and from then on it became the official insignia of the SAS. This was January. The colours of light and dark blue were chosen because in the original unit there was a representative of each of the Oxford and Cambridge boat race crews – J.S. Lewes, Oxford; T.B. Langton, Cambridge.

Members of the original SAS will not be entirely happy with the description of their badge as a 'winged dagger'. It was meant to symbolize Excalibur, the legendary King Arthur's sword, and thus represent a sword which would win freedom from the invader.

Wings were worn after qualifying in seven parachute jumps. Normally they were worn on the right arm but if a man particularly distinguished himself on an operation he might be awarded 'operational wings' – the right to wear them on his left breast. Stirling made this award for the SAS and later Jellicoe made it for the SBS; it was more prized than a decoration. Although quite unofficial it was a powerful morale-builder.

The wings themselves have an Egyptian appearance and in fact were taken from the fresco in the foyer at Shepheard's, where there was a symbolical Ibis with outstretched wings. This caught the eye of Lewes who removed the Ibis and substituted a parachute.

In the early days for a short period the SAS wore white berets. It was not a very happy choice for it irritated other soldiers and led to violent disagreements. Wisely, the present sand-coloured beret was substituted.

---

* According to Malcolm Pleydell, the badge was designed by Corporal Tait, later Squadron Sergeant Major Tait, MM

In 1944 when the SAS came under 1 Airborne it was decreed that the SAS should wear the Parachute red beret. Mayne never relinquished his SAS beret and is a conspicuous figure in group photographs. The beige beret was restored in 1957.

The party set out for Bouerat on 17th January. The LRDG contingent was fourteen strong and the SAS party eventually numbered seventeen including two members of the Special Boat Section, and an RAF officer and a Flight-Sergeant. On the way they were attacked and lost the wireless truck with its three operators. This was bad enough, but even worse was the fact that the truck carrying the canoe had an accident in which the canoe was rendered useless. The Special Boat Section, which became a part of the SAS a year later, was an independent unit which had originally been used by Layforce to recce beaches and harbours. In the event there was no need for the canoe as there were no ships in the harbour. Fortunately there were plenty of installations to blow up and they included eighteen petrol carriers of which the Germans were already desperately short. The SBS detachment, which consisted of an officer and a corporal, also blew up the local radio station. It was a successful night's work, although with a different target from those which had originally been envisaged. The return journey was made somewhat less hazardous by a sandstorm; this fortunately obscured them from the inevitable aerial pursuit which, as it happened, was more thorough than usual.

What no one realised at the time was that Rommel had no intention of falling back on Bouerat, but had mounted a massive counter-attack with the intention of retaking Benghazi. It was a complete surprise to the Allies and he regained not only Benghazi but also a good portion of ground further on – in fact the LRDG had already had to evacuate Jalo.

This sudden reversal of the position meant that Benghazi – if it could be reached – was a primary target, not only because of the cluster of airfields around it, but also because of the harbour. The Benghazi opportunity put Stirling in a difficult position. On the one hand he knew he had insufficient time and men for the right sort of balanced force; on the other here was a golden opportunity to show that the SAS was not merely a raiding group for putting time-bombs on enemy aircraft, but was the nucleus of a well-balanced force which would deal with shipping, destroy harbours, and even dislocate industry. For this enterprise he had a small, mixed party which included several members of the Special Boat Section, an Arab interpreter and two Senussi soldiers; it set off on the night of 28/29th March 1942. One of its members was Lieutenant David Sutherland (Black Watch and SBS), but on this occasion he did not progress very far. Some way short of Benghazi the captured German staff car in which he was travelling was blown up by a thermos mine;* he was wounded and had to return to Siwa. When the party came to the outskirts of Benghazi they found themselves on a good tarmac road and proceeded to drive along it at 70 miles an hour with lights full on. There were clearly going to be differences in procedure and timing here. On a desert airfield the approach was silent and the time bombs were fixed with varying length fuses so that nothing would go off before the job was completed. Shooting up any suitable target was a bonus which could only occur if and when the major task was completed. Towns and harbours were a different story. Installations would probably be more carefully guarded, and boats would be more difficult to reach than aircraft had ever been.

In the event, on this raid, the wind was too strong and the water too choppy for the canoe. Nevertheless, for practice they tried to assemble it; all attempts to do so proved useless, as the canoe, not designed for the rough treatment it had experienced in transit, could not be properly fitted together. The No. 1 rib, and the bow and stern posts had all been broken and, although they were mended to the best of their ability with limited stores, they were far from perfect. Furthermore the skin was distorted through heat and

* Small mines which looked like thermos flasks.

bumping. With the canoe unusable – even if it had not been damaged – and with no other obvious targets, there was no alternative but to treat the raid as a reconnaissance, depart without arousing suspicion, and return again another day. Stirling put a few charges on a railway track on the journey home, but Benghazi – not for the last time – was going to prove a frustrating experience. It was not a very productive period; the only real successes fell to Mayne who destroyed fifteen planes at Berka. Stirling, however, never ceased cogitating on the plan to destroy enemy shipping. He therefore allotted Captain Fitzroy Maclean (Cameron Highlanders) the task of solving the boat problem. Fitzroy Maclean* had extricated himself from the diplomatic service by saying he wished to stand for Parliament, but had first joined the Army. In Cairo he had run into Stirling and been recruited to the SAS. His first task now was to find a transportable boat which would be suitable for getting to lethal assignments with enemy shipping. Initially he was not very successful, but eventually – with the help of Captain Cumper – he acquired some Royal Engineers reconnaissance boats, small, black and easy to inflate. To prove the efficiency of waterborne night-ops they tied empty limpet mines to all the British ships they could find in Suez harbour. It seems that their presence was not detected till Stirling telephoned the next day and asked if he could now have the empty mines back. Like the RAF in the Heliopolis incident, the Navy sucked their teeth, but took it in good part – and tightened their security.

Another notable recruit to the SAS at this time was Randolph Churchill, son of the Prime Minister. He had Commando experience but none of parachuting and he acquired the latter in a qualifying jump in which his parachute did not open properly; after this bruising experience he was allowed to accompany a Benghazi raid –

---

* Now Sir Fitzroy Maclean, MP. In the Benghazi raid he bluffed his way into the dockyard by demanding to see the Guard Commander and rebuking him for his sentry's slackness.

which did not involve parachuting. His knowledge of Italian was very useful in getting the raiders past sentries and into the harbour area, but once again the boats failed them, this time presumably from punctures. The expedition did not do much damage but showed what confidence and a fluent command of the enemy language could accomplish. Unfortunately, on the way back they had a bad car crash which put Fitzroy Maclean into hospital for three months and damaged Randolph Churchill's spine so badly that he had to be invalided home.

In *Eastern Approaches* Fitzroy Maclean (on page 194) describes some of the activities of the SAS:

'Working on these lines David [Stirling] achieved in the months that followed, a series of successes which surpassed the wildest expectations of those who had originally supported his venture. No sooner was one operation completed than he was off on another. No sooner had the enemy become aware of his presence in one part of the desert and set about taking counter-measures than he was attacking them somewhere else, always where they least expected it. Never has the element of surprise, the key to success in all irregular warfare, been more brilliantly exploited. Soon the number of aircraft destroyed on the ground was well into three figures. In order to protect their rear the enemy were obliged to bring back more and more front-line troops. And all this was done with a handful of men, a few pounds of high explosive, and a few hundred rounds of ammunition.

Training was based on practical experience. Physical fitness was clearly of the utmost importance. For days and nights on end we trudged interminably over the alternating soft and jagged rocks of the desert, weighed down by heavy loads of explosive, eating and drinking only what we could carry with us. In the intervals we did weapon training, physical training and training in demolition and navigation.'

So far the SAS had taken an independent rôle, doing as much damage as possible on targets they chose themselves. In June 1942 it was called upon to play a more specific part. Malta had for long been under attack but, during this summer, pressure on its defences had been steadily increased

44

and the supply situation was becoming desperate. A convoy was due to reach Malta in June with an urgently needed cargo and was bound to suffer heavy enemy attack. Stirling was summoned to HQ in Cairo and informed of the position; his assignment was to reduce the strength of enemy air attack as much as possible. Consequently he briefed eight five-men patrols, three for Benghazi, three for Derna, one for Barce and one for Heraklion on Crete; four of the patrols would be drawn from the Free French contingent which had recently joined but had not yet taken part in any raids, and other Frenchmen would accompany the English patrols. The Free French had been in training for some time and were keen to use their experience. As their assignment would take them through areas swarming with Germans they had attached to them members of the SIG – the Special Interrogation Group. This latter was composed of Germans of strong anti-Nazi views, but unfortunately at this time also included two prisoners-of-war who were thought to be trustworthy; it was commanded by Captain Herbert Buck, MC, an officer from the Punjabis. Not knowing the correct password made progress difficult, but eventually the party reached its destination. Before it could do any damage it was over-whelmed by Germans, having been betrayed by one of the two former German prisoners-of-war. Fourteen of the fifteen Frenchmen were killed or taken prisoner, but not without giving spirited battle against a German company.

The disaster which overtook the French party was partly avenged by the successes of the others. Stirling's own party consisted of three men only, but by moving adroitly they were able to place bombs on aircraft, in hangars, on spare engines, and in workshops. The resultant destruction was enormous. A feature of this raid was the stealth and speed of the party – an art which Stirling had developed in earlier days deerstalking and which – to a lesser extent – he still possesses. Mayne, although a large, powerful man, could also move like a cat and was a great hunter.

The other parties, although less successful, did consider-able damage, partly by bombs and partly in pitched battles.

They blew up a number of aircraft and stores but the Germans were soon alerted to the situation and turned out a considerable force to track the raiders down. In making their exit the SAS ran into different problems, but one of the most interesting escapes was that of Sergeant Lilley. Looking for a way back he wandered inside the perimeter of a large German camp. After a short time he realised that it would be impossible for him to slip unnoticed through the German lines so he stood up and walked for two miles. He was dirty and dusty and no one noticed he was not a German until he met an Italian outside the perimeter; the latter unwisely tried to arrest him but had his neck broken for his trouble. Lilley kept on walking. A dozen miles later he ran into other members of the expedition, and soon after linked up with the LRDG at the appointed rendezvous.

At this point the party should have returned home. However, before they set out, Stirling and Mayne decided it might be a good idea to have a last look at the extent of the damage. As their own transport had been destroyed they had to rely on the indulgence of the LRDG to let them use a truck which was supposed to be used for transport and reconnaissance only; the commander of the LRDG was Captain Robin Gurdon who agreed to lend the truck on the solemn promise that it would be returned intact. It seemed an unlikely contingency, as the area was full of Germans still looking for the raiding party.

Undoubtedly this last throw was asking for rather more luck than they were likely to have, but it produced two interesting lessons, apart from the further damage it inflicted on the Germans. The first lesson came when the party was stopped at a road block within a few hundred yards of the airfield. As all were in British uniforms in a British truck the position was a delicate one, and not even a fluent stream of abuse from one of their German-speaking members seemed likely to alleviate its dangerous possibilities. The situation was resolved by Mayne who cocked his revolver as the nearest sentry peered into the truck. The man decided it was in his best interest to pronounce them genuine Germans and have the barrier raised. Lesson number one was to take action before the opposition really knew what to make of the situation.

Once through, the party made no further efforts at subterfuge. Whatever they came upon they shot up. They decided that entering the town would be pressing their luck too far and instead kept to the dark road outside, where there were plenty of targets. On the way out they were nearly intercepted by a German truck but it gave up the chase when they reached very rough terrain. As they drove on, now looking forward to a leisurely breakfast after two successive nights of raiding, they suddenly heard a shout warning them to jump for safety. The rough ride when they were trying to shake off the German truck had activated one of the time-bombs; the back of the truck had still a goodly load of these and other explosives. Seekings and Lilley,* who were the nearest, both heard the click as the acid finally ate through the time pencil and yelled the warning to leap for safety. They leapt. A second or so later the bomb went up destroying the truck completely. The journey was continued on foot. After a few miles they encountered some Senussis who kept a look-out for Germans and sent a message to the LRDG, who then collected them.

The second lesson was that if you pick the right men who are then trained to be permanently alert to the slightest unusual sound or happening you may well survive unexpected disasters. The key to success and survival was clearly speed of reaction; though this had never been overlooked, its tremendous importance had not – up to this time – been so fully appreciated.

So much for the land raids; equally important was the one on Crete. This party was under the command of Commander Bergé of the Free French; his second in command was Earl Jellicoe, son of the famous Admiral. Jellicoe had not been with the SAS long, but he knew Crete well and also spoke

---

* Some say Cooper was the first to react but everyone is very modest about this story.

fluent French. After only three days preparation and practice they approached Crete by means of the Greek submarine *Triton* and landed by rubber boats. Progress was slower than had been anticipated; the route through the mountains was very rough and their load very heavy. After two nights' marching they reached the airfield but had to wait till the next night before attacking. There were over sixty Junkers 88s on the field.

Getting on to the airfield was not easy, as it was wired and guarded. Fortunately for the SAS an RAF plane chose that moment to drop a stick of bombs across the runway, and in the resultant confusion the SAS party planted bombs on twenty-one planes and a number of other targets. They slipped away from the airfield without casualties and later in the night were able to look back and see their bombs exploding. Another twenty-four hours took them to within a few miles of the beach, where they concealed themselves until they could be taken off. Jellicoe and their one Greek guide – Lieutenant Costi – went off to a nearby village to make contact with a Cretan who would signal to the submarine. Unfortunately, in the meantime, the party's hiding place had been accidentally discovered by a party of Cretans and betrayed to the Germans. The result was that Bergé suddenly found himself the objective of three separate German patrols. Although he decided to fight in the hope that he might escape after dark, the party, already heavily outnumbered, had only Tommy guns which soon ran out of ammunition. All were killed or captured. When Jellicoe returned with the information about the rendezvous for being taken off he could find no trace of Bergé's party. He soon enquired from nearby peasants what had happened and learnt that Bergé and the other prisoners had been taken to Heraklion. Jellicoe embarked three days later with twenty refugees. It had been a disaster, but it had also been a victory, for the Crete expedition had destroyed more than the other two parties combined.

In spite of the raids, the Malta convoy took a tremendous hammering, losing fifteen out of seventeen ships; nevertheless the two ships which did get through carried enough supplies to tide Malta over till the next convoy, or part of it, arrived. Whether the thirty-seven aircraft which the SAS destroyed in their raids that night might have sunk the remaining two ships is anyone's guess but there was no doubt in the minds of the German command that this steadily increasing destruction of valuable aircraft was dangerous as well as humiliating and must be stopped at the earliest possible moment.

Meanwhile, in every other way, the campaign was going superbly for the Germans. Tobruk, with its vast supplies, surrendered to them, and the whole of the British army was falling back towards Alamein. German troops had already crossed the Egyptian frontier and although their advance was not without loss it seemed to many as if their next stop would be Cairo. There was considerable alarm in what had been thought to be secure rear areas; documents were burnt and all the morale-destroying programme of evacuation was in full swing. But morale, in some people, is an unpredictable and effervescent substance. This dramatic change in the military situation presented the SAS with an emergency rôle for which it was not entirely suited, but also gave to Stirling the opportunity to acquire vehicles and armaments which were ideal under any conditions. These were 'jeeps',* the small American GPs – general purpose trucks – which were fast, mobile, manoeuvrable, inconspicuous and uncomfortable; and Vickers K guns. Vickers Ks were aircraft guns which had formerly been mounted in the Gloster Gladiator fighter aircraft. As this plane was now obsolete the RAF had spare supplies of Vickers in their workshops and Stirling, who had come across them by accident, laid his hands on all he could acquire. They were mounted in pairs at the front and rear of the jeeps, and later supplemented with a .50 Browning. The Vickers could be electronically controlled, but whether used singly or in pairs their effect was devastating. An average rate of fire was 1,200 rounds a minute, and the noise was so

* See appendix IV.

shattering that it virtually contributed to the firepower. A truck caught by a Vickers K would disintegrate. Occasionally the Vickers jammed, but meticulous maintenance reduced such hazards to the minimum.

The whole of the SAS became mobile. All the supplies which could possibly be taken were loaded on to three-tonners, twenty in number. By this means their programme could be more flexible; and they could stay in the desert for approximately three weeks, barring accidents. All that remained was to obtain a full report of the general situation, be briefed on the most desirable targets, and go.

However, there were accidents. The sand was too soft for the heavily laden lorries and, after numerous delays, many of the supplies were abandoned and the party reduced drastically in numbers. The remainder drove on; it was not clear where they would find a hole in the enemy lines but they would find out by looking. And they found it. Navigated by Gurdon of the LRDG they travelled 150 miles without encountering enemy opposition and then linked up with another LRDG party under Timpson, also of the LRDG. These two highly capable and experienced LRDG officers would then be available to pilot the SAS parties to whatever targets were thought suitable.

On this occasion the raiding plan was based on the somewhat optimistic assumption that the British army, having retreated this far, would now turn and take the offensive. In the event the offensive proved abortive but the SAS gained some useful experience. Mayne was given the task of destroying planes on the Bagush airfield while Stirling established a road block and ambush on what had been predicted as being an important enemy supply route. The traffic failed to materialise, but Mayne succeeded in reaching the airfield and planting bombs on forty aircraft. Much to his irritation half the bombs failed to explode, having become damp, and it seemed that some eighteen aircraft would have to be left intact on the airfield. At this point Stirling decided to see what the new Vickers Ks could do. He and Mayne drove around the perimeter of the airfield and shot seven aircraft to pieces. Clearly the new guns could do as much, and more, than had been expected. The other parties had had varied fortune, chiefly because the airfields they raided were now being much more carefully guarded. Even so, the bag amounted to some seventeen aircraft and a larger number of trucks. The return journey was hazardous but the only casualties were to their transport. By this time the SAS were highly experienced in dodging enemy aircraft or – if destruction was imminent – abandoning the vehicle and making a run for it.

As soon as they had taken stock the SAS were off again, this time in five parties. They had varying fortunes. Mayne's was the most successful, destroying fifteen aircraft; a good part of Mayne's 'luck' was probably due to quicker thinking and greater experience, but some people do seem to be luckier than others and they make good commanders. The greatest loss on this expedition was that of Gurdon, who had been killed by enemy aircraft – which he was trying to shoot down. Although not a member of the SAS – he was just about to transfer to them – he had, as a member of the LRDG, made a tremendous contribution to its successes.

By this time it was necessary to obtain more supplies; both food and ammunition were running low. A resupply party consisting of three jeeps and eight trucks was organised and included Lieutenant Scratchley, well-known to the peace-time world as a steeplechaser. In the event it turned out to be his roughest ride ever.

By now the Germans had established themselves in the areas through which the SAS had previously passed without difficulty; it was therefore necessary to go back through the Qattarra Depression which had one track of doubtful firmness across it; the remainder was salt bog with a thin crust which would not bear the weight of a vehicle.

The crossing was made by day, which meant that the heat haze concealed the party from patrolling aircraft, but they were exposed to intense heat of the most unpleasant kind. Owing to the roughness and uncertainty of the track, progress was slow – a few miles an hour – and periodically the convoy had to stop to change a tyre. Conditions such as these would have been insupportable for men less fit and experienced, and without high morale. This was the sort of situation where moral courage takes over from physical and raises the limit of endurance. Less torrid conditions have produced heatstroke and mental disorder among men who, although sound enough, simply had not the requisite experience and morale. As an example of the latter one of the trucks was set alight by an enemy air attack early on the trip. While it was burning three men removed the wheels because, as they put it, 'the tyres might come in useful'.

Within eight days the resupply party had returned with twenty jeeps, Vickers Ks and stores of all varieties. With this new equipment it was planned to make a straightforward attack on Sidi-Enich airfield, which was reputed to be crammed with aircraft of every variety. On this occasion it was decided that a different technique was needed. The Germans were not submitting tamely to the destruction of their planes and had adopted every measure possible which did not involve the large scale use of troops. They had begun by making a man sleep beneath the wing of every plane. When this proved unsatisfactory the perimeter was more carefully guarded, searchlights were mounted, and armoured cars were attached to some of the larger fields. The new method the SAS would therefore employ would be to arrive with such fire-power that the defences would be overwhelmed. Stirling planned the raid like a drill movement. The three leading jeeps would clear the route ahead as the party moved down the runway and the other jeeps would give their attention to the planes parked alongside. The raid was carefully practised in darkness. With the jeeps five yards apart it was important that formation should be strictly maintained, otherwise some of the bullets would find the wrong targets. Navigation was in the hands of Sadler who was meticulously accurate in spite of rough going and obstacles. They arrived at the airfield on time.

To their surprise the airfield was not in darkness as they expected but brilliantly lit. The runways were in full use, with

52

planes landing and taking off. Into the well-organised scene suddenly appeared a force of eighteen jeeps, all but one of which were positioned to use their four Vickers K guns. Consequently the firepower of this little convoy amounted to some 68 guns, each capable of firing 1,200 rounds a minute. As it moved down the middle of the airfield it created a scene which almost defies description. Formation was rigidly maintained, and the sweep of destruction reaped a harvest beyond the most optimistic dream. In a few moments the crowded airfield was so full of blazing and exploding planes that the SAS men had their hair singed and faces scorched. The Germans were caught completely by surprise – one plane was destroyed as it landed – but a mortar and a Breda soon began a steady but not particularly effective response. Having gone through the middle of the airfield the jeep party paused, reformed and made a sweep around the perimeter. In the last round they added a number of Junkers 88s and some stores buildings to their total. It was a classic display of ingenuity, control, firepower, skill and surprise. Every plane on the airfield had been destroyed. It was the sort of demonstration which does enemy morale no good at all.

Casualties were light. Three jeeps were lost, one man was killed on the airfield and one on the way back in an air attack.

It was, of course, an enormously successful raid and showed what could be done in this sort of surprise attack. It also gave a good indication of the fire power of the Vickers guns which, used in this way, could overwhelm and silence any emergency defence the airfield could put on. Everyone seemed pleased except Stirling. He gave a swift but damping debrief; the raid had been good but by no means good enough, the firing was too wild, some people had wasted ammunition and run out – which might have made the homeward journey very tricky – others had lost their formation in the darkness and excitement. It was a timely little dash of cold water for in the excitement of the success the mistakes might have been forgotten. Next time those mistakes might prove fatal. But one aspect of the raid was unusual. On the way back the party which had gone to Bagush to stage a diversion had the extraordinary experience of capturing two German prisoners who had landed in that area to have a look at what they thought was a deserted battlefield. One of them was a doctor. Both refused parole and had to be guarded. Malcolm James Pleydell in his book *Born of the Desert* recounts some of the conversation he had with them; he had a little difficulty in convincing them that Germany, whose troops were within forty miles of Alexandria and who had overrun Europe and much of Russia, was going to lose the war. In spite of their refusal to give parole the prisoners were not very carefully guarded and one night they slipped away and were not seen again. It might have been thought that that would be the last heard of them but that did not prove to be so.

This was not the first or the last time for the SAS to be at risk through being too trusting with prisoners, but there can be no question of the rightness of their policy. If the SAS took a prisoner they took responsibility for him. If subsequently he gave them information, or helped them as the doctor did, so much the better; if, however, a prisoner – like Bruckner – proved to be playing a double game and betrayed them, so much the worse; units such as the SAS are not suited to carrying around prisoners but would do so well aware of the liabilities or assets which might be attached.

The loss of the prisoners coincided with the recall of the SAS to Cairo. There were a number of detachments out when the order came, so the main party had flown back before they returned. They had enjoyed considerable success among the enemy transport. Their route back was through the ill-famed Qattara Depression. On this occasion they planned to return by night, but in the process lost so much time on the first attempt that they had to return and lie up in hiding for a day. The next night was equally hazardous in a different way. By mischance they found themselves in the middle of the quagmire and only by sacrificing certain vehicles were they able to cross to safety.

The recall to Cairo proved dangerous to the SAS but in a manner different from anticipated. Earlier, Stirling had made several attempts to prove that the SAS could raid more than desert airfields: hence the attempt on Benghazi harbour. Now Benghazi harbour was vital to the offensive which the Allies knew Rommel was planning. Tobruk was an equally important target. However, Stirling, who had spent many months trying to convince HQ planners that the SAS was an essential unit, was now irritated to find that the 'back-room boys' were now going to try to allot it tasks for which it was neither equipped nor suitable. This running battle with authority, the attempts to obtain approval for plans which men in the field know are reasonable, is one which will be familiar to many soldiers, whether in special forces or not. But equally frustrating, even disastrous, is the allocation of the wrong task through Staff Officers not having the right 'feeling' for the situation. The classic example was Passchendaele 1917 when the Higher Command did not realise that troops were up to their knees – sometimes to their waists – in mud. Fortunately, this sort of isolation is much less prevalent than it was.

The task on this occasion was to raid Benghazi and Tobruk simultaneously, using SAS forces from the land side, and naval and commando units from the sea. The aim was maximum destruction in a short but overwhelming raid. The two destroyers, *Sikh* and *Zulu*, a number of MTBs, commando troops, signals, sappers and the LRDG would all take part. The Tobruk party would be under the command of Colonel John Haselden (who was killed, as were many others in his party).*

There were several snags in the scheme as far as the SAS could see. It was a large scale raid; the whole basis of SAS success was that small numbers were used – three or four being ideal. Anything larger might be detected by air reconnaissance, by informers, or by enemy spies. It was also a combined op. There would be a preliminary bombardment from the sea, commando landings, infantry operations by the

* A full account of the naval side of this operation is given in *Assault from the Sea* by Rear Admiral L.E.H. Maund (Methuen 1949).

Sudan Defence Force to try to retake Jalo – useful as a staging point on the return journey – and last, but not least, an attack by the LRDG on Barce airfield. The LRDG, of course, had occasionally mixed it with the enemy but their vital use was reconnaissance and the reporting of enemy movement; they could fight as well and, in fact, a good deal better than many other units but this was not their best employment. Lastly, the SAS was asked to include in its ranks an extra hundred and twenty men who could not – by any stretch of the imagination – be adequately trained in the time available. There were other disadvantages too – such as the number of vehicles involved; these could hardly fail to be observed. The distance was about 1,500 miles each way. But this sort of situation is always difficult for the leader of a unit which has won goodwill in the face of considerable difficulties, after a long period, and is then offered a challenge. Stirling – and others – knew that the SAS were now being drawn into an operation which was quite different from their normal rôle, and which was full of risks which he could not properly calculate. Stirling was happy to take risks but only those which had an ultimate point and purpose in them. But he was given less than a month to prepare men for an enterprise of which the outcome was less predictable than any he had previously entered on. Eventually Stirling had 200 men, 40 jeeps, and 40 supply trucks.

This, of course, was in itself conspicuous enough, but there were reasons for supposing that it might be detected whether it was conspicuous or not, for too many people seemed to know too much. Service men are all familiar with the experience of being told by a civilian where they are going – and later finding out that he was right. In the event they escaped unscathed on the first stage of the outward journey although their escort of tanks – to deal with road blocks – failed to get through the sand sea. The second stage was less happy. An Arab guide, of dubious record, was detailed to pilot them but lost the way, intentionally or inadvertently. When the SAS got back on to the right path they were ambushed on a road which was heavily mined. In the ensuing battle the SAS with its experience and concentrated firepower was more than a match for the ambushers but the fact that surprise had obviously long been lost made the enterprise futile and, reluctantly, Stirling gave the order to return. The return journey was considerably more hazardous than the outward one. They were strafed from the air and lost eighteen jeeps and twenty-five trucks. Jalo was still in enemy hands, but they were fortunate enough to be able to borrow enough petrol from the Sudan Defence Force to get them back to Kufra. Not only had the raid been a failure but in men, time, and materials it had been costly.

The Tobruk enterprise had been worse. The aim had been to secure a bridgehead so that the seaborne invasion could proceed without difficulty. The plan was based on an ingenious scheme of using the SIG (Captain Buck's anti-Nazi German soldiers) as 'escorts' for eighty soldiers dressed to look like prisoners of war. These would pass into the town without difficulty and capture a fort, harbour defence guns and a wireless station. Meanwhile the RAF would bomb the area sporadically in an effort to divert attention from the main enterprise. When the bridgehead was secure the Commandos would then be landed from MTBs.

Unfortunately the shore party had too much on its plate to be able to signal to the naval craft waiting outside until an hour and a half later than the planned time. When the signal did go the Germans were not long in realising that something unusual was happening, with the result that only two boats managed to come in. The small force which had managed to land was soon captured, and the German and Italian air force and navy went after the naval landing party. Casualties on land and sea were high; most of those engaged were killed or taken prisoner and out at sea four MTBs and two destroyers were sunk. Like the Gazala raid, it had proved a disaster, and an expensive one, but it had made clear to everyone that this sort of raid and organisation was not the right use of the SAS.*

* The SBS part in this enterprise is related later.

When the party was disengaging from heavy counter attack, by aircraft machine-gun fire, a man fell off the jeep in which Mayne was travelling. Mayne ordered the driver to keep on till they found cover, then went straight back on foot, found the man and brought him in on his shoulders.

However, although the Benghazi raid was a setback for the SAS, the unit found this an encouraging time in other ways. General (later Field Marshal) Alexander decided that the SAS should be given the status of a regiment. No longer would the SAS need to live from hand-to-mouth, even though it had done very well in the process; it would have an establishment, be recognised for what it was, and not be in perpetual danger of misuse or disbandment.

However, all was not plain sailing. The Director of Military Operations informed Stirling that his HQ link would be the department known as 'G Raiding Force' which was in charge of Colonel 'Shan' Hackett.* Colonel Hackett was a first-class soldier with a first-class brain, as his career, militarily and academically, showed. Hackett was sympathetic to Stirling's plans and together they went to see General Montgomery, who at that time commanded the Eighth Army. Stirling was hoping to be able to recruit extra numbers from the Eighth Army but his proposal received a strong refusal; it was, of course, hardly surprising. For the SAS to have had a free pick from the units the General was going to take into battle a fortnight later was asking rather much.

General Montgomery was well aware of what the SAS had achieved with small numbers but considered that its uses were limited; he said that the SAS had failed at Benghazi – as indeed they had – but was unaware that the disasters of the latter occasion were not the fault of the SAS and would not have occurred if Stirling's own views had been respected. He could not see any justification for allowing Stirling to pick men out of regiments which would be used in the forthcoming offensive. This was a blow for the SAS who had

* Subsequently General Sir John Hackett, GCB, CB, CBE, MC, BLitt, Principal of King's College, London.

reached their present pitch of efficiency by superimposing their own training onto previous training and experience. There was now no Layforce to recruit from and Stirling would have to pick his men from freshly-arrived troops. As he was convinced that a training programme of at least three and a half months was necessary, the prospects for mounting continuous offensive against Rommel's communications in the near future did not look encouraging. However, he kept the SAS in action by sending a squadron of experienced men, commanded by Mayne, up to Kufra, with instructions to raid along the coastal communications, and himself supervised the training of the recruits. Mayne, as may be expected, made full use of his opportunities and blew up many trains and sections of track. The regiment was now divided into two squadrons, Mayne, now a Major, being in command of A. He had set out on the 7th October 1942 with eighty men. One of his party was a man called David Sillito, at that time a private, although commissioned later. Near Tobruk, a small group which included Sillito was laying charges when they were seen and attacked. Sillito found himself on his own and had three courses open to him: he could surrender to the nearby enemy, he could hide with friendly Arabs and wait till our own forces came nearer, or he could try to walk back to his base, which was a mere 180 miles across the desert. He had no food and only enough water to last a day. For direction he had a compass, for protection he had a revolver. Yet after eight days he limped into a wadi, where he was found by a patrol, and two weeks later had completely recovered from his ordeal. Sillito set down his account soon afterwards:

The first night I just kept slogging on, with nothing to eat and nothing to drink. Occasionally I came across piles of empty petrol tins upon which was collected dew, and was able to wet my tongue on them. There was not much of it.

Then, in a wrecked tank, I found a tin of bully beef but when I opened it and tried to eat the meat I found that I couldn't as my tongue had become like dry putty and mastication was out of the question. I threw the meat away but kept the tin.

It came in handy for holding my urine, which I then started to drink. It stopped me from desiccating and drying out altogether. Of course it was acrid and unpleasant, but it was better than dying of thirst. I kept this up for seven days – marching on the bearing in daylight and using the stars at night.

During the hottest part of the day I used to lie on my back and use a greatcoat as a tent till that became too heavy to carry.

Eventually I hit a wadi called Hatiet Etla, which was the one we had rested in prior to setting off on the final stage to the railway and I knew that the LRDG had a store of emergency rations of biscuits, bully beef and water hidden in a broken down three-tonner they had left there.

I hit the northern extremity of this wadi – it was about a mile long by about one hundred yards across. At first I thought I was at the wrong place and followed some jeep tracks for several miles until I found a haversack. It contained nothing of use to me, so dragging my blistered feet I returned to the wadi. Just as I got there it began to rain. Oh what a joy! What a relief.

Shortly afterwards he collapsed completely but was then discovered, as mentioned above, by a group of SAS men.

By now the tide of war was turning. Although Alamein was only the first of many battles, the long sequence to German defeat had now begun. In these circumstances the task of the SAS would broaden and perhaps change considerably. It was already expanding.

After Alamein it was clear that Rommel would try to stabilise his position around Agheila, as this was the point in which the Germans would be in a better position than the Allies for obtaining supplies. The more the SAS could disrupt German communications in this area the better it would be for the Allies. Mayne therefore went with a squadron to Bir Zalten, which lay about 150 miles south of Agheila, and was soon joined by Stirling with an enthusiastic but inexperienced group whose training would therefore be completed in the field. Jellicoe was allotted the important but somewhat tedious task of staying at the base and supervising training.

Stirling's description of the following weeks is as follows:

We undertook at this stage to maintain continuously a patrol covering off over a 40 mile section of the enemy's coastal communications from Tripoli to Marble Arch.* This required the establishing and supplying of 16 sub-bases from which 16 patrols could operate against the coastal communications at least two or three times a week within their own allocated 40 mile sectors. This meant a minimum of about three or four raids every night somewhere on the enemy's main coast communications between Tripoli and Agheila. In practice the operation went very successfully east of and including the Bouerat area. North of the Wadi Zem Zem the country was very much more difficult for operations due to its dense population, and the SAS patrols, although very successful to start off with, were mostly driven off or rounded up after three weeks. However, we certainly succeeded in stopping enemy transport movement by night for a considerable period, thus forcing transport movement by day which provided the RAF with good strafing † targets. By the middle of January we had shifted our activities westwards and were mounting patrols and continued raiding on enemy communications as far north as Sfax in Tunisia (incidentally this is where I was captured by a German Reconnaissance unit).

The area in which the SAS operated at this time was well known to their companions of the LRDG. General Sir Roderick McLeod, who as Brigadier R.W. McLeod commanded the SAS Brigade in 1944, had this to say of the LRDG:

This unit specialized in obtaining information, and for eighteen months they operated continuously against the enemy rear areas, based on the oases of Kufra, Siwa and Jalo. There was one coastal road along the Mediterranean shore which was used by the Axis armies in the Western Desert for almost their entire supply. It can be imagined how much it was in use, and what great value there would be for GHQ, in a census of the traffic that went up and down it. That is precisely what the LRDG provided. For four and a half months from April 1942, and seven vital weeks in the autumn during the

* By this time the SAS had trained their own navigators and no longer had to rely on the LRDG - who, of course, had other tasks.
† Strafing = punishing. In World War I the Germans were said to have drunk the toast 'Gott strafe England'. The word soon became English slang, and tended to mean destroy rather than punish.

Alamein offensive the LRDG kept watch on it. Week after week, twenty-four hours a day, there was a two-men post on the road near Marble Arch, a few hundred yards from it by day, and a few hundred feet away at night. Every Army vehicle, every tank moving up or down the road, was counted or logged and the information was quite invaluable to Intelligence in Cairo.

The combination of the LRDG, who were the desert experts, and the SAS, who were experts on demolition, proved highly successful. When the SAS made a number of most successful attacks against the railway between Tobruk and Mareth those in Cairo whose business it would be to provide for the 8th Army when it advanced, began to be worried over the destruction that was being done to the railway lines, signal communications, and the like. A signal was sent *'Leave the railway alone, we may need it.'* It was rare to get a reply from the SAS but this time it came quickly: 'Very sorry. Railway blown up at X, Y, and Z. Couldn't resist it!'

Like the SAS the LRDG were experienced walkers and would think little of completing a watch by walking a dozen or so miles back to camp. It should be borne in mind that they carried warm clothing, which was bulky, and arms which were heavy. The Tommy gun was in widespread use at this time; it was heavy in itself and its clips or drums of ammunition, which could be shot off in a few minutes, weighed very heavily indeed. And, of course, like the SAS they carried grenades.

Conditions in the desert may be bakingly hot or freezingly cold. It can rain continuously. These factors at times seemed so important that men forgot they were not taking a census for the Ministry of Transport on a Bank Holiday and were surprised to find themselves the object of unfriendly enemy attention. On more than one occasion patrols of the LRDG and SAS found their hide-up surrounded by an enemy convoy – on one occasion a Division – and if it rained would get into the dry under an enemy vehicle. The quality most required on these patrols was a blend of familiarity and alertness; the familiarity enabled them to move around casually and naturally without arousing suspicion but the alertness was very necessary in case they did.

For the raids Stirling's base was considerably further west than Mayne's, at a place called Bir Fascia, at the end of a very rough route. The first attacks took place on the night they arrived. For this operation each of the eight jeeps carried two men, and would launch an attack – of one kind or another – every three days or oftener. Everything stationary would be blown up, and mines would be left to greet new arrivals along the road. In the event it was not only the journey which was a rough passage but also the operation. The initial attacks were successful, and surprisingly easy, but the German Area Commander was clearly a man of some resilience and the raids were followed by intensive air search. It was obvious that the raiders could not have gone far, and might be found. Air patrols were reinforced by land parties; which included armoured cars and tanks. It was a tribute to the damage the SAS was causing, but – to say the least – inconvenient. A jeep has many advantages but few of them amount to anything when it confronts an armoured car. The area in which they were operating was too confined, the time in which they were supposed to complete the operation was too short, and the opposition – including Rommel himself – were prepared to go to a lot of trouble to deal with the SAS, even if only temporarily.

This sort of situation was an occupational hazard but was contrary to the best way to employ the SAS, which, as we have seen, was to use stealth, surprise and speed, to slip in and out, not to indulge in heroic though pointless suicide attacks, but to make the best possible use of men and materials. The SAS never believes its troops are expendable – although individuals have been known to feel this about themselves. However, heavy though SAS losses were on this occasion the results and dislocation caused to the Germans justified them.

There was one unexpected occurrence at this time. Major Oldfield had done a lot of damage before he was captured, so when the Germans counted it up they decided he should be shot. At this stage – in the desert – war was fought with chivalry – as between gentlemen. Later, in Europe, when control was exercised more closely by Hitler, orders were issued that all captured SAS men should be shot and, of course, many were. Of that, more later. Major Oldfield probably would have been shot, but he had been wounded and in the hospital was looked after by a doctor who was a friend of the German doctor who had been captured in the desert and had escaped. Doubtful about his ability to convince others that Oldfield should not be executed summarily – as Hitler had ordered – he smuggled him into Tripoli where he was forgotten, and survived. Today he is a senior partner in the firm of Knight, Frank, and Rutley, Estate Agents.*

In January 1943 the strength and constitution of the SAS was as follows. The 1st SAS – as 'L Detachment' had been officially named in October 1942 – had an establishment of five squadrons, a total of 50 officers and 450 other ranks. Of these 40 officers and 350 other ranks were on the strength. The remainder would be made up from Middle East Commando, which had been handed over to Stirling in November 1942. At the time this unit consisted of 30 officers and 300 other ranks; of these Stirling intended to select 10 officers and 100 other ranks. It will be noted that the proportion of officers to men, one to ten, was exceptionally high, and also that many of the NCOs and men were themselves of officer quality. The SAS has often been criticized for the high proportion of officers and NCOs, as well as first-class men, which it absorbed, and the answer must invariably be that used in this way they caused far more damage to the enemy than they would have done if they had been with other units. The main drawback to this officer/NCO/soldier ratio was that if a party was killed or taken prisoner the enemy scored a success well out of proportion to the numbers involved.

Under Stirling's command were the following units:

---

* Incredibly, the SAS encountered the same doctor again in Germany when he operated on an SAS man in Oldenburg and saved his life; Oldenburg was still behind the German lines at the time.

1. The French SAS squadron, referred to earlier. This, it was hoped, would be the nucleus of a French SAS regiment which would be invaluable in the invasion of Europe:

Officers 14 Others 80

2. The Greek Sacred Squadron

Officers 14 Others 100

3. The Folboat Section (Special Boat Section). This had had a separate existence up till August 1942.

Officers 15 Others 40

4. 1 SAS (Establishment of 50 officers and 450 other ranks but short of this figure. Strength would be made up by selection from disbanded Middle East Commando).

Officers 40 Others 350

The only unit which had failed to develop was Captain Buck's German unit. This had now ceased to exist because of the difficulty in obtaining reliable recruits.

Most of the men who were under Stirling's command at this time were qualified parachutists but those who were not were in the process of training. The comments of these men were illuminating. Some said they were quite pleased to do it because they had always disliked heights and it was therefore a challenge, others said they were terrified from start to finish and were glad when the training was over; among this latter group were men whose enterprise and daring on other occasions was quite remarkable. Nowadays when parachuting and free-fall parachuting are popular sports this original attitude may be hard to comprehend. The answer is probably psychological. To travel by any conveyance at 50 miles an hour in the 1850s – if it had been possible – would have been a terrifying, and probably hazardous, experience; to travel on a main road at 50 miles an hour these days is to make one liable to be accused of dawdling. However, psychological or not, there are very few people who actually enjoy parachuting; to most it is a challenge and that is that.

To return to 1943. General Montgomery's next push forward was timed for mid-January. The SAS was therefore briefed to attack in four main sections: between Sfax and

Gabes, between Mareth and Tripoli, at Mareth, and in northern Tunisia. This last was an attempt to link up with First Army, where Stirling's brother, Lieutenant Colonel William Stirling would be operating with the newly formed 2 SAS. It was felt that if the SAS were the first unit from the Eighth Army to link up with the First Army it would help to reinforce the growing official view that the SAS was an essential unit. Stirling – always thinking ahead – considered that the moment would soon be ripe to split 1 SAS into two regiments and therefore with 2 SAS have the necessary components for a brigade.

Not long afterwards there would be an SAS brigade but David Stirling would not be available to command it. The only snag – and it turned out to be a big one – in the plan was that the territory over which Stirling planned to take his party was virtually unknown. In the event it proved difficult country. The LRDG had had experience of negotiating all types of sand, from soft dunes which you had to race up but stop sharply on the crest to avoid going over a precipice, to places in which one might suddenly sink to the axles. On this trip they encountered the Grand Ergh Sand Sea which consisted of narrow ridges and was impossible to negotiate without acute discomfort. North of it lay Lake Djorid and between that and the sea lay the Gabes Gap. The route had been found by the LRDG and was one of their many valuable contributions to Allied success during the desert campaign. However, the going was appalling and at times speed was down to one mile per hour. The route alternated between soft sand and rocky valleys. To make matters more interesting, the area was full of enemy transport.

It was not, by any stretch of the imagination, ideal raiding country. It was full of enemy movement, hazardous by day and difficult by night, and the local population was not the type to be helpful. Nevertheless the SAS managed to mine the Sfax-Gabes railway line and shoot up a number of trucks. The Germans were now fully alerted to the threat posed by the SAS and had imported a special regiment for the sole purpose of countering them. The SAS decided they had a better chance of avoiding interception if they split up into small parties, but this unfortunately did not avail them much. Their luck ran out. Stirling's party was caught by the German anti-SAS company when the latter were on a training exercise. The German unit had co-opted several hundred other troops to take part in a cordon and search exercise of a wadi (dry watercourse). Having stationed men at each end they sent a search party through the middle. Two members of this party came on Cooper, Sadler and a French soldier called Taxis. For some unaccountable reason the Germans failed to recognise their enemy and moved on. So, as soon as the Germans had gone out of sight, did Cooper, Sadler and Taxis. Stirling, in a nearby cave, was less fortunate. Like the others, he was taking a brief sleep at a time when daylight travel would have been impossible. He woke up suddenly to find himself staring into the muzzle of a revolver. As his captor seemed nervous and likely to shoot by accident if not by design, Stirling obeyed orders and awaited the opportunity to make an early break. However, when he came into the open he discovered that he was surrounded by some five hundred German soldiers.

Ironically, Stirling's captor was not really a soldier but a dentist who had been put into the search party to make up the numbers. However, dentist or soldier, he had certainly drawn the fangs of the SAS for the time being.

The following night Stirling managed to escape, but was not at liberty for long. Having neither food, water nor weapons he was bound to make contact with the local Arabs, who in this part of the world were seldom friendly and in any case would be tempted by the large reward the Germans were offering. He was eventually discovered by an Arab shepherd who pretended to be friendly but led him straight into an Italian search party. It was numerous and well equipped with machine-guns. After this he was so thickly surrounded by guards that he could not escape again.

But the SAS did achieve a link up, and very appropriately one party that did this contained Sadler of the LRDG, Cooper and Taxis, the French soldier. They had a hazardous journey, having no arms, food or water, and were lucky on more than one occasion to avoid being murdered by Arabs intent on robbery. There is of course a wide variety of Arabs, and not all speak the same language. A few, such as the Senussi, were friendly to the British but large numbers were friendly to no one but their own selves and would rob and murder at the slightest opportunity. Happily also, four men from the French patrol led by Lieutenant Martin linked up and this was something to offset the bad luck the French had had in previous raids.

Stirling was eventually imprisoned in Italy, but escaped four times for short periods. His liberty was brief because an escaped prisoner can disguise almost anything except his height. Even so, the Axis decided to take no further risks and eventually transferred him to Colditz. He ended the war with one DSO to which was subsequently added an OBE. It is, of course, somewhat ridiculous that Stirling who had seen more action than many people had even read about should have so little recognition, but the services have an understandable rule that senior officers have to be – if not actual witnesses – close enough to be aware of the circumstances justifying an award. Undoubtedly there were many senior officers who would have been very glad to have removed their red tabs and accompanied the SAS raids, but the exigencies of the service dictated otherwise. However, even when Stirling was in prison his mind did not cease planning the future of the SAS.

The early days of the SAS must strike the reader as being an extraordinary mixture of the practical and the wildly improbable. Wildly improbable ideas win wars if they are worked out with sufficient care and attention to detail to make them practical; but if they are not tied to competent administration they may lose battles. It is not reasonable to expect a man to march 40 miles across a desert without boots or 800 miles with them, but if the right sort of training and attitude precedes these emergencies there is a chance a man will succeed. Preliminary training had cut down water consumption to half a water-bottle a day; during the night men marched thirty miles and would usually, to avoid enemy air reconnaissance, hide up by day. Water would be drunk in small sips. Lewes' theory of leadership was: 'Never let anyone try to do something unless you have done it first and proved it to be possible.'

To the best of their knowledge [Malcolm James Pleydell says]: nobody had ever jumped out of a Bombay* aircraft before and when they landed on the gravel desert surface a thousand feet below it did not take them long to find out why this was so. For the tail of the Bombay was set too low in relation to the fuselage to allow safe parachuting, and it had ripped great gaps in the silk canopies of some of the chutes as the men jumped out of the plane. This is but an example of the way the unit had to learn each point from practice; there was no experience on which to base their experiments and it was only by good fortune there were not many accidents to mar those early days.

The Lewes bomb, which was the basis of their successful attacks on airfields, was invented by Lewes after numerous experiments. The problem was to make a portable time-bomb with incendiary after-effects.

Fuses for these bombs were called 'time-pencils' [Pleydell records]; they worked on the principle of acid eroding through a metal wire, thus releasing a spring which resulted in the explosion. The acid was stored in a small glass phial which could easily be broken before the bomb was placed on the target; variations of wire thickness resulted in bombs with fuses of anything from half a minute to half an hour. Although they did not always work exactly to time, they were invaluable for their purpose; and with the aid of an engineer were soon being made in adequate numbers.

Pleydell, the unit doctor, often considered the motivation of men who like himself volunteered for the SAS. It was not entirely a spirit of adventure, although there was something of that. In the Second World War some men were well content to fall into dull jobs along the line of communication; others could not bear inactivity and volunteered for

* This was doubtless meant to be a Valentia.

69

everything which came along. One man who later went into the SAS volunteered for everything in the early days of the war and as the enterprises which attracted him were so hush-hush had little idea of what he had volunteered for. One day he was suddenly called away, trained as a saboteur, and landed on an enemy coastline via submarine and boat. He was in Albania – at that time in Axis hands. He never discovered which particular piece of volunteering took him there. Today he is back in routine again – in SAS administration! There were many like him. But in the desert monotony and boredom were far worse than in most other theatres. As Pleydell put it:

The cloudless sky which might have been painted over your head for month after month; the way the sand would snake and hiss across the uneven hummocky ground; the thought of four long days till your next wash; the way the sweat dried on your body leaving little white sinuous tracks; the digging of a slit trench at every conceivable halt. Waiting for the next meal; driving into the leaguer each night; dispersing with the dawn; standing to; wondering what the devil was getting your mate down these last few days. Tapping the sand off your biscuits; skimming it off your tea; combing it out of your hair; picking it out of your ears. That was the glamour which the desert gave to the ordinary soldier and which was so seldom mentioned in the communique from Cairo.

However, even after joining the SAS the sand was still with them, and there were other unpleasantnesses too. Hard training which takes you to the limit of physical and mental endurance can be enjoyable but there were certain misadventures which were not really amusing. One was 'ringing the bell': this meant that when jumping through the hole in the floor of a Whitley bomber to parachute you caught your face on the far side. Broken noses were not uncommon.

There are, of course, numerous misconceptions about the desert. In the early days of World War II there were many people – in positions of authority, too – who believed that men could not fight in either the jungle or the desert. Subsequently it was proved that not only could one fight in both types of terrain but also that British troops who had been brought up in urban areas could learn to be as good as if not better than most other people in those conditions. Among the more prevalent misconceptions was that the desert was always hot, whereas it might freeze any night from December to March; that there was no wind, whereas there was usually some sort of breeze but it did not necessarily whip up the sand with it; it did this in much used areas – where the armies were – because the sand had been loosened. A real sandstorm would blot out everything and was so noisy that speech had to be by shouting. The most extraordinary feature of the desert was the ability of flies to appear from nowhere:

My God! How we grew to hate those flies [Pleydell remembered]. And what a trial they became at sick parades, clustering round the desert sores or the exudate that had seeped through the dressings and bandages. Sometimes you would see a man waiting his turn, quite unaware of the black, rosette shaped cluster of flies that had grouped round his sore, until, suddenly noticing their activity, he would slash at them in his fury and start the ulcer bleeding afresh. And the irritating tickling as the flies ran over your back, up your arms, and round your lips and eyes, while you were bending over trying to adjust a dressing or tie a bandage.

Unfortunately the SAS were so exposed to air observation that it would have given their position away if they had dug adequate trenches or been able to burn all refuse at a distance.

In spite of its drawbacks SAS men developed a fondness for the desert and an appreciation of its beauties and special qualities:

The desert was vast; our fading marks could not long defy her immensity. But as for us – we always had our recollections. Happy they might be or bitter as gall, but they remained and could not be touched. And with us we took our memories of heat and cold; of early dawn fresh as the dew on a petal; of the glory and splendour of many tinted sunsets.

Our time had not been wasted for we had gained resourcefulness and knowledge from our own haphazard and natural way of living, and we realized the true worth of our own insignificance. In this way we had matured, we had known greater mental sufficiency, had

71

discovered our fears and reaction to danger, and had tried to overcome them. We had become familiar with hardship and with the submission of the body to rigid control, so that it became at last a mere discipline of the mind.

Recounting the excitement and success of the raids, the adventure and the hairbreadth escapes it is sometimes forgotten that some men were not lucky and were killed, and there were few who did not have a painful experience at one time or other. If you were wounded when out with the SAS you were very unlucky. Pleydell describes one occasion:

A second inspection of this leg confirmed my earlier impression. There were, however, the following points to be considered before deciding on any form of treatment; we had another seventy or eighty miles to travel before reaching the rendezvous; there was the period of the attack on Benghazi when I should have to leave him; and if the attack was not successful then we would have to bring him over the eight hundred miles of rough country back to Kufra. I thought he would recover more quickly if his leg were amputated, both bones were already broken into splinters and lay tangled in the charred skin and clothing ...

We found it hard to drive behind that lorry and watch the wounded men rolling and bumping about. For at each irregularity in the ground the lorry would bounce up like a live thing, bumping and shaking the patients; and from where we were we could see the three legs and one stump fly up into the air and fall back asprawl the stretchers with a sickening jolt. We stopped our vehicles and bound the men's legs down to the stretchers with some more rope ...

There were good days and bad days. Pleydell tried to describe the 'family life' that went on inside a unit:

The SAS was made up of such a fine group of men that even now I find it difficult not to daydream about past experiences. But perhaps the critical reader [of his book *Born in the Desert*] will ask exactly what the SAS did achieve in the desert. 'All this is very interesting,' he may say, 'it is most diverting to read of the way you dashed about the desert in jeeps like a crowd of overgrown schoolboys. But what precisely are your results?' So to them and to those who love statistics, I can only quote the following figures: we destroyed a total of approximately four hundred enemy aircraft in the desert; A Squadron, during the autumn of 1942, demolished the enemy railway line on seven occasions; while between September 1942 and February 1943 forty-three successful attacks were made against German key positions and communications. Our raids then were more than mere pin-pricks; and there were occasions when we must have diverted enemy forces and upset their road convoy system considerably; while the steady drain on aircraft probably exercised an influence on the course of the desert war.

The opinion that the SAS raids had an influence on the course of the desert war was held not only by Pleydell but also by GHQ Middle East and also by the German Higher Command – particularly by the latter. They had good reason to. Before the Battle of Alamein they had 350 serviceable aircraft in Africa, plus 225 bombers based in the Mediterranean area. They also had 300 transport aircraft. By this time the SAS had destroyed nearly 400 of their best aircraft, as well as hangars full of spares, and workshops. Repairs had been delayed, trucks and telegraph communications blown up, and hundreds of men diverted from important military tasks to try to guard scattered airfields and vulnerable lines of communication. The coastal railway between Tobruk and Dorba had been cut in various places and had been out of action for thirteen of the twenty days immediately preceding the Alamein battle (23rd October 1942).

Hitler had no doubts at all. 'These men are very dangerous,' he said in a Special Order. 'They will be hunted down and destroyed at all costs.'

# CHAPTER III

# The Special Boat Service

So David Stirling, who had founded the SAS and given it a unique philosophy, disappeared from the scene in early 1943, but the SAS was by this time so firmly established that it continued to grow. Before leaving Stirling it is appropriate to consider what sort of a person he was – and is. A lot of this has come out in the story of the SAS so far, but his achievements are so remarkable that it is useful to take another look before moving on. He was endowed with a very strong personality which could inspire others. He knew how to handle other individualists, and knew what to concentrate on and what to ignore. He was extremely brave because he was often afraid. When I asked him what it felt like to jump out of the aircraft from which the last two parachutists had been killed, he said: 'Well, I had to; it was a moral obligation. But I was horribly scared.'

Neither Stirling nor Mayne were insensitive, as they were so often thought to be. Mayne was very fond of poetry and much troubled about the ethics of war, greatly though he enjoyed the excitement of fighting. Stirling had a passionate patriotism and was an artist and dreamer in many ways; unlike many artists and dreamers he put down his ideas and translated them into action. At Cambridge he had begun to read for a Tripos in Architecture and at one point after leaving Cambridge he had thought very seriously of studying painting, at which he had considerable talent. He no longer paints because he finds this particular activity more exhausting than anything else and, as he lives at a great pace, almost constantly on the move, that is a surprising statement.

Stirling believes that leaders are born, not made. He did not, as has been said, enjoy killing; he did so because he had to. This recital of his assets and virtues may give the impression that he is an aloof intense personality; on the contrary he is cheerful and modest, has a lively sense of humour, and makes mistakes like anyone else, though perhaps not so many of them.

There must be many people to whom the above description would be reasonably appropriate, apart from the biographical details. The unique quality of Stirling was that having devised a brilliant plan for helping to win the war he had the drive to implement it, the gift to influence men at all levels to help him in his task, the leadership to build up morale, whether he was present or not, and – most extraordinary of all – the ability to make an apparently disastrous setback the stepping stone to a further leap forward. It has been said that his great achievement was to add a new regiment to the British army. That was no mean feat, but vastly more important was the fact that he took warfare several decades ahead of his time. What Stirling thought and did in Africa in 1942 had effects in France in 1944, in Malaya in 1954 and Arabia in 1959 and in Borneo in 1964. Before Stirling, men behind the lines were safe from anything except bombing or perhaps a long-distance shell. After Stirling nobody, whatever his rank or situation, would ever be safe again.

But it was not the loss of Stirling which caused the SAS to change course in 1943; it was the progress of the war. For several months after Stirling's capture the SAS continued their harassing raids behind the German lines. Eventually the 1st SAS Regiment was reorganised as the Special Raiding Squadron under Major R.B. Mayne, and the Special Boat Squadron under Major the Earl Jellicoe. Each unit contained about 250 all ranks. The two units came under the command of Brigadier Turnbull and were designated Raiding Forces, Middle East, which also included Middle East Commando.

In May 1943 a new SAS Regiment came into being. This was 2 SAS under the command of Lieutenant Colonel W.S. Stirling, brother of David Stirling. It was part of 62

Commando, a raiding unit which had recently been sent out from England.

These units then took part in a number of raids on the Dodecanese and Greek islands, Sardinia and Crete. SRS and 2 SAS temporarily came under the command of 1 Airborne Division, this arrangement being made to make the best and most economical use of available troop-carrying aircraft. 1 SAS did not long remain under its title of Special Raiding Squadron and by the end of 1943 was again 1 SAS; we shall therefore refer to them as 1 SAS (SRS).

The future raids were to be a different type from those which have been described above. The new type was in many ways similar to two previous raids which are often attributed to the SAS, though in fact they had no connection. Both had been 'failures' in that they did not achieve their main objectives but both had provided experience which would be extremely useful later. One of these was Operation 'Colossus', February 1941, the destruction of a viaduct in Italy, the other was the Rommel raid, the attempt by 11 (Scottish) Commando in October 1941, to eliminate General Rommel. The former of these is most easily confused with an SAS raid because it set out under the name '11 Special Air Service Battalion' and consisted of troops from No.2 Commando. Although it failed to achieve its main objective, which was to inflict great damage on the water supplies of the province of Apulia, southern Italy, and therefore affect morale in the Italian forces serving abroad in theatres such as North Africa and Albania, it was successful in that it did very considerable damage. The difficulties of such an operation in those days when airborne units lacked the experience and facilities necessary for this type of raid were considerable. However the objectives of the raid could only be reached by this type of expenditure; bombing was not sufficiently accurate and the distance from the coast made any sea assault too long and complicated. Intelligence knew that the most vulnerable point on the supply line of water to Apulia was the Tragino aqueduct. Eventually a party of 36, commanded by Major T.A.G. Pritchard, Royal Welch Fusiliers, set off, after appropriate training, on 10th February 1941. Included in this party was Lieutenant A.J. Deane-Drummond,* Royal Corps of Signals, who would later be known for a series of near miraculous escapes and adventures, including standing thirteen days in a cupboard in a house occupied by German troops after Arnhem. Lieutenant Deane-Drummond later commanded 22 SAS in the Oman.

The party set off in six Whitley bombers which were accompanied by two other Whitleys carrying bombs which would be dropped at Foggia marshalling yards, thereby creating a diversion from the main purpose of the enterprise. The parachutists were dropped from 400 feet and the nearest was within a few hundred yards of the aqueduct; the farthest was well away from the area and its troops did not arrive on the scene in time. The aqueduct was blown with approximately 800 pounds of explosive but unfortunately the water supplies in the area were maintained from reservoirs while it was being repaired and the principal objective was therefore not achieved. Nevertheless, the raid had a number of useful secondary effects: the Italians were greatly alarmed and for years afterwards they took entirely unnecessary and wasteful precautions against a repetition; airborne forces learnt much useful technical information as a result of this raid; and there was an effect on enemy morale although it was not as great as had been hoped for.

The party should have been recovered by submarine four days later from a point fifty miles away. As their presence was known, and the uniform conspicuous, they had to move by night through extremely difficult country. Eventually they were seen and captured without bloodshed through a piece of remarkable psychology. They were surrounded by village dogs and children, by women, and ultimately by Italian soldiers. Had they opened fire they would have killed the women and children.

The 11 Special Air Service Battalion did not retain its title for long. In September 1941 it became 1st Parachute

---

* Now Major General A.J. Deane-Drummond, DSO, MC.

Battalion, which was a part of 1 Parachute Brigade. 1st Para retained a goodly number of the men who had joined No.2 Commando under the impression that they were going to land by sea and would have been astonished to learn that subsequently they would find themselves floating down by air instead.

The second raid which is often thought to have been an SAS project was what became known as the 'Rommel raid'. In fact it was a venture by Layforce, the command of Lieutenant Colonel R.E. Laycock* and was timed for 17th/18th November 1941. The raiding party was nearly double the size of the 11 SAS party which had blown up the aqueduct, and numbered 59, of which six were officers. They were drawn from Scottish Commando and were led by Lieutenant Colonel Geoffrey Keyes. Their aim was to land far behind the German lines and capture General Rommel, dead or alive. They were taken to the selected beach in two submarines and landed by rubber boats. Bad weather made the landing extremely difficult, and continued to make the march inland thoroughly unpleasant over the rough terrain. Eventually, with the help of Arab guides the Commandos reached the house which was alleged to be Rommel's headquarters. This raid had been thought to be something of a suicide mission before it started and now it seemed as if the forecasters had been correct. The occupants of the house were surprised but did not take long to recover. Although the raiding party inflicted heavy casualties their own losses were severe. One of the first to be killed was Lieutenant Colonel Keyes. He was awarded a posthumous VC. As it happened Rommel was far away and had never used that particular house, which was merely the HQ of supply services. Laycock and Sergeant Terry subsequently managed to reach safety at Cyrene after forty-one exacting days. Their return journey, during which they lived on what they could find, included the sort of experiences well known to SAS men later.

* Subsequently Sir Robert Laycock, KCMG, CB, DSO; he became a Major General at the age of 36, the youngest in the Army. In 1954 he was appointed Governor of Malta. He was the first Colonel Commandant of the SAS.

The British and German versions of the events immediately before Keyes' death make an interesting contrast. The British version is that Keyes opened various doors and looked inside rooms; they were empty. He then came to a door which had a light showing beneath it. Inside were about ten Germans. He fired a few rounds from his Colt, but slammed the door shut when Campbell said: 'Wait, I'll throw a grenade in.' Keyes held the door shut while Campbell pulled the pin out of a grenade. When Campbell said 'Right', Keyes flung open the door and Campbell rolled the grenade in. Sergeant Terry fired a short burst from his Tommy gun and Keyes shut the door. Before he could close it the Germans fired and killed Keyes.

The German version says that there was a sentry outside the room – in the dark passageway. The Commandos ran into this tough German soldier who was not easily disposed of. In the struggle he fell against the door, giving the alarm. The Germans opened the door and looked for a target. Meanwhile Keyes was throwing two grenades into the room. The Germans opened fire, but without hitting Keyes. The bullet which killed Keyes came from the gun of Lieutenant Kaufholz, the German orderly officer who had just run down the stairs. He shot Keyes, but was himself shot by Campbell. Before dying he fired one more shot and wounded Campbell. The sentry who had given the alarm and spoiled the surprise was only lightly wounded. He was a Military Policeman and there is no record of his name, but his contribution to events was considerable.

Although this raid is usually dismissed as an expensive failure the verdict is unjust and unwarranted. There was no opportunity to obtain all the detailed information that was needed; and it might not have been obtainable at all. There was no previous experience to go on, and this particular enterprise was not one for which Commandos were specially trained or suited.

But the idea was sound, and the ambition of it was highly commendable. Wars are not won by avoiding risks. The SAS were able to draw on this experience for their successful attacks on German posts in the Aegean and Northern Italy in particular, but in many other situations too. The essential was never to wait for the enemy reaction but always be creating situations to which there could be no reactions at all, or – if there were – would occur after the raiders had moved. The ideal – and it happened – was to leave one sector in the dark, both being under the impression they were attacking the raiders.

According to Hitler's orders all those captured should have been shot, but Rommel decided otherwise and they were treated as prisoners of war. Considering that the raid had been aimed specifically at Rommel, to kill or capture him, the reaction of the German leader was – to say the least – chivalrous. Two years later an SAS man used to frame Rommel in the sights of his gun as he took early morning walks in France. The explanation why he never pulled the trigger was that Rommel's strategy, tactics and reactions were well known to the British General Staff so that they always knew what counter moves would be necessary – and had planned them in advance. Had Rommel been killed, his replacement would have been an unknown quantity and therefore a much more difficult opponent.

The above two raids were not made by the SAS although some of those who took part later became members of the SAS. However, as one took place before the SAS was formed, and the other when it was in its earliest stages, there is no difficulty about drawing the distinction. After Stirling's capture, when 1 SAS was divided into the Special Raiding Squadron and the Special Boat Squadron to make up Raiding Forces, Middle East it could be said that both were still SAS or that, temporarily, neither was. The Special Boat Squadron wore SAS berets and to all intents and purposes were as much a part of the SAS as was the Special Raiding Squadron. Technically, however, the SBS had become a separate unit. Had Stirling not been captured this separation would not have occurred, to the benefit of everyone concerned except the Germans and Italians, but Stirling was in a prison camp and, as he freely acknowledges, he had kept too many of his plans in his head and when he disappeared from the scene SAS development suffered a temporary setback.

The period following Stirling's capture saw the successful conclusion of the fighting in Africa and the beginning of a new rôle. But they were difficult days. GHQ, which had not been over-helpful in the early days of the SAS but had learned to appreciate its worth in the desert, could not now visualize a future for it elsewhere. Mayne had had to argue long and hard for it to continue at all. The first employment 1 SAS (SRS) was offered was to go to the Caucasus. The object of this particular exercise was to disrupt the German line of communication in that area.

This idea had been in force for some time. It will be remembered that Captain Fitzroy Maclean had played a valuable part in the Benghazi raid and was a linguist of considerable skill. In September 1942 GHQ Persia and Iraq had decided that if the Germans came through Persia an SAS-type force might be able to cause damage to their communications. Accordingly, Fitzroy Maclean was sent to Baghdad to discuss the formation of a suitable unit. It was decided that it should consist of 150 volunteers and was, for operational purposes, to be known as M detachment, SBS. Like the SAS it was directly responsible to GHQ and was as Maclean puts it 'my private army'. It would be trained in parachuting and other methods of infiltration. Maclean spent some time in reconnaissance, recruiting and planning, but it was not long before he got his first job. This was the successful kidnapping of General Zahidi, who was suspected, and later proved, to be in touch with the Germans who were ready to stage a coup d'état in Persia. The General was kidnapped without bloodshed. It was not entirely an SAS operation for Maclean had the assistance of a platoon of Seaforth Highlanders although the latter – to their disappointment – were not called upon to do any serious fighting. Following this success, M Detachment continued to train at Isfahan where they were joined by Lieutenant Scratchley and Captain Cumper who brought a convoy of well-equipped jeeps. More useful recruits were acquired, among them a piper from the Seaforths whose performances encouraged his friends and disconcerted any Persians who might have mistakenly thought that the Germans would win the war, and should be assisted; they found the sound of the pipes sinister and intimidating, it seems. Another valuable recruit was Sergeant C. Button who had fought in World War I. He began his parachuting in his late forties.

However, the German defeats at Alamein and Stalingrad effectively removed the threat to Persia. Fortunately this did not cause an interruption of Maclean's activities for the experience he had gained in Persia was recognized by General Wilson to be of value elsewhere. Eventually he went to Yugoslavia where he performed notable feats, though not under SAS auspices. Before this happened M Detachment had been training with the Special Boat Squadron at Athlit, Palestine and later in Zahle in the Lebanon. This latter move was for training in mountain warfare. Fitzroy Maclean was then briefed for a raid on Crete. 'Large scale maps and air photographs were procured, and we settled down to the detailed planning. We soon felt as if we had known that aerodrome and the rocky gullies by which we should have to approach it since our earliest childhood.' However the raid was called off because the Germans were no longer using the aerodrome which was the objective of that particular raid.

But Maclean was not left to kick his heels for long. Although he had never before been in Yugoslavia he was chosen by the British government to be dropped in that country as head of a Military Mission to assist the Partisans. There were two groups of people who were resisting the Germans in Yugoslavia. They were General Mihajlovic and the Cetniks, and an unknown called Tito who had some followers called the Partisans. The British Government had just decided that of the two forces Tito's was the one with the greater possibilities. Germany had invaded Yugoslavia in 1941 and the resistance movements had gone into operation immediately. At first they had worked together, although the Cetniks consisted mainly of officers and men of the Royal Yugoslav army, and the Partisans of peasants, most of whom were Communists. Soon a rift developed, both sides alleging that the other had betrayed their positions to the Germans. The core of their conflict was that the Cetniks wished to limit German retaliation and destruction, possibly by reaching a compromise, while the Partisans' answer to retaliation was to redouble their own efforts against the invader. When they met the Cetniks they fought them also. Eventually the Cetniks were passive, or in some cases supporting the Germans, while the Partisans were inflicting tremendous damage on Cetniks and Germans alike. Fitzroy Maclean was sent to the Partisans as they were clearly the most effective force operating against the Germans. By 1943 they numbered 150,000, possibly more. The British Government did not like their political views but approved strongly of their fighting qualities.

The Germans launched seven offensives against them, each using at least ten divisions, but this availed them nothing. Fitzroy Maclean's task was to head the Allied Military Mission which would see that Tito received the supplies and assistance he needed. It was a complicated situation. The Cetniks, with whom we would have preferred to co-operate had they been as effective as the Partisans, were being assisted by the Germans; the Germans thought they could use the Cetniks to gain complete control of the country, the Cetniks on the other hand thought they could use the Germans to enable them to dispose of the Communist threat posed by the Partisans. Fitzroy Maclean was sent in as a soldier/diplomat, and although the SAS looked with approval on the fighting record of their former member at this point he disappears from this history; the rest of his adventures appear in his book *Eastern Approaches*.

So much for M Detachment. It now follows that we should trace the story of L Detachment, the command of Major T.B. Langton, a man with a great reputation in Cambridge and Henley rowing circles in the years immediately before the war. It was a somewhat different organisation from the original L Detachment which had developed into the SAS, but in its way had a potential little less deadly. The third

83

detachment of the Special Boat Squadron was S, commanded by Captain D. Sutherland. The squadron itself was commanded by Major the Earl Jellicoe, DSO.

The Special Boat Squadron had a curious history and was to have an even more curious future. When the first Commandos had begun their training in 1940, there was formed a small detachment of canoeists whose task was reconnaissance and small scale sabotage. At the time an invasion of Pantellaria, a small island lying midway between Tunis and Sicily, was contemplated. The proposed invasion was cancelled at the last moment; instead, an invasion of Rhodes was planned, to be undertaken by Layforce. This, as we have seen, brought the founder members of the SAS to the Middle East, and with them came the Folboat (Canoe) Section which was attached to No.8 Commando. No great future was envisaged for the Folboats, for if they were damaged they could not be replaced overseas. However, as we have seen, German successes in Greece consigned the Rhodes invasion plan to the wastepaper basket and Folboats, who now had no obvious present, let alone a future, were transferred to HMS *Medway* to work with the submarine flotilla. Among its duties would be landing spies and agents although soon its members were engaging in the more interesting activity of blowing up enemy railway lines, bridges and other acceptable targets. Their biggest assignment came with the Rommel raid of which the other parts are described earlier. Folboats landed from the submarines and did the preliminary reconnaissance, and then guided in the raiding party, who were in rubber boats.

The submarine returned a few nights later, ready to take off the raiders who, of course, by this time had all been captured or dispersed. No signal came from the beach so Langton and Feeberry went in to have a look. Their joint weight was 28 stone and, not surprisingly, the light craft overturned in the surf. They reached land but the lights and landing signals they saw did not appear to come from their own troops. Treating them with suspicion – very rightly – Langton returned to the submarine and observed from its periscope;

the beach was occupied by Germans and there was, of course, no sign of the SAS.

Up till this point Folboats had hardly been thought of as having a separate existence but before the end of the year Courtney, their pioneer and commander, returned to England and formed the Special Boat Section. This sub-unit practised landing on inhospitable coasts, and climbing and descending rugged cliffs; the experience gained would come in very useful later.

Courtney was succeeded by Captain M. Kealey. Folboats continued to have interesting experiences, such as experimenting with attempts to destroy enemy destroyers in Navarino harbour; of these and other SBS raids there is a full account in John Lodwick's* book *The Filibusters*. Not least of them is the occasion when Captain K. Allot paddled a canoe, in rough seas, through enemy patrolled water, from the Ras-el-Tin headland to the Gazala inlet – a distance of 150 miles.

But the SBS was too hazardous a service to remain intact for long. During the next few months its successes in sabotage were paid for by the numbers of its members killed and captured. But some survived. Among them were Allot and Sutherland.

These two took part in a raid on Rhodes in September 1942. They were taken to their destination by submarine and put ashore by Carley floats and a Folboat. Subsequent progress, on land, was much slower than anticipated. It is one thing to look at a map and see a gentle slope, but quite a different thing when you reach it and find it covered with thorny scrub and full of deep crevasses which have to be climbed into and climbed out of again. The guides turned out to be useless and were dismissed on the grounds that no guide is better than a bad guide. However, in spite of unexpected setbacks the party reached its target and destroyed a number of aircraft and store dumps. The raiders had accomplished their mission.

---

* Lodwick was killed in a traffic accident in Barcelona in 1959.

Getting away was, not surprisingly, even more difficult than getting in. There was a large garrison and all possible escape routes were swept by searchlights. Allot's party were detected, surrounded and captured. Sutherland and Duggan were several times within seconds of being discovered but each time were passed by the searchers. From one hiding-place they had the mortifying experience of seeing an Italian MTB discover and tow off the craft in which they had landed. Eventually, after five days without food and two days without water, they obtained a reply to their recognition signal, very faint, but a reply none the less. They then swam two miles and were picked up by the submarine HMS *Traveller* which had been standing by for two hours in a situation of acute peril. Both men were suffering from exposure and took some time to recover.

On these bare facts it might be assumed that the gains of this raid scarcely balanced the losses but, in fact, the Marizza and Calato airfields which they had attacked were severely damaged and partly out of action for several weeks; Mediterranean convoys benefited considerably from the consequent easing of pressure.

At this point the SBS was too crippled by losses to merit a separate existence so it joined forces with, and became part of, the SAS. With it went a troop from the Greek Sacred Squadron. Sutherland took most of the SBS to Syria where they continued training, while Langton took the remainder to the Tobruk harbour raid of 1942. This, as we have noted earlier, was part of the combined operations on Benghazi, Tobruk and Barce. (The last, a diversionary attack by the LRDG, was the only success; they destroyed thirty enemy aircraft.) This large-scale raid was, as we have already pointed out, contrary to SAS principles and was an overall failure in spite of local successes. However, the SBS part of it merits more than a passing reference.

Langton was given the task of signalling in the MTBs, but when he went to the beach, had little success; two had already arrived, the others could not do so. The Germans, who had been expecting the raid and were fully prepared, were out in force, sweeping sea and land by searchlight and making full use of their gunners. Langton went to one of the MTBs which had landed, but found no one on board. He was however soon joined by four other men; they included Sillito (of the desert walk) and Private Watler who would soon be known as 'the man the Germans could not hold'. Watler was a mechanic and tried to start the ship's engines, but his attempts proved unsuccessful. It was abundantly clear that the raid was a failure, if not actually a disaster. One of the supporting destroyers was towing the other – badly crippled – out to sea, fierce fighting was going on between German and British troops inshore. Langton and his party thereupon embarked in one of the assault boats and paddled sedately around the harbour. The Germans were so astonished at this apparently suicidal gesture that emotion affected their marksmanship. On the far side of the bay Langton deemed it reasonably safe to land and, after crossing two minefields, discovered twenty survivors of the raid. From them he learnt what had happened. Haselden, who had commanded the land party, had done considerable damage before his small force ran into a German battalion. Haselden was killed by a grenade while leading a charge.

Langton now had a party numbering twenty-five. Although this split up, all but Langton and Privates Watler and Hillman were captured. These three walked for 78 days, much of the time barefoot. In the early stages they had had to dodge enemy patrols and nearly died of hunger and thirst; in the latter stages exposure and exhaustion had nearly put paid to their chances.

On 1st April 1943 the SBS established themselves at Athlit, south of Haifa. We have already seen what happened to Fitzroy Maclean's M Detachment; it remains to be seen what would happen to L under Langton and S under Sutherland. Each detachment contained six patrols, each thirteen strong including the officer commanding. With essential administrative troops at the base the entire force numbered 250. As we have noted, it was commanded by Major the Earl Jellicoe.

Brigadier Laycock of 'Layforce' was now in England

commanding the 1st Special Service Brigade. When 62 Commando was disbanded he sent two very useful officers to the SBS: one was an Englishman named Philip Pinckney, of whom more later, the other was a Dane named Anders Lassen. At the outbreak of war Lassen was in England and had joined the British army. He was soon sent to Arisaig, West Scotland, to be trained as a Commando. While up there he showed – among other qualities – that he could approach and kill a stag with a knife. He could move so swiftly and silently that a witness said he 'moved as if without touching the ground'. His abilities were noted by Captain Gustavus March-Phillips who, with Captain Geoffrey Appleyard, had in 1941 been given permission to select and train a raiding unit. Up till this point Lassen's training – although he did not know it – had been designed to prepare him for eventually being parachuted into Denmark. Instead, fate took him on an entirely different course which ended in his being killed in Lake Comacchio, Northern Italy, within a month of the end of the war. He was awarded a posthumous VC. Before he died he had killed or captured a very considerable number of Germans, and his presence in an area had even affected enemy strategy, a remarkable and rare achievement.

His first assignment was a raid on the West African coast where German merchantmen were lying in Vichy French waters close to Dakar. It will be recalled that the Vichy Government was a puppet French government maintained by the Germans after the fall of France. It was, naturally, detested by the Free French, and the Resistance, as well as by large numbers of French who were unable to do any more than produce passive non-cooperation. March-Phillips' party, known as Small-scale Raiding Force (62 Commando), sank two German merchantmen with limpets and sailed off with the third. Lassen, a lance corporal up till this point, was commissioned for his part in the raid. The raid is often described as SAS, but was in fact purely Commando. Most of this splendid and enterprising unit, including March-Phillips himself, were killed in the Boulogne raid of the spring of 1943. At this point it should be mentioned that although the SAS joined with the SBS from Layforce, this was not the only SBS in existence. For example, No.2 Commando had an SBS which not merely conducted reconnaissance of enemy coasts, but also carried out raids on its own account.

Pinckney, who had joined the SBS (SAS) at the same time as Lassen, was posted to 2 SAS in the summer of 1943. After serving in Sicily he was parachuted on to the Brenner Pass. There, after he had blown up a railway tunnel, he was captured and shot by the Gestapo. His execution was, of course, a crime under International Law. Just as the endurance walks of Keith, Sillito, Langton and others had established that an SAS man can (probably) walk his way from anywhere to anywhere so Pinckney established the fact that an SAS man could live on anything almost anywhere. He was a food expert, and delighted in collecting slugs, snails, grasshoppers, and strange unhealthy looking leaves and insects which many men would dislike to touch, let alone eat. Few commanders have ever inspired such awe and terror in their men, who never knew what they might be required to swallow next. However, not all Pinckney's diets were bizarre and he chose a blend of rations which would be reasonably satisfactory in any area. This eventually became the standard SAS operation ration.

After Fitzroy Maclean had left the SBS, his place was given to Captain J.N. Lapraik, MC, who brought with him Lieutenant D. Stellin. Lapraik would later command 21 SAS; another notable recruit was Captain W. Milner-Barry who had already had a successful career in Shell-Mex in Palestine. Apart from their considerable ability as soldiers, Milner-Barry, and another officer named Lieutenant J.S.F. Macbeth, played a notable rôle as diplomats when – as often happened – the SBS trod on the toes of allies and potential friends. Small independent units who live a rough carefree life often tend to be impatient with protocol and precedence, although well enough aware of the necessity of such matters in the services. Massive injections of tactful diplomacy are often required to soothe tempers which may have been aroused unintentionally but are then derided; the job of fighting men in large or small units is to be at odds with the enemy and friendly with one's own side, however obstructive, petty and jealous some of its members may appear. It may be a bore to suffer fools gladly, but it may at times be necessary, for fools can often exercise control of such vital matters as supplies, reinforcements and even employment.

In June 1943 Crete was again raided. The aim on this occasion was to destroy as many German aircraft as possible so that the Germans would have that many less to ward off the coming invasion of Sicily. The assignment was given to Sutherland. He took three 4-man patrols led by Lassen, Lieutenant K. Lamonby, and Lieutenant A. Rowe and a base party. Lassen tackled Kastelli aerodrome which contained Stukas and Junkers 88s, but was heavily guarded. Accompanied by Gunner Jones, he decided to create a diversion to the west of the airfield while the remainder of his party, Sergeant Nicholson and Corporal Greaves, got to work on the aircraft on the eastern side. Lassen bluffed his way past sentries, distributed a few shots and grenades, and retired. He was soon back and laid charges himself. Meanwhile the other pair destroyed every plane they saw. The essence of the success of these raids was that it was dark, the raiders could move swiftly and silently, they only had to get to their target for a few seconds, and physically they were more than a match in personal combat for anyone who tried to stop them. Against this was the fact that they were in an area they did not know, they were heavily outnumbered, they had to be careful not to kill their own side and they had a considerable load to carry. Once the alarm went, escape from the area was difficult. On this occasion Lassen was chased into the mountains by German soldiers and had to hide for eighty hours without food.

Rowe found nothing on his target, Timbaki, and returned to base. Lamonby found no planes at Heraklion but blew up a huge petrol dump. With considerable astuteness the Germans wasted little time and effort on chasing the SBS in the mountains but placed large forces along the areas from which they would be likely to embark. Meanwhile Cairo radio and newspapers had loudly proclaimed the safe return of the SBS; unfortunately the Germans treated this false news with scepticism, rightly suspecting it was yet another twist of British cunning. Eighteen days after landing the raiders were still on Crete. Nevertheless, on the night of the 10th July they were taken off by HM Motor Launch *361*, but not before Lamonby had been killed and two German prisoners taken.

Escorting the two German prisoners through Cairo, Sutherland and Lassen decided they were thirsty and would like a drink. They stopped at Groppi's which was the great centre of social life – and probably also of every sort of intrigue and spying. They could not very well leave their prisoners unguarded in the truck parked outside so they took them into the bar and bought them a drink. Groppi's was full of uniforms of a number of different nationalities but no one appeared to notice, let alone object to, these two latest additions.* There is another war-time story of a man dressing up as a German officer and walking around all day in London; he was frequently saluted, but never challenged – so the unauthenticated story goes.

The next raid was more complicated and less successful; at times its incidents seem scarcely credible. By August 1943 it was obvious that Italy had had enough of the war and would gladly come to terms with the Allies if allowed to do so. The fly in the ointment was the German interest in keeping Italy in the war, a procedure that was likely to be facilitated by a swift German occupation of areas the Italians would be only too glad to hand over to the Allies. Not least among these was the island of Rhodes, which was considered with some rightness to be the key to the control of the Dodecanese Islands which were garrisoned, though thinly, by Italians. Rhodes, whatever happened, must not be allowed to fall into German hands, and therefore its Italian Governor, Admiral Campioni, must be persuaded, by force if necessary, to accede to the Allies. Unfortunately the forces at our disposal for this

* Unfortunately someone did and Sutherland was subsequently reprimanded.

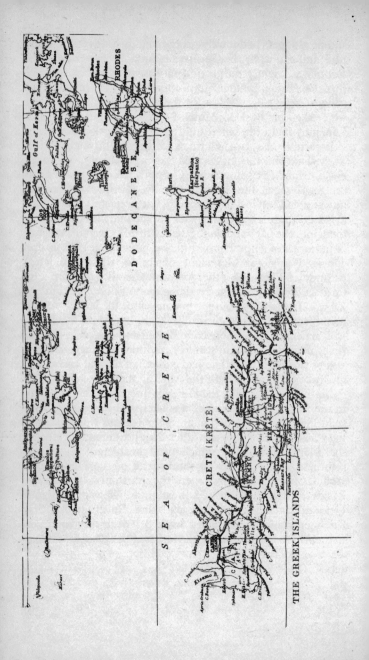

large-scale enterprise were sadly small. Coercion would therefore have to be preceded by bluff. The entire SAS, SRS (1 SAS) and as much of the LRDG as could be brought in, would be employed. These forces would seize and hold strong points until 8th Indian Division could land and occupy.

The key to control of the island was Admiral Campioni. If he agreed to hand over to the Allies many lives would be saved; if, on the other hand, he decided to wait and see, the Germans would almost certainly take over Rhodes before the Allies could arrive. The SAS task, therefore, was to encourage him to join the Allies. Sutherland therefore occupied the island of Castelrosso nearby and a persuasive mission dropped on Rhodes itself. This expedition consisted of Jellicoe, Major Dolbey, who was an Italian interpreter, and Sergeant Kesterton, who was a signaller. Dolbey, who was approaching middle age, had never parachuted in his life and unfortunately landed in the dark on a road and broke his leg. Unable to move and in severe pain, he was discovered by an Italian search party. The others had been scattered by the breeze and Jellicoe, believing he was surrounded by Germans, had eaten the letter General Maitland-Wilson had given him to deliver to Admiral Campioni. It was apparently neither succulent nor digestible, took an hour to eat, and left him with a raging thirst the next day.

However, in due course, they were taken to Admiral Campioni, Dolbey now on a stretcher. It was 2 am. Campioni was surprised to hear of the armistice and was well aware of the presence of some 10,000 well-organised German troops on the island. British troops, on the other hand, could not arrive in less than six days. Jellicoe radiated confidence, but could not quite take the Governor with him as the latter was only too conscious of the proximity of the large German forces who were about to give him an ultimatum. Eventually Campioni decided the German threat was too great and too immediate to be disregarded, and he capitulated. Rhodes was lost but Jellicoe decided that the Dodecanese should not follow. On 11th September 1943 he went out to take them over. The circumstances of this adventurous journey were somewhat unusual. Admiral Campioni was still wavering on the 10th but had assured Jellicoe he intended to resist. Jellicoe had doubts, but reluctantly accepted the argument that the presence of SAS men on the island prejudiced any bluffing of the Germans that the Admiral might hope to do. Jellicoe put it thus:

I then agreed to embark that night in a MAS* for Castelrosso. It seemed to me on reflection that if the Governor was genuine in his policy of temporisation my further presence in Rhodes might well be an embarrassment to him and that if he was not genuine there was in any case no point in staying longer. Before leaving I asked that all the available intelligence on the minefields in the Aegean and of the Italian defences in Rhodes should be put at my disposal and this was done. We accordingly left the Governor's Palace shortly after dark loaded with a curious assortment of kit which included our wireless gear, two bottles of Rhodes wine and an excellent picnic basket.

They were given as escort the Admiral's Chief of Staff, one Colonel Fanetza. Unfortunately the Italian Colonel fell into the water on arrival at Castelrosso when he was otherwise tending to be extremely dignified; Jellicoe smiled and in consequence diplomatic relations suffered a setback.

Nevertheless, although Castelrosso, Cos, Samos and Leros were successfully occupied by eighty men, two motor launches, and three caiques Jellicoe considered that a vital opportunity had been lost at Rhodes. He felt that Admiral Campioni, though not a strong character, was sincere in his efforts and that if the Allies had made a great effort to introduce a force of approximately three thousand, Rhodes could have been taken; consequent savings in Allied shipping, aircraft and soldiers would have been considerable.

In this story there is a sequence of acts of cool, isolated courage but even in this Dolbey's stands out. To make one's first parachute descent on a windy night in the dark on to a hostile island might make the most adventurous thoughtful;

* A MAS is a Motor Anti-Submarine boat – a fast motor launch.

to break one's leg, to be in acute pain and then to conduct difficult negotiations in the early hours is not a task many men would relish.

The war in Africa being over the next target was Sicily. However, it would not do for the opposition to realise the exact direction of the Allies' next thrust, so a diversionary attack was planned for Sardinia. This was allotted to Langton's squadron who would also supply some members to be dropped with 2 SAS in Sicily. Langton was ill at the time and his command was taken over by Captain John Verney. Verney, who is now a well-known author and painter, describes this operation in *Going to the Wars*. All embarked on – Verney says 'squeezed into' – the submarine HMS *Tiber* on 27th June. It was not a pleasure cruise; the party suffered from malaria and claustrophobia. It was discovered that if highly-trained and energetic men are kept inactive in cramped conditions the results are worse than they would be with people of less developed physical efficiency. On this particular 17-hour dive the situation was exacerbated by the fact that many of the men had already contracted malaria. As the submarine subsequently developed engine trouble and had to return after having landed only a proportion of the raiders, it may have been that the air-conditioning was below standard; certainly the degree of lethargy and dullness went far beyond what might have been expected.

When the submarine returned to port, Verney suggested that parachuting should now be used. The plane allotted to take them somewhat inconveniently dropped them through the floor, a method which they had not previously experienced. But as Verney put it, 'the RAF staff were very efficient, and helpful and kind, like doctors and nurses before a serious operation.'

They carried light weapons and six bombs 'which weighed one pound each and looked like small Christmas puddings' and detonating fuses. The latter had been put in their left breast pockets on the basis that 'if one did get broken in the fall, at least the man would hardly be aware of it'.

But they landed. Verney comments on a problem which faced all raiders:

It is always interesting, arriving in a new country which one has studied carefully beforehand from photographs, maps and books, to see how far the mental picture tallies with the real one. In the past fortnight I had studied Sardinia very thoroughly in various topographical surveys and in air photographs. But what can you really learn about a country from such things? The landscape varied, so one guide book had said, between 'high and wild mountain ranges where the only vegetation is *maquis* or thorny scrub; undulating rocky pastureland for goats and sheep; populous fertile plains yielding rich crops of grapes, fruit, olives, corn and so on'. The only features common throughout the island appeared to be the *nuraghe*, a prehistoric type of conical stone hut, and the Sardinian peasant in his long black woollen cap and white stockings. Now here we were, after so little effort, standing on Sardinian soil when three hours before we had been in North Africa.

By moonlight, the landscape resembled nothing I had imagined. We were on a plain, but parched, rocky and barren, stretching away in all directions. Not a *nuraghe* nor a black-capped white-hosed peasant to be seen. The landscape was so bare we had difficulty in finding bushes thick enough to conceal our chutes.

The group was split into two, Verney leading one and Captain Brinkworth leading the other. Verney's party made a successful attack on an airfield, destroying aircraft and petrol dumps. They then set off for the coast where they hoped to be picked up. Their adventures from that point became somewhat bizarre. Verney, although in British uniform, succeeded reasonably well in passing himself off as a German officer – and remained tramping around the island for eleven days. At one point he took a lift on an Italian convoy. Brinkworth displayed similar aplomb and remained at large for seventeen days. Brinkworth usually marched his men along the road, singing German songs, and treating the Italians as if they were dependable, though rather inferior, allies. On one occasion when Brinkworth was about to be arrested he calmly shook hands with a worried policeman and walked off. When they were eventually captured half the island's garrison was out looking for them. The Germans took no further chances with this unpredictable pair of officers and sent them straight to prison camp in Italy.*

The remainder of the party were not hastened into captivity so fast, and arrived at their Italian prison camp just in time for the armistice. They promptly disarmed their guards and set off to join their comrades further south. One of them, Lance Sergeant Scott, by chance ran into Lieutenant McGregor of 2 SAS, near Pescara and about one hundred miles ahead of the Allied lines. These two, in company with others of the SBS party, and some from 2 SAS then proceeded to make life difficult for the garrisons in their area. Eventually Scott, who appeared to lead a charmed life, had to escape in a rowing-boat.

Another remarkable character thrown up by the fortunes of war at this time was Corporal R.A. Summers, who had the unusual nickname of 'Safari' from the endless treks in which he had taken part. He was in the small group of Langton's squadron which, not being needed for Sardinia, had been dropped in Sicily. They wandered around happily, living off the country, cutting telephone wires, blowing up roads and bridges, and generally committing such acts of sabotage as occurred to their fertile minds. As, on the way back to their own side, they had to pass through the enemy front line which was full of alert fighting troops, their days were not without their difficult moments. And, as often happens, they had an unnerving experience when they made contact with their own side, who suspected them of being enemy spies. His account of this operation is given in the Appendix.

Enterprising though these ventures were they were outclassed by the audacity of Jellicoe's activities in the Dodecanese. The islands were commanded by Italians but these had the assistance – and embarrassment – of German troops in the vicinity. As many of the Italian commanders had wives and families in parts of Italy still occupied by Germans

---

* Brinkworth went on to Germany, but Verney was kept in Italy from which he subsequently escaped. He rejoined the SAS and fought in Germany.

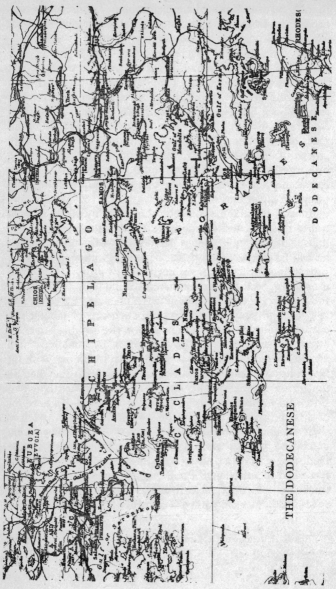

they were in a difficult position and usually handed prisoners over to the Germans in case of reprisals on their own homes. Those Italians under no such pressure usually threw in their lot with the British. The result was that the islands were under a divided command although unfortunately for the Allies the Germans possessed valuable airfields on Rhodes. Jellicoe took over Cos and Leros without great difficulty and these were subsequently reinforced. Major J. Lapraik and Anders Lassen had a similar bloodless victory in Simi and made the island a centre for raiding German bases on Rhodes. Lapraik had six caiques to assist him in warming up the Rhodes situation. Lassen landed at Calchi, close to Rhodes, which was garrisoned by twelve carabinieri. He gave them stores, trained them and warned them that if when the Germans came they did not fight like tigers he would come back and deal with them. When the Germans came they did fight like tigers although sustaining many casualties! Such is leadership.

Sutherland took Samos, and was relieved by a company of the Royal West Kent Regiment. He then moved to a less satisfactory task at Calino. All this was in September 1943.

But in October the Germans fought back. With the advantage of a strong base at Rhodes they were able to launch a powerful attack on Cos, using their air superiority. They won after considerable bloodshed on both sides. Losses on the British side would have been much higher had Milner-Barry not landed on the island, kept back the Germans by demolitions, and evacuated 105 British supporters.

In Milner-Barry's patrol was Private Watler who had shown something – although not all – of what he was capable in the long march after the Tobruk raid. He became separated from the rest of the patrol and was captured. Watler escaped when he was bored, which was very soon, was recaptured and then escaped again. He wandered around for a while sabotaging everything he could find, and then made his way back to his own side. In the course of his adventures he swam two miles down an unknown coast.

The Germans pressed on. Simi was their next objective.

They had every advantage and began well. However, the combination of SBS, well-led Italians, and the overall encouragement of Lapraik and Lassen made the task considerably more difficult than what they had first envisaged. Eventually they withdrew after heavy casualties. The island was subsequently heavily bombed. In spite of its spirited defence it was decided that Simi should not be held, so in the second half of October it was evacuated; essential stores were then transported to the base on the mainland. However, in view of the previous experience, the Germans were reluctant to occupy the island. Calino was also evacuated and the struggle now centred on Leros. There were now three British battalions on the island, an anti-aircraft battery, and a number of Italians who had decided to join the Allied side. The SBS, under Sutherland, was given the task of dealing with any attempt at airborne invasion.

For the first two weeks of November Leros was bombed steadily in an attempt to soften it up. Then came the invasion. The sea landings gave the Germans a foothold by early morning and by midday the expected airborne assault arrived. Six hundred parachutists were dropped while Messerschmitts bombed and harassed the ground defences. By well-directed fire and steady sniping the SBS prevented the container parachutes being recovered by those parachutists who had managed to land intact. The Germans fell back into cover, planning to emerge after nightfall and recover their missing supplies, but when they did so they found the containers empty.

Further German troops were then landed from the sea. A fresh consignment of parachutists was not so lucky. Four of the transports were shot down and, as weather conditions had worsened, some of the parachutists fell in the sea while others were dragged over the rocks. A number of parachutes failed to open; of the 200 who dropped only about twelve reached the ground in a condition to fight.

Elsewhere conditions were not so fortunate for the British. Heavy and continuous bombing took its toll of the strength of the defence; there was no air cover and not much space for manoeuvre. Even so the Germans lost $2\frac{1}{2}$ times as many as the British – 1,000 to 400 was the ratio finally recorded in the cemetery. Leros was surrendered after five days' gruelling fighting and the SBS were able to slip away before the Germans caught them. One man, Balsillie, had to be left behind, as he was suffering from acute dysentery. A day or two later he felt sufficiently recovered to steal a German boat and row himself across to Turkey – about 60 miles.

With Leros gone, Samos could not but follow. The Germans now controlled the Dodecanese. They had won them by intelligent and serious fighting; it now remained to see whether they could enjoy and make use of their gain or whether the SBS could whittle away the advantages the victors should have possessed. At the outset the Germans could scarcely have thought of an SBS threat. They soon had a division in Rhodes, 800 men in Casos and Saria, 4,000 in Leros, 2,000 in Cos, 200 in Stampalia, 150 each in Simi and Piscopi. The remaining small islands were garrisoned in turn at roughly the same strength as Simi and Piscopi. The total number of German troops involved in these dispositions in the Aegean amounted to six divisions. It was not therefore merely a matter of the SBS giving these troops an unhappy time, it was Allied policy to immobilize and isolate this large number of men so that they could not be withdrawn and used against the coming Allied invasion of France. Accordingly, SBS efforts would be assisted and supplemented by air attacks from Cyprus bases, submarines would blockade the ports of Portolago, Piraeus and Heraklion, and coastal forces from the Navy would patrol the shores, land and disembark and do a considerable quantity of harassment of their own. Needless to say they would not find their tasks easy. The Germans had large numbers of seaplanes, lighters, barges and caiques. These latter – which were also used extensively by the SBS – were eminently suited to navigating tricky waters. With their fleet the Germans hoped to control, supply, and defend the islands; with theirs the SBS hoped to make the islands anything but a terrestrial Paradise for their new occupiers. A typical manoeuvre would be to lure a respectable contingent of German troops to an island by an irruption of sabotage and then to make it extremely expensive for them to get away when they realised they had been bluffed into weakening their other dispositions. The Turks obligingly bent their neutrality to allow British forces to use their territorial waters just as generously as they allowed German warships to sail through their waters from the Black Sea. The Germans tried to protest against British use of Turkish shelter in the Aegean but as their only evidence came from reconnaissance planes which had violated Turkish air space to take photos of the SBS the Turks merely laughed at them. However, just in case the Germans decided to aim bombs instead of take photographs the British ships took care to be well camouflaged, to move discreetly but frequently, and not to do anything provocative when in Turkish territorial waters.

For people who are born hunters, and who accept any risk in pursuit of their most cherished activity, this was an ideal situation. They were, of course, in an enviable position. They were living on boats, were surrounded by highly trained and entirely trustworthy companions, and had considerable freedom, both in the adventures they undertook and the lives they led. Any danger they encountered was highly personal, and if they met violent and messy ends would at least be fighting in the process, not merely at the receiving end of quite impartial high explosive. They were more congenially employed than many of their comrades-in-arms in other theatres but it must be said, in fairness to both sides, that few people were equipped to make a success of the life they were leading, and the number who would have chosen it was limited.*

Of those who wished for nothing better were Anders Lassen, and his aide, Guardsman O'Reilly; O'Reilly, incidentally, was forty-two. These two opened proceedings with a brisk raid on Calchi. The party numbered seven in all.

* Even on those who did, it was a tremendous physical and psychological strain.

There were only six German supporters on the island but while the SBS were there a German motor launch came into the harbour and was promptly captured.

The next raid on Stampalia was on a bigger scale. This took place in January and the weather was as bad as might have been expected in that area in that month; the gales being frequently Force 6. Nevertheless, a small party blew up a seaplane and four caiques. An even smaller party then proceeded to blow up telegraph stations and shoot up German billets. The rest of the garrison were so unnerved that they took totally unnecessary precautions. Similar harassing raids were executed on Patmos and Archi. On one of these a captured boat had a cargo which included six cases of champagne, ten of Pilsner beer, thirty kegs of Samos wine, and twenty-five radio sets. It was sent to base under the command and care of one man, Marine Smith, who had instructions to sink it if likely to be captured; it was not captured but some of the cargo evaporated shortly after it reached port. These raids were typical of many others. Some were amusing, though the enemy may not have thought so; there were, however, occasions when the Germans displayed a touch of whimsy that was entertaining and sometimes disconcerting. However, the SBS were not easily bluffed. For example, the German CO on Piscopi dressed up two of his privates in British battle-dress, gave them pipes to smoke and turned them loose to find the British patrol which he suspected lurked on the island. He assumed that pro-British Greeks would direct them. They found the patrol – or rather were found by it – and unwittingly gave away the German password for that night. With that valuable information the SBS were able to move in close to the German billets and take a heavy toll on men and installations. This all sounds delightfully light-hearted, and to those who were neither killed nor wounded it probably was. One cannot but sympathise with the German sentries who on this, as on other occasions, were executed for neglect of duty; they were like amateurs who inadvertently get involved in a punch-up with professionals; they were out of their class and they suffered

103

severely and ignominiously for a fault which they could not remedy. Tempting though it is, there is no space to give a full account of these raids in these pages. All we can do is to single out some which were typical and some which were remarkable by any standards.

However, it should not be assumed that life in the Aegean was one glorious succession of hit and run adventures. Each operation needed careful planning and logistics. Inevitably this meant that some SBS members could not be used. They were sent off to ski at the Middle East Ski School. It seemed a far cry from their beloved canoes and caiques, and they said so, although knowing full well their views would be heard courteously and dismissed promptly.

There is an apt proverb 'Man proposes; God disposes'. To the SBS this must have frequently seemed to have been their position in the Aegean, with GHQ acting as God. Unfortunately for the SBS they were not the only Allied force operating in the area. As on most coastlines around occupied Europe there was a brisk activity in the movement of agents, and the landing of supplies to resistance movements. This traffic took precedence over SBS who would be warned to lay off an area which was needed for other activity. Frequently the restrictions went well beyond the area concerned simply through each minor official adding a bit on to his own liking. Soldiers will be familiar with this mental process for they will have had the experience of being told to parade at 0900 hours and yet be standing to since 0730 as every minor cog in the wheel down to the Lance Corporal will have added his preliminary parade and inspection. It is a point which goes unrecorded on recruiting advertisements, but is rarely omitted in conversation among former soldiers, whose influence on recruiting is often greater than Higher Management appears to think.

In the Aegean the mental process of adding a bit often resulted in the whole area being put out of bounds to the raiders. However the SBS were usually allowed to recce. Reconnaissance can, of course, easily land a party in trouble and as trouble was what the SBS were secretly hoping for it is not surprising that there were occasional lapses, followed by angry words from GHQ.

The Germans were not by any means the easy victims that the successes recounted against them might suggest. Many of them were excellent fighting troops and when they were caught unawares they were well aware that they had only themselves to blame and preferred to fight to a finish rather than surrender. Lassen in particular was an adept at exploiting surprise. He could slip past sentries and then methodically walk from room to room in a billet tossing a grenade or two in each. The unfortunate drawback to many of these exploits was that while dead British would be buried by the Germans with full military honours, live Greeks who were suspected of having assisted the SBS were shot. For some time the SBS were puzzled that garrisons could be taken by surprise so easily but eventually discovered that this was because the Germans carefully suppressed news of raids in other areas. It seemed a high price to pay for security. In the Cyclades thirty-nine SBS men killed forty-one of the enemy, wounded twenty-seven more, and took nineteen prisoners. Their own losses were two killed and three wounded.

However, success on such a scale could not last, and before long every area had had a taste of the SBS and was much more prepared. Furthermore the garrisons were reinforced, and sentries increased and better organised.

The Greek Sacred Squadron took an increasing part in these raids; at Calino the SBS was put under the command of a Greek Major (he had fourteen Greeks and eleven SBS in his party). This raid ran into much more trouble than had been anticipated and had heavy losses, but in return created much destruction and alarm among the enemy.

For some time the SBS had been meditating on the possibilities of a return raid on Simi which the SBS thought had been surrendered too easily. (It could probably have been held a little longer but in the circumstances of that time its loss was inevitable and to have held on longer would probably have inflicted crippling losses on the SBS.) The main snags to making landings on Simi were in the shape of two German destroyers. However, these two snags were eliminated by an expedition of Royal Marine Boom Commando troops who sank them with limpet mines while they lay at anchor in Portotago harbour, Leros.

With the destroyers out of the way the main hazard to landing had been removed, and accordingly a force of 220 (81 SBS and 139 Greek Sacred Squadron) landed on 13th July. They were split into three sections. After fierce fighting the island was retaken and general celebrations held. This was necessarily a somewhat temporary arrangement, for the Germans, once they had realised what had happened, were bound to launch in substantial forces from neighbouring bases. The SBS decided it would be sensible to withdraw before the overwhelming odds arrived but before doing so destroyed vast quantities of German stores and installations; they also took away some useful prisoners.

This was the SBS swan song in the Aegean, for the Greek Sacred Squadron were now well enough trained and equipped to take over that area. It was, of course, appropriate that Greeks should harass the Germans in their own country and, when the time came liberate it. The SBS thenceforward would mainly be used in Italy, Yugoslavia and Albania. However, Lapraik and Harden were left to assist the Greeks.

Lapraik, who was awarded a DSO, OBE, and two MCs was a Doctor of Law and a top-class middle-distance runner; he was also a very capable swimmer. This was a remarkable record by any standards, but all the more so because at the age of eight he had contracted TB of the knee and been a cripple for five years; two of those years he had spent with his leg encased in plaster. He had rebuilt his health by perseverance. In the early days of the war he had been in 51 Commando (then commanded by Major H.J. Cator, who later joined the SAS); this unit established a British Army marching record of 52 miles in 14 hours – mainly over rocky desert country – in which only one man fell out. This, and similar experiences, convinced Lapraik that thorough and enlightened training was the best service that any officer could do for his men. 51 Commando included in its ranks a number of Jews and Arabs who worked together in perfect comradeship and never quarrelled.

The thoroughness of SBS training was a significant factor in keeping their own casualties low. They could collectively move in or out of a town within minutes, however dispersed they might be when the signal was given. They used an amazing variety of weapons, mostly captured. They managed Bredas very well, but had a particular affinity for the Schmeisser. Although the Schmeisser is an automatic not designed for single shot some of the SAS were able to use it as such by lightness on the trigger. Controlled firepower was an essential of success. Some caiques had as many as nineteen machine-guns on board and this enabled them to take on overwhelming odds on occasion – for a few minutes. At Stampalia an HDML – a Harbour Defence Motor Launch – met an enemy destroyer. Two orders followed in rapid succession: 'Open fire: abandon ship'. But enough damage had been done to the destroyer to make the brief exchange eminently worthwhile.

Unfortunately all this expertise was wasted when the SBS, like the LRDG, was badly misused in the northern Adriatic. Because of their excellent fighting reputation they were thrown in against hopeless odds in situations where their own qualities were at a discount. Used properly the SBS had a variety of ways of inflicting damage and alarm on their opponents, who at one time included the notorious 999 (Penal) Division. Having very few people and a large area to cover they used every device they could muster. One was to set up PIATs outside enemy camps, which in late 1943 were surrounded by barbed wire. The PIAT was fired by a simple but ingenious device involving a time-pencil. Targets could therefore be attacked simultaneously, causing much confusion, not least to those trying to estimate SBS numbers.

SBS intelligence was extraordinarily effective. Every island had a signal post transmitting information of enemy movements. One of these was on top of the German Commandant's house on Santorini. It was manned for fifteen months and never detected. How close intelligence agents were to sources of information emerged when it was reported (accurately) that two German Commandants, one on Simi and the other on Kalimnos, had had the misfortune to lose their testicles. One's had fallen to a rifle bullet, the other's to a fragment of a grenade.

A typical SBS action took place at Thira in April 1944. On hearing that a mixed force of 48 Italians and Germans were billeted on the first floor of the Bank of Athens, fourteen SBS decided to winkle them out.

We succeeded in getting the main force into the billets unobserved in spite of barking dogs and sentries [reads a first-hand account]. The living quarters comprised 12 rooms and it was our intention to take the troops there prisoner. This idea had to be abandoned and will have to be abandoned in similar circumstances in the future until raiding parties are issued with good torches. Casualties were sustained during the general mix-up in the dark. Instead, the doors of the rooms were kicked in, a grenade thrown into the room, and two to three magazines of TSMG and Bren emptied into each room. Lieutenant Casulli was killed almost instantaneously and Sergeant Kingston seriously wounded by shots fired either from the rooms or the sentries outside. Two other slight casualties (Privates Trafford and Harris) were also caused in the same way.

During the engagement a German patrol challenged us from outside, but were heavily engaged by Sergeant Nicholson with a Bren fired from the hip. One Italian jumped from the window – a drop of forty feet.

At approximately 0245 hours, and when I was satisfied that all the enemy were killed or wounded, we left the building, carrying Sergeant Kingston. Shots were exchanged with stray enemy during the withdrawal. We returned to the cave to find Lieutenant Balsillie waiting for us with eight prisoners; he had completed a neat job.

Sergeant Kingston was fully conscious when we left the building. He himself, as a medical orderly, considered he was not dangerously wounded. The next day the local doctor was called and on his recommendation we decided to leave him by the roadside for the Germans to pick up, as he had suddenly taken a turn for the worse. He died before this could be done. Arrangements were made with the local doctor for him to be buried with full military honours. The same request was made about Lieutenant Casulli and I have every reason to believe that this was carried out.

As there were still Germans on Crete, on 23rd July, 1944, it was raided once more. 165,000 gallons of petrol were destroyed as well as a number of trucks and staff cars: thirty-two Germans were killed. SBS losses were two men captured; subsequently these two escaped from a prison in Serbia and rejoined the SBS 134 days later. Revisiting Crete was Gunner Jones who had worked with Lassen on the earlier raid; on this occasion he was in a team with Summers, who had now become a Sergeant.

Lodwick relates that Summers, having laid all his bombs, then crawled up to the German guardhouse. He peeped inside and saw some Germans; several were asleep, but one was reading a newspaper. Summers left a heavy charge of explosive on the window-sill and slipped away. He felt that this would round off the raid neatly. It did; it destroyed not only the guardhouse but also set the surrounding vegetation alight.

The new SBS headquarters was at St Angelo and the unit's employment was to be along the Adriatic. While the events described here were going on the rest of the SAS were busily engaged elsewhere, but, for the sake of clarity, it is easier to continue the SBS story and pick up the other threads later.

Proceedings along the Adriatic opened with Lassen taking a patrol to destroy the railway bridge at Karasovici, Yugoslavia. The bridge was destroyed but not without opposition, in fact a mixed force of Germans and Ustachi, numbering four hundred, nearly surrounded the raiding party. However, Lassen cleared a path with grenades and the SBS withdrew safely. The Ustachi (Croat Fascist Nazi supporters) were greatly disliked opponents, for their first activity on capturing a prisoner was to emasculate him – or so it was said.

The opposition which the SBS now encountered came as much from their Allies as from the enemies. The Partisans, who had so far done well with little help, felt that, given time, they could finish off the job perfectly satisfactorily by themselves and resented the sudden incursion of British into their area when the battle – so it seemed to them – was nearly won. They were so suspicious that it was unwise to tell them of plans – in case they should obstruct them. The complete answer to the Partisan philosophy was Lieutenant McGonigal (no relative to the Lieutenant McGonigal who had been killed on the very first (Gazala) SAS raid). He ignored the Partisans completely. In consequence they often followed him into action. The terror and uncertainty created by these raids completely upset the Cetniks who had formerly supported the Germans; in consequence there were soon numerous Cetnik desertions causing dislocation of German plans.

For anyone looking at this scene twenty-five or thirty years later it would naturally appear that with France invaded, Italy half-retaken, and the Russians on the offensive, the war was all over bar the shouting. This was unfortunately not true. A few mistakes, a new weapon or two, and the war could swing the other way again. For people in London the advent of a new terror weapon in the shape of V1s and V2s was enough to destroy any growing complacency and fighting soldiers abroad were only too well aware that a careless move could make them as thoroughly dead as at any time earlier in the war. The Germans might be evacuating certain areas but the end of the war was a long, long way off. Fighting men do not necessarily lose the habit of killing the enemy even if they are retreating; sometimes they can be even more deadly on the retreat than ever they were in the attack.

In September 1944 the Germans were shortening their lines, which meant the evacuation of southern Greece and the Peloponnese. The SBS felt that this gave them a great opportunity – to cut off large numbers of the retreating army, and also to make a thrust across the country to Salonika. This operation was called 'Bucketforce' and was under the command of Jellicoe, now a Lieutenant Colonel.

Patras, the jumping off point, was bluffed into surrender by Major Ian Patterson, an ex-Parachutist who had joined the SAS some time before and shown remarkable gifts for raiding work. Although tough and firm he was worshipped by his men and his death, later, was greatly mourned. Patterson had

110

a mere sixty-two men to compel the surrender of 865 Germans, and 1,600 members of a Greek collaborationist force that was euphemistically known as a 'security battalion'. He switched his 62 men from one point to another with such frequency that the enemy thought they were being attacked by numbers equal to their own. The Greek battalion was persuaded to surrender on the basis that they would not be handed over to their own side (also known as partisans but somewhat different from the Yugoslav bearers of that title). Jellicoe gave his undertaking and obtained a promise from the Greek partisans that there would be no reprisals on the 'security battalion'. Patras was then captured by a total of twenty men, drawn equally from the SBS and the RAF Regiment. The Germans withdrew, and the SBS, amazed at their good fortune so far, decided not to relax but to pursue and cut off the retreating enemy; not least of their ambitions was to harass the enemy so that they would not be able to carry out systematically the demolitions they had planned.

The SBS bluff worked very well for a considerable time. At Megara, however, the Germans began to realise there was something badly amiss. They sent patrols on counter-attack. Even then the bluff did not give way, for the SBS were much more experienced than their opponents at patrol work and captured a number of German prisoners. As the sands were running out, it was as well that a company of the 4th Para brigade had been ordered to drop behind the SBS and reinforce them. Unfortunately the drop coincided with gale force winds and only two-thirds of the parachuters landed safely. The sight of this drop was, however, enough to send the Germans out of Megara.

Athens was clearly the next objective. With Patterson's experienced company, with Milner-Barry, and an American correspondent, Jellicoe set out for Athens in a caique. They landed at Scaramanga, on the outskirts. The Germans were evacuating and the only transport available was two bicycles. Appropriately, Jellicoe, the architect of victory, and Patterson, his chief instrument, rode them side by side into Athens. They were soon followed by 55 members of the SBS. It was not the orthodox way for conquering heroes to enter a city, but these two had no mind to be heroes though they were fully intent on conquering, and it seemed, in the circumstances of their unorthodox progress, quite a suitable mode of entry. Their swift arrival saved much bloodshed for Greece was on the brink of civil war in which many innocent Greeks would have been killed and the only people to profit would have been the Communist Party.

But they did not stay among the rejoicings in Athens for long. Two days later they were on the move, keeping contact with the retreating enemy. Between being delayed by German demolition work, and dodging bombs from our own pilots who mistook them for German stragglers, they made slow progress. When they caught up progress was even slower, for the Germans were retaliating with well-directed machine-gun and mortar fire. And so it went on, SBS and 4 Para pressing, the Germans retreating and hitting back; finally they stood on the Yugoslav frontier, beyond which progress was forbidden.

Sutherland was now in Albania, and Milner-Barry joined him in the town of Korce. Lassen, much to his discontent, which he once but only once voiced to Jellicoe, found himself raiding the remaining coast and islands from the sea; he thought it lacked purpose and excitement, which of course it did. However, no one successfully questioned Jellicoe's dispositions.

But, Lassen was soon in business again and heading for Salonika. He thought the Partisans were displaying too apathetic an attitude towards the Germans and stirred them into more vigorous measures. At first they had tried to restrain him but soon decided it was better to support him however wild the demands he made on them. Eventually Lassen was on the outskirts of the city. His presence and the general harassing, not to mention short severe engagements with the German rearguard, gave the impression that large numbers of British troops were following up, and these were the forward reconnaissance parties. Consequently the Germans hastened to evacuate Salonika before being pinned down in a major battle which might decimate their shrunken forces.

But Crete was still in German hands in November 1944. 13,000 German troops still remained on the island and, although they withdrew into the north-west corner, holding an area of 240 square miles they could, if they wished, make a considerable nuisance of themselves still. Their area included Maleme airfield. Here they were rather inefficiently blockaded by Greek Andartes (Guerillas). It was clear that, apart from one night attack which a joint Greek and SBS force put in, the Greeks were more concerned with an internal power struggle than getting rid of the remnants of their late conquerors. The two main parties were ELAS (Left Wing infiltrated by Communists) and EOK (Right Wing) and each was now hoping to fill the power vacuum it saw in Greece. The Allies had been arming anyone who was prepared to fight against Germans, but as the German threat had disappeared a date (8th December 1944) was fixed for return of these varied weapons. Instead, ELAS decided to make a bid for power. It was a story which later would become all too familiar elsewhere, particularly in the Far East. The resistance group, which had been lavishly supplied with arms, money, food and assistance, had little effect on the enemy, but had stored up supplies for future use. When they staged a coup d'état the resultant government bore little resemblance to the democracy that had been so ardently professed but instead had all the marks of a mean and savage dictatorship. The ELAS, realising that the SBS and the Paras might interfere with their plans if their orders told them to do so, decided to disarm them; their efforts however failed except for one patrol. The SBS then had the unpleasant, but necessary task of restoring order. Exactly one month after the coup d'état, order was restored and the situation was back to normal.

In December 1944 Jellicoe, now a Brigadier, was posted to Haifa for a staff course. His command was taken over by Sutherland, whose S Detachment of the original SBS had rarely been out of contact with the enemy since M, L and S Detachments had been given their separate designations.

Sutherland had ambitions in Istria where he felt a heavy toll might be taken of enemy transport, but instead he had to operate against German held islands in the Adriatic; his base would be Zara, an Italian town which had been cleared of Germans and was now mainly occupied by Yugoslavs. The Yugoslav government and its executives tended to be haughty and obstructive, a characteristic which probably had its roots partly in the temperament of people who had been brought up in conditions of the utmost rigour, and partly in the indoctrination they had been given about the evil intentions of Anglo-American imperialists.

The SBS were well aware that theirs was not a task to be undertaken light-heartedly. The Germans who occupied the islands in the northern Adriatic were soldiers of some experience and many of them had been in the Aegean area. There was nothing casual about their attitude to the expected attacks and every likely target was well guarded, wired and mined. The sea was also full of mines, which had been laid by all sides for different reasons. Any ship which moved through these waters was therefore at considerable risk – as they frequently and disastrously discovered.

One of the raids was on a German strongpoint on Lussin. Casualties were higher than usual and it was not one of the more successful attacks. One of those wounded was Lieutenant Jones-Parry. He was caught in a machine-gun burst but managed to kill the firer and subsequently walk the two miles back to the boat. On being asked how he felt he admitted he did not feel too good. This was hardly surprising as it was then discovered that his right arm was broken and another bullet was lodged in his spleen!

An attempt to destroy the bridge linking the islands of Cherso and Lussin was beaten off by the Germans after heavy fighting. The Germans numbered eighty and the SBS thirty-eight. The SBS showed great skill and determination but lost about half their number; this was a waste of highly trained men on the wrong task and objective. It was clear, after these ventures that the SBS would lose less men and kill more enemy if they temporarily abandoned attacks on strongly held points and instead used their mobility to lay ambushes. These, and the attacks which had preceded them, began to have an effect on enemy morale and soon there was a trickle of desertions. The final reduction of the islands came soon after, when British naval and gunnery support, combined with the assistance of the Royal Marines, enabled a substantial force of partisans to get ashore and compel the islands' surrender.

The SBS was then free to carry out its ambition to move from Istria to Trieste and link up with the Eighth army. This, if it could be accomplished, would be as valuable as the SAS link with 1st Army in the Western Desert days.

Sutherland sent Captain Daniel Riddiford into Istria on 11th March 1945. Istria, although an Italian possession, was populated almost entirely by Slovenes, who disliked Italians, Germans and their Partisan Communist neighbours, with equal impartiality. They would have been happy to have been occupied by an Allied force, with all the material benefits that such an administration would bring. This coast, incidentally, was being watched by the Long Range Desert Group which, following its brilliant activities in the desert had gone on to fight and watch elsewhere. They were now noting the type, speed and course of all enemy ships in the area; this information enabled the RAF to sink large numbers of enemy craft with methodical deadliness.

The SBS main party landed, not without some difficulty, on the night of 12th April 1945. An unexpected hazard was a sudden but vigorous naval battle which took place between a small force of motor launches against a flotilla of German lighters. The ML party was commanded by Lieutenant Commander Timothy Bligh, DSO, DSC, a dashing and intrepid warrior who distinguished himself in the Navy during the war and later rose with speed to the higher realms of the Treasury; unfortunately he died just as he was at the height of his powers. As one bunch of professionals looking at another the SBS admired the brisk and effective determination of this naval action of which they found themselves the surprised witnesses.

In Istria, as in Greece, politics played an important though irritating part. The Yugoslavs longed for control of Istria but realised that if their prestige were ever to amount to anything they must liberate – or appear to liberate – the country themselves. Sadly for them, they had not the military strength to do so. Their only policy was to take over areas which the Germans deemed it fit to relinquish. In this interesting situation the SBS, which seemed quite happy to conduct vigorous guerilla warfare against German units, was something of an embarrassment. The Yugoslav government therefore wished the SBS to refrain from harassing the Germans; it was a request which would bear deeply on any unit, and particularly did it do so on the SBS. Unfortunately politics now seemed more important than war. To their disgust the SBS were evacuated with none of their ambitions fulfilled. Their only consolation was seeing Lieutenant Commander Bligh, referred to above, accept the surrender of forty German craft. As he had only two motor launches and one fighter aircraft at his disposal at the time, and the skippers of the craft were inclined to blow him and then themselves to bits in their despair, this piece of naval diplomacy was a comfort if not entirely a consolation.

The next SBS employment was in support of the Commando Brigade near Lake Comacchio. The Allied offensive seemed to be spent; it was certainly checked. A spring offensive was planned but in the meantime there was stalemate. One way of paving the way to success would be to outflank the enemy. The only way to do this was to drive up between Lake Comacchio and the sea, where there was a well-mined and well-defended spit of sand. This was the area the Commando and SBS were briefed to break through. The lake is about four miles across but only about two feet deep. Eventually on 9th April 1945 this exceptionally difficult crossing was made. Two VCs were won that night, one by a Corporal in the Royal Marine Commando, the other by Anders Lassen; both were killed. Lassen's death, as he advanced along a road silencing first a machine-gun and then four pill-boxes, exceeded anything which he had done previously.

116

In the citation appear the following paragraphs:

. . . machine-gun fire started from the [German] position, and also from two other blockhouses to the rear.

Major Lassen himself then attacked with grenades, and annihilated the first position containing four Germans and two machine-guns. Ignoring the hail of bullets sweeping the road from three enemy positions, an additional one having come into action from 300 yards down the road, he raced forward to engage the second position under covering fire from the remainder of the force. Throwing in more grenades he silenced this position, which was then overrun by his patrol. Two enemies were killed, two captured, and two more machine-guns silenced.

By this time the force had suffered casualties and its fire power was very considerably reduced. Still under a very heavy cone of fire Major Lassen rallied and reorganised his force and brought his fire to bear on the third position. Moving forward himself he flung in more grenades which produced a cry of 'Kamerad'. He then went forward to within three or four yards of the position to order the enemy outside and take their surrender.

Whilst shouting to them to come out he was hit by a burst of spandau fire from the left of the position and he fell mortally wounded, but even whilst falling he flung a grenade, wounding some of the occupants, and enabling his patrol to dash in and capture this final position.

Major Lassen refused to be evacuated as he said it would impede the withdrawal and endanger further lives, and as ammunition was nearly exhausted the force had to withdraw.

By this magnificent leadership and complete disregard for his personal safety Major Lassen had, in the face of overwhelming superiority, achieved his objects. Three positions were wiped out, accounting for six machine-guns, killing eight and wounding others of the enemy and two prisoners were taken. The high sense of devotion to duty, and the esteem in which he was held by the men he led, added to his own magnificent courage, enabled Major Lassen to carry out all the tasks he had been given with complete success.

Lassen was so very much the ideal SAS soldier that it will be of interest to see if any useful lessons can be deduced from his career.

In his schooldays Lassen had shown himself to be

117

intelligent though not over industrious; he was a good all-round athlete and the fastest runner in the school. He said, and it was doubtless true, although only meant as a modest disclaimer of his ability, that he reacted faster than anyone else to the starting gun. He came of an aristocratic family but was adventurous and wanted to see the world; therefore he took a job as a cabin boy and was on a Danish ship when war broke out. In the first six months of the war the Germans sank 29 Danish ships (345 killed or drowned) but Lassen saw no action. Denmark was invaded on 9th April 1940 and was, of course, unable to withstand the Germans. From then on Lassen sailed in a British ship, which saw plenty of action. Lassen was, however, mainly impressed by Londoners, whom he met while in hospital for a short time in 1940.

They are an admirable race [he wrote], these Londoners, who don't care a damn about bombs or Germans. In hospital I was in the same ward as two old fellows whom I considered to be between seventy and eighty. They had both been dug out from the ruins of their bombed houses. They only made a joke of it – and when there was an air raid the possibility they might be hit again didn't even cross their mind.

Lassen's subsequent career in the British army has already been outlined in these pages, but there are a few points which require to be added. During the commando training, which is usually enough to occupy the minds of most people – it included jumping across moats filled with barbed wire, marching 120 miles in four days, and doing boat exercises in vile weather conditions – Lassen was always thinking of additional ideas of damaging the enemy. He was very keen to use a bow and arrow and wrote a letter to the War Office to encourage them to the same way of thinking.

Bow and Arrow used in Modern Warfare [he wrote]: the thought may appear ridiculous, even stupid, to those who are not aware what a wonderful weapon it is.
That we should continue to use in 1941 the same weapon which won victory for the English in the Hundred Years War may seem

118

impossible when one compares the bow with the machine-gun or a tommy-gun.

However, after having attended different training schools and according to what I know about guerrilla warfare, scout patrols, raiding patrols and all that sort of thing I have no doubt that bows and arrows would in many cases prove of great value. [He went on to list the advantages]:

1. The arrow is almost soundless.

2. The arrow kills without shock or pain, so it is unlikely, shall we say, that a man would scream or do anything like that.

3. A well-trained archer can shoot up to fifteen shots a minute.

4. The arrow is as deadly as an ordinary bullet.

5. Actually one does not aim, which at night would be a great advantage – it is more like the way one throws a stone.

He mentioned the disadvantages, one being expense, the other that archery is extremely difficult and requires a great deal of training and interest.

No one would query the bow's deadliness or the need for incessant practice, but arrow wounds were said to be so excruciatingly painful that if a man did not cry out it was because he was paralysed by shock. Lassen's figure of fifteen shots to the minute is 25 per cent faster than the performance of the average trained mediaeval archer who, of course, did little else but practise.

Eventually Lassen received two bows and arrows from the War Office and shot everything from sparrows to stags with them. His addiction to the bow is not as odd as it might seem – it is a hunter's weapon, silent, effective and economical.

According to Lassen's sister Suzanne, he was transferred to the SBS at the request of Jellicoe, who met him while on a short visit to England; Brigadier Laycock agreed to the move. He learnt to parachute in the Lebanon. Although he revelled in all the other arduous training, parachuting was not greatly to his taste; however, he soon qualified.

When in action Lassen behaved with nonchalant calm interspersed with bursts of lightning action. When Simi was

119

being bombed he was caught in the middle of a pulverising air attack. As the bombs crashed around him, and it seemed as if everything would be obliterated, he turned to his companion and enquired plaintively: 'Do you know a remedy for my hair? It's all falling out.' His companion reminded him that his worries looked like being ended summarily, but he ignored what appeared to him to be irrelevant rudeness, and went on: 'I've also lost some teeth. If I go on like this there won't be much left of me.'

Needless to say, Lassen was greatly admired by his men, and he, in his turn, spared no effort in looking after them. However he was never familiar. It might be thought that an officer living in such close contact with his men would soon become on familiar terms with them. This easily happens, and often enough the officer's authority seems to become shared out among the men, leaving him with the ultimate responsibility for decisions he may not have been alone in making. It did not happen with Lassen. Authority never slipped from his grasp, not merely because he was an officer but because he was clearly the best, and the leader.

Lassen became a close friend of Colonel Tzigantes, leader of the Greek Sacred Brigade. The Greeks had gone to Leros to strengthen the defences against the expected German attack. The 'Heros Lokos' had been in existence, though not continuously, since 379 BC and had a long experience of fighting for freedom. It had distinguished itself at the battle of Alamein. Its badge was a sword surrounded by a wreath and its motto 'Return victorious or dead' – said to be the words Greek wives used to their husbands on the eve of battle.

Lassen's ability for leadership was equalled by his capacity for friendship.

Andy had a quality which overshadowed even his physical and moral courage [Jellicoe wrote] and which will always stand out clearest in my memory; that was his sympathy for those who were less fortunate than himself and the love he inspired in them. Whether it was a poor Greek peasant or a Yugoslavian refugee, wherever he went one felt this deep sympathy for the unfortunate, and the affection which these people he had befriended or helped felt for him was quite extraordinary.

120

A British officer wrote of him:

I got an impression of his style when one day his jeep pulled up beneath my office, and the following second he stood in the doorway. It was so terribly silent and quick that I thought, 'By God, that must be the way you appear at the German headquarters; not a sound, just standing there, filling the doorway.'* To get to me he had come twenty paces along a gravel path, up four steps and along a wooden floor. He wore rubber-soled boots but there wasn't so much as a rustle from his clothes – and he had on a crinkly gas cape against the rain ...

The VC has been awarded twice to soldiers who were not British nationals; on both occasions they were Danes.

There are numerous stories about Lassen: his habit of befriending disreputable and smelly dogs, the occasion when he suddenly stood up in a boring conference with senior officers and announced 'I go now' (which he did, leaving them dumbfounded), and the devotion he inspired in his men. But the final word on him should go to Colonel Lapraik, in whose M Squadron – after the departure of Fitzroy Maclean – Lassen fought:

Many people think of Andy as a hit-and-run adventurer, superb as a raider but no more. In fact he was a lot more. He could have commanded a battalion with distinction, and perhaps gone higher. His attention to the welfare of his men was exemplary. He was outstanding in every way but completely unassuming with it.

Inevitably the question will be asked: 'What was there to show for all this romantic activity in the Aegean, Greece, and the Adriatic? Was it just a welcome break from normal regimental training for those taking part, or did it do anything constructive towards shortening the war?'

This question has been partly answered already. Small numbers of men can cause damage and despondency over a wide area if they are properly trained to the task. This is what

* He would not. The SBS trained men never to frame themselves in doorways when raiding.

happened in the Aegean, tying up large numbers of enemy troops who would otherwise have been used elsewhere. Such forces can establish contacts with, and supply, reliable elements in, resistance movements. Had the SBS not been pressing into Athens the enemy could and would have done what the Japanese did in the Far East, that is, hand over their weapons to subversive elements which would give us endless trouble in the future, or if not us, potentially friendly governments. Sometimes – as in Greece – the fact that our own men are in the area and know where to go, can avoid long-drawn and expensive operations later. It is, of course, unthinkable, that any enemy should be allowed to occupy a vulnerable area and be allowed to stay there unmolested. In the Aegean, Adriatic and Greece they were much more than merely molested; they were attacked, bewildered, driven back and slaughtered. Here, as in the desert and France, a few dozen men could, and did, immobilise thousands.

Few units can have achieved so much with so little as the SBS. They inflicted casualties, blew up dumps and destroyed stores, made the Germans use scarce shipping to safeguard routes and eventually, by their presence, stopped civil war and chaos occurring in various parts of the country.

# CHAPTER IV

# A Footing in Italy

For the sake of clarity we have followed the SBS up till one month from the end of the war in Europe. It is now necessary to return to the beginning of 1943 and look at the experiences of SRS (SAS) which was Major Mayne's command. At this time existing formations were liable to be allotted new names and numbers, while unorthodox formations, known to their cynical fellow soldiers as 'funnies' were created at short, irregular intervals. This complex of new and unfamiliar names was designed to confuse and dismay the enemy; if it confused them half as much as it did our own nationals and allies the process must have reaped a rich harvest indeed. Still under its name of Long Range Desert Group that enterprising unit was watching the sea and engaging in whatever fighting it could find. There were a number of other anomalies in 'Land Forces Adriatic', and many nebulous and secret formations whose real point and purpose is to this day shrouded in obscurity. Not least compelling of the arguments for reviving the SAS from its post-war disbandment was that all these mysterious units could be better and more efficiently run if they came under one umbrella in peacetime, and the most practical way of doing that would be to incorporate them all in the SAS.

As the African campaign drew to an end – it was officially over on 12th May 1943 – plans were made for the next phase of the war. At the Casablanca conference in January 1943 Roosevelt and Churchill had agreed that although the quickest and best way to end the war in Europe was to drive straight through France to the heart of Germany the time for such an attack was not yet. Much had to be prepared before an invasion of the Continent could be a certain success. The date of the invasion of France was settled for May 1944 – it eventually took place on 6th June 1944 – but in the meantime it was accepted that the capture of Sicily would safeguard the vital Mediterranean sea route, tie down German divisions, and probably cause the collapse of the Fascist regime in Italy; Mussolini's hold on the country had been loosened by the loss of his African Empire and it was thought that another blow might topple him from power and probably take Italy out of the war.

The forecast that a successful invasion of Sicily would probably end the rule of Mussolini was correct but the Allies underestimated the German reaction. As we have seen in Rhodes and the Aegean they showed no inclination to yield territory without severe fighting, and in Italy they acted equally promptly, occupying Rome and other vital points. The German forces in Italy were commanded by a general of great resilience in the person of Field Marshal Kesselring and, in consequence, Allied progress, even with overwhelming air superiority, was painfully slow. Kesselring was an expert at dogged resistance and built a series of formidable defensive lines; the most notable were the Gustav Line which went through Cassino and the Gothic Line just north of Pisa. The 'quick collapse' of Italy consequently dragged on for the best part of another two years. In the latter part of this time many of the Allied resources had been taken away to be used in the invasion of France and the troops left in Italy shared with the 14th Army in Burma the feeling that they were a 'forgotten army'.

However, it was abundantly clear that this situation of a slow advance over rugged country offered very considerable opportunities to a unit such as the SAS. It could be used to prepare the way for an invasion, and once that had taken place, create destruction and despondency in the enemy rear areas. What it was neither capable of, nor suited for, was being sandwiched in between enemy reinforcements and their front line. It had neither the numbers nor the equipment nor the logistic support for such a task. However, not for the last time, this wasteful use of highly-trained specialist personnel seemed a distinct possibility. All too often in military history we see specialists used on tasks where their special abilities are wasted, or even more frequently, disbanded and never used at all. It was with some relief therefore that the SRS having been training as skiers in addition to their other accomplishments found themselves chosen to land in Sicily at Cape Murro di Porco, which is on the south eastern corner of the island – even though it was a commando operation. In July 1943 the Raiding Squadron, only three hundred in number, had captured three batteries, cleared the Cape area, and captured five hundred prisoners; their only losses were one killed and two wounded. The story of this operation is given in *These Men are Dangerous* by D.L. Harrison, who took part as a lieutenant. The title of that book was taken from Hitler's personal directive which ran '*Captured SAS troops must be handed over at once to the nearest Gestapo unit. These men are very dangerous and the presence of SAS troops in any area must be immediately reported. They must be ruthlessly exterminated.*'

While the SAS were paving the way for the landing in Sicily, the SBS raid on Crete – already reported – was going ahead under Jellicoe, and Verney and Brinkworth were busy on Sardinia. The success of these raids may be judged by the fact that Harrison did not see a single German aircraft as the invasion – code named 'Husky' – sailed for Sicily.

After the success at Cape Murro di Porco the SRS re-embarked on their transport, the *Ulster Monarch*, and after a somewhat eventful night were put off at Augusta. To their surprise they met very little opposition. At the conclusion of their task they were taken off in two destroyers. In the event the real battle for Augusta was still to take place, for there were large German forces in the area. Nevertheless the initial probe had destroyed enemy equipment and created considerable alarm and disturbance. From then on the SAS waited – but in vain – for an assignment. Jobs which they had been allotted were suddenly swept away at the last moment in case they should become entangled with our own advancing troops. They waited, and trained.

The Sicily campaign was over in 38 days. It was a great

Allied success, the only drawback being that it was a great German success also. Owing to the large numbers of German anti-aircraft guns in the area, and the brilliance of their ferrying and general disposition, the Germans managed to evacuate 60,000 men and took off the island more equipment than they had put in. It was a foretaste of the sort of opposition the Allies might expect on the Italian mainland.

The next SAS task was to land at Bagnara on the mainland, seize the town, and so disrupt the German line of communication that they would be less likely to make a stand in what is known as the toe of Italy. As every schoolboy gratefully knows the outline of Italy is easily remembered as it looks like a human leg kicking a little football – Sicily.

The scene on arrival was one with which all SAS and SBS troops became familiar later. After a swift and silent landing the British would be seen and recognized by the local people, whose joy would know no bounds. Their pleasure would be freely and loudly expressed, much to the horror of the SAS who were well aware that their presence might only be temporary and the enemy would wreak substantial revenge on the local people for the welcome they had provided. Even worse was the fact that after their presence had been given away the SAS would still be hampered by this embarrassing but premature welcome as 'liberators'. This might become serious if the Germans decided to put in a strong counter attack. Fortunately, on this occasion the Germans put up very little opposition, and as other British units came into the area quickly the SAS task was soon over.

The next assignment was Termoli, a port on the Adriatic. During September the Germans had occupied Rome, and Skorzeny – an operator whom the SAS regarded with ungrudging admiration – had liberated Mussolini in a daring raid. Otto Skorzeny was an Austrian in the German army who had ideas very closely related to the SAS concept of warfare. In addition to kidnapping Mussolini from what was thought to be a secure area he had also whisked away Admiral Horthy from Russian control and kept Hungary in the war; he also organized the infiltration and deception tactics of the

126

Germans in the 'Battle of the Bulge' in the Ardennes in 1944. At the beginning of October the Americans had captured Naples but the main factor in the war was that the Germans were well dug-in with heavily prepared positions. Later the SAS would be used in a more appropriate rôle but here, as in Sicily, the unit was a small-scale commando, as its temporary name clearly indicated.

On 3rd October 1943 the SRS, in company with No. 3 Commando, and 40 Royal Marine Commando, were detailed to capture the port and town of Termoli. This would upset German defence plans. No.3 Commando was allotted the task of landing and building up a beachhead through which 40 Royal Marine Commando and the SRS (SAS) would move in. No.3 Commando successfully accomplished its task without meeting opposition; this state of affairs would not last long, and there would be plenty of fighting later. The SAS were briefed to seize and hold a vital road junction which lay two kilometres south east of the town. This was where Highway 16 joined Highway 87, linking Naples and Termoli.

Although the initial landing had the advantage of surprise it did not take long for opposition to rally. From this point onwards it was a desperate battle in which the SAS, like the other units, took heavy casualties. 207 had landed, and out of them twenty-one had been killed, twenty-four wounded, and twenty-three taken prisoner. These last had been encircled by the First German Parachute Division.

Mayne was reported to have conducted a minor war single-handed. He was observed to have killed twelve Germans early in the fighting and then, when a truck-load of men – twenty-nine in all – had been killed by a German shell he went off on an expedition of his own. He gave no account of what had occurred but it was thought that he had exacted some adequate revenge for the incident. However, it seems unlikely that he would have wiped out 29 men single-handed.

Mayne's exploits were often so devastating that accounts of them may appear to exaggerate. He seemed to have a charmed life, but possibly some part of his 'luck' was his amazingly quick reaction. Those who fought with him and knew him

127

well said that he was born in the wrong century. In the distant past he would have been one of the great warrior kings whose exploits in battle are thought to have been exaggerated by the chroniclers, a man who wielded weapons which no one else could handle, who inspired devotion in his followers and who was also renowned for his intellect and culture. Accounts of such supermen – Charlemagne, de Courcy, Godfrey de Bouillon, Richard I, Edward IV – are often dismissed as exaggerations, but not by those who went to battle with Mayne, or even watched his performance in the boxing ring or Rugby football field.

The Termoli assignment, like previous engagements in Sicily or Italy, was obviously not the sort of operation for which the SAS was organized and trained. Nevertheless, it proved certain points. One was that the SAS could cope with entirely different types of fighting if needed, another was that if there was no obvious employment for the SAS in its proper rôle then it could be very useful in others. It follows that if the SAS was used in Commando type operations in Italy it was right that they should be used in similar tasks in the Oman. Nevertheless the logic of this is unlikely to prevent the SAS deploring their wrongful use, nor other units lamenting that the SAS is capturing jobs that properly belong to other formations.

The Sicily/Italy campaign brought Lieutenant Colonel W.S. 'Bill' Stirling into conflict with higher authority; his idea was to drop small parties of SAS men in Sicily and Italy and play havoc with German communications. Especially did he wish to drop the SAS into the triangle enclosed by Spezia, Bologna and Florence, where they would be able to do massive damage to the railway tracks over which the Germans were rushing reinforcements to the front. In the event twenty men only were permitted to drop, but they managed to derail fourteen trains. Unfortunately many more men would have been needed to keep the lines out of action for any length of time; a party of this size simply could not cover the necessary ground.

It was a foretaste of what was to become a bitter dispute,

leading to the resignation of Lieutenant Colonel W.S. Stirling. To him, and to the SAS, it was crystal clear that the sensible and economical way to use SAS troops was far in the enemy rear; to higher authority this was too loosely controlled and they preferred not to have small parties of legalised bandits roaming around far behind the enemy lines. Subsequently the Higher Command realised that where there was a rear area this was the ideal employment for SAS but, unfortunately, by that time rear areas were becoming much more crowded, and a lot of very good opportunities had been missed.

However, that nebulous body called the 'Higher Command' contained certain senior officers, who understood the SAS and spoke highly of it. Among them was Lieutenant General M.C. Dempsey, who commanded 13 Corps. He described the SAS work at Cape Murro di Porco as brilliant and mentioned that the Termoli operation – in which, of course, the SAS men were in company with the Commandos – had caused the Germans to switch the 16 Panzer division from the west coast to the east coast and in general eased the way for the Allied advance.

In my military career [said Dempsey], and in my time I have commanded many units, I have never met a unit in which I had such confidence as I have in yours. And I mean that.

He went on to give what he considered to be the six reasons for the SAS success:

Firstly you take your training seriously. That is one thing which has always impressed me about you.

Secondly you are well-disciplined. Unlike some who undertake this specialized and highly-dangerous job you maintain a standard of discipline and cleanliness which is good to see.

Thirdly, you are physically fit, and I know you well enough to know you will always keep that up.

Fourthly, you are completely confident in your own abilities – yet not to the point of over-confidence.

Fifthly, despite that confidence you plan carefully.

129

Last of all, you have the right spirit, which I hope you will pass on to those who may join you in the future.

While SRS (SAS) was busy with the events described above, 2 SAS under Lieutenant Colonel W.S. Stirling, was operating with the 1st Army. It had begun in North Africa but had found the going difficult, partly because of rugged terrain and partly because the enemy positions were static. However just as 1 SAS had been fortunate in being able to draw in high quality experienced men from Layforce so 2 SAS had a similar bonus in recruiting from 62 Commando. Their experience enabled them to mount raids on Pantellaria, Lampedusa, Sicily and Sardinia. 2 SAS trained at Philippeville, where they were joined by Major Roy Farran, later to win fame in Italy, France and elsewhere. In *Winged Dagger*, he describes the training as follows:

Before a recruit was accepted he had to run to the top of a six hundred foot mountain and back again in sixty minutes. Failures in this final test were returned to the Infantry Depot on the other side of the hill.

There were long route marches with sixty-pound packs, practice in night infiltration and various schemes to encourage self-reliance in the men. It was emphasised that the method of approach to the operation area was of secondary importance. That which really mattered was what you did when you got there. We were trained to land by sea in fast surf using West African dories, to infiltrate overland by foot or in jeep, and in the normal parachute drill in an old fuselage. We experimented with all kinds of sabotage devices, and close-quarter shooting was taught in a style which would have shocked old instructors in the Small Arms School at Hythe.

For the first ten days my body ached so much that I could only listen with open mouth to the tales of the old hands in the Mess, but gradually I became fit enough to be restored to my normal low intelligence. My seniority gave me a post as second-in-command to Sandy Scratchley, who was commanding a newly-raised squadron then in training for a landing in Sicily. About a fortnight before the Allied landings in Sicily, Bill Stirling revealed the exact nature of our task in a lecture in the Operations Hut. We were to land a short time ahead of the Highland Division to seize a certain lighthouse which was suspected of housing a number of machine-guns so sited as to be able to sweep the beaches on which the landings were to take place. He showed us an air photograph of the island on which the lighthouse was situated and left us to work out our plan. He had a great knack for appreciating the crux of a problem, and we readily agreed to his wise modifications. At the time most of the unit was much more concerned with large parachute operations in Northern Sicily, Sardinia and Italy, so that we were left very much to ourselves in our minor tasks.

Immediately before the operation the unit moved to Msakin, near Sousse. Unfortunately the lush surroundings at Philippeville had contained malarial mosquitos, and at the new camp the effects were soon seen. Thirty-two out of forty-five were out of action within two days, and the casualties included Scratchley. By the time the landing party embarked most of the remainder were affected.

In the event, the landing on the tip of Cape Passero was unopposed, and the lighthouse was occupied without resistance. Italian morale seems to have been destroyed by the weight of the Allied bombardment. With its original mission accomplished the SAS filled in time picking off machine-gunners further inshore, and awaiting orders. These came via Randolph Churchill, their liaison with the Highland Division. He strolled up unconcernedly through a stream of bullets and informed the SAS they were to return to Bizerta for a fresh assignment. However, the land battle for Sicily went well, and 2 SAS were not needed for the time being.

Although lucky in their initial recruitment 2 SAS were on stonier ground when it came to expansion. Much of the material they had to accept from the Infantry Depot was far below the required standard. Of the better quality volunteers many had their transfers blocked by COs. And all the time the General Staff was looking at the SAS and wondering whether it should be in existence at all. Assignments were minor commando-type operations, which the SAS cheerfully accepted, hoping they would pave the way to more suitable employment later.

September brought the Taranto landing, which was uneventful. On the way in the convoy heard that Italy had surrendered but that Mussolini had been snatched out of Allied hands. However, even if the Italians wished to retire from the war the Germans had no such intention, nor were they prepared to let their unwilling allies go.

After finding the town clear of opposition the SAS pushed inland along the main road. Their task was to find the Germans, test the resistance, and if possible infiltrate their rear areas. Small groups of enemy were encountered, engaged, and killed or captured. A complication was the enthusiastic welcome which the Italians gave to their liberators. Jeep crews were literally pelted with presents. The enthusiasm of the liberators soon wore off after they had been struck several times with grapes, walnuts, apricots and even, on one occasion, with wet fish.

The party moved from Taranto to Ginosa, and thence to Riverella. At the latter town they linked up with Canadians of the 8th Army who had come up from Messina. Between Riverella and Grassano it became obvious the Germans were ahead in position and there was a chance of infiltration. Moreover the Canadians were advancing in strength and there was no further requirement for the SAS in that area.

The next move was to Bari, where the unit came under command of 4th Armoured Brigade. Bari had been captured by 'Popski's Private Army'.* In a village called Stormarella there was half a day's street fighting.

In the last dash [Farran wrote] I found myself crawling across a dung heap with three other officers and no men. A Schmeisser was chipping the plaster from the last house behind us, its bullet ricocheting off with a whine to the other side of the street. In the odd glances I obtained between crawling through the barbed wire and throwing myself down in the dung, it appeared that the firing was coming from the corner of a fig grove. Most infuriating of all I had lost my Luger. Peter Jackson threw a grenade and then we all stood up and poured a fusillade into the suspected bushes. They were the last shots of the skirmish for the German withdrew from the area.

* See *Popski's Private Army*, V. Peniakoff, London 1950.

132

Jackson was the grandson of a double VC. On the way to Foggia the party ran into heavy German fire. Jackson's jeep was set alight but he kept his guns going as the others withdrew. When the flames reached the petrol they hopped out and ran into the woods under cover of the black smoke. The Germans gave pursuit but abandoned it after a time. Jackson and his two companions ran for three miles then borrowed a pony and trap to complete their journey. Jackson was killed a few months later in a jeep accident.

Foggia, which the Germans did not contest, was a rich prize. Around it lay valuable airfields which the Allies proceeded to use with much effect. They gave the Allies the opportunity to make full use of their local air superiority and to push the bomber offensive into southern Europe.

Advancing from Foggia the SAS were engaged in skirmishes of varying severity. In one of these Farran was wounded:

There was an enormous explosion. We threw ourselves trembling on the ground fearing that our presence was known; it flashed through my mind that we must have exploded a trip mine. And then clods of earth and bricks came whistling down from the sky above. I was hit on the side of the face by a large lump of masonry. Blood poured over my shirt and I thought my jaw was broken. The others helped me into the shelter of the vines. I felt ill – very ill. Someone produced a hip flask and poured neat cognac down my throat for I could not swallow.

Nevertheless Farran did not relinquish command and was much cheered to learn that his party of twelve had actually taken the town of Lucera.

In reading about battle, privation, and sudden death, the reader might naturally feel that seasoned warriors who seemed to thrive on discomfort, hardship and danger, were unaware of any other sort of life and values. This would be far from the truth.

There were handsome white oxen carving furrows in impossible slopes; peasant women in bright kerchiefs were bent over their hoes;

133

here and there the brown earth changed to green where the grapes grew; some of the stony ground was shaded by orderly lines of olives; and from the crests of the hills neat white cottages looked like rosettes sewn on a patchwork quilt. This was a land of peace. If war is civilization, you can keep your flush lavatories, your nylon tooth-brushes and your vulgar motor cars. Give me rather a two-roomed casa with a strong wife, salami sausages hung from the rafters and strings of onions from the windows, two pigs in a sty, three oxen in my stable, and a plot of land which is my own. (Winged Dagger)

And then it was back to Bari, and a rôle more in keeping with SAS possibilities, though not, as it happened, a particularly successful one. There were a number of escaped British prisoners roaming around behind the enemy lines and it was the SAS task to find them and get them out. The plans were to drop parachuters within appropriate areas, locate the ex-prisoners, and then guide them to the beaches where the Navy would pick them up. The hazards were the Germans who were liable to scatter the parties before they could be rescued, and the difficulty of making an accurate landfall on a featureless coast. The enterprise went on for two somewhat frustrating months.

Thence to reunion with SRS (SAS) at Termoli. There they met the Commando Brigadier, J.F. Durnford-Slater, and his Brigade Major, Brian Franks. The latter would command 2 SAS later and also be largely responsible for resuscitating the regiment from its post-war disbandment. Farran, who could scarcely be described as excitable, said of this occasion:

The building had been hit only a few minutes before by a shell which killed the Staff Captain. Brigadier Durnford-Slater, and especially the Brigade Major, Brian Franks, struck me as being incredibly cool amongst it all. When we were led out of a position in the windows of the hotel it was humiliating that I felt forced to duck at every shell, whereas Sandy only half-ducked and Brian Franks walked on, as if nothing had happened.

Franks, like Verney, Jellicoe and Sutherland, was an Etonian. One feels that the SAS could have been invented by John Buchan, for most of its leading characters would fit

134

perfectly into his novels. Scottish aristocrats, Etonians, brilliant athletes – Mayne, Lewes, Langton and Rowe – famous riders – Scratchley and Hislop – public schoolboys who had led lives of bizarre adventure all over the world – these settled down and worked in perfect harmony and friendship with much less startling personalities. It was, as has been pointed out, not so much a regiment as a way of life – and it still is. But, of course, the secret of it all is that nobody cares who you are or where you come from but what you are, what you can do, and where you are going.

The last operation performed by 2 SAS in Italy was an entirely satisfactory SAS employment. Sixteen men embarked on an MTB, landed by rubber boats and cut the railway line between Ancona and Giulianova. There were various alarms and discomforts, such as a German submarine recharging its batteries just off the point at which they wished to land, and torrential rain which made movement difficult. At one point they decided to check their bearings by pretending they were German, and enquiring the whereabouts of the nearest cross-roads from an old Italian. He escorted them – and then said good-bye in English. They blew the line in sixteen places and also demolished seven telegraph poles and an electric pylon.

The return journey – of seventy miles – was extremely difficult as the rain had made all the mountain paths so slippery that ascent was almost impossible. One of the party – Corporal Clarke – was a little too well-covered to be much of a marcher and it was said that he rolled further than he walked. However, his contribution to morale was tremendous as he commented on his own and others' misfortunes with dry witticisms. On this – and on many other occasions – the return journey would not have been possible without assistance from friendly villagers who housed, fed and advised the raiders.

Like SRS (SAS) these Italian adventures of 2 SAS came to an end in 1943. In March 1944 they went back to England, and rejoined the rest of the SAS in Ayrshire.

# CHAPTER V

# Reorganisation and the North-West Europe Campaign

By 1944 the successes of the SAS in the Western Desert, Italy and the Aegean, had convinced the Higher Command that SAS units should be continued rather than dispersed. The decision was based not only on the activities of the SAS but also the performance of the LRDG and Wingate's deep penetration groups in Burma. Accordingly, in January 1944, approval was given for the formation of HQ, SAS Troops, under Lieutenant General Browning. Brigadier R.W. McLeod, who would later become General Sir Roderick McLeod was appointed commander of a brigade made up of 1 SAS, 2 SAS, 3 and 4 French Parachute Battalions and a Belgian Independent Parachute Squadron which later became the Belgian SAS Regiment. F Squadron GHQ Reconnaissance Regiment (Phantom) was attached, under command, as a brigade signal section. The brigade strength was 2,500.

In order to make the best possible use of the new brigade a special branch of the staff at HQ Airborne troops was established under Lieutenant Colonel I.G. Collins,* who was very experienced in planning commando and SAS operations, and also in co-ordinating them with the activities of special agents. Agents in occupied territory were the sphere of SOE or Special Operations Executive. Lieutenant Colonel Collins managed to carry out his onerous task approved by one and all, although in the early stages there were many who forecast that the difficulties would be insuperable and that his

---

* A pre-war Davis Cup tennis player.

task would be impossible. It will be appreciated that effective use of SAS troops depended on co-operation from many quarters and necessitated a close and understanding relationship with the exiled government in whose countries the SAS was proposing to operate.

It will be noted that the SBS was not included in this command structure. This is hardly surprising as its theatre of operations was in south-east rather than north-west Europe; it therefore came under Land Forces Adriatic. Nevertheless, although going its separate way, the SBS still felt itself to be SAS and wore the beige beret and badge. Subsequently Lieutenant Colonel David Sutherland, MC, of S Section SBS, commanded 21 SAS when the TA regiment was re-established in conjunction with the Artists Rifles. Nowadays there is a Special Boat Section in the Royal Marines and it is therefore thought to have a connection with the old SBS; there is however no direct link although it will not be forgotten that the SBS derived from a wartime commando unit.

The task which fell to Brigadier McLeod was an exacting one. Both 1 and 2 SAS resented being put under the command of 1 Airborne but had no wish to create any difficulties over the matter. There were a few internal tensions, such as the fact that members of 1st Army and members of 8th Army were such rivals that they were scarcely on speaking terms, but this was as nothing to the two French battalions who were prepared to fight each other on sight. There was also a little problem of what is now called community relations. The local landowners, although delighted to welcome the SAS into their area, were slightly nonplussed at finding salmon fishing practised with grenades and sheep liable to disappear into the cookhouse. Brigadier McLeod had difficulties at all levels and on all sides with the highly individualistic troops which formed his new command, and it seems doubtful if either his difficulties, his efforts, or loyalty were properly appreciated by those under his command at the time.

The most unfortunate event of this period was the

resignation from the SAS of Lieutenant Colonel W.S. 'Bill' Stirling. The initial employment visualized for SAS troops was that after D Day they should be dropped just behind the landing area between the enemy infantry and his armoured reserve. It was not so much that this was a near suicidal mission which angered the SAS but that it was an ineffective form of employment; there would be no time to organise proper damage to the enemy, and greater opportunities elsewhere would be missed.

This was a serious situation for a volunteer unit [Farran put it], since our main allegiance was to our Colonel, in whom we had the greatest confidence. I knew the full facts and contemplated resigning, since I fully supported Bill Stirling's views over our proper rôle. If I had decided to go, almost all the regiment would have gone with me. As it was, Bill Stirling took the broad view and asked me to stay under Brian Franks, whose behaviour I had so much admired during the battle of Termoli. I was very keen to fight with the SAS in France and, as far as I am concerned, what Bill Stirling says goes. I agreed to stay. I have never regretted it since, for Brian Franks proved to be one of the best commanding officers one could wish for, and at least we knew that we were to be finally employed in exactly the way Bill Stirling had visualized.

In the event the SAS employment was never entirely strategic and towards the end of the war was inevitably purely tactical.* In France, Belgium, Holland and Italy SAS parties attacked rear headquarters and destroyed communications, gathered and relayed information, and co-operated with local resistance groups but in Germany they were employed on reconnaissance, harassing attacks, counter-intelligence and the capture of war-criminals.

Needless to say the diversity and difficulty of many of the SAS tasks required high standards from the planners as well as from the men on the ground. Parties which were operating behind the enemy line might be required to take on additional

* Brigadier McLeod fought a continuous battle – which was largely successful – to ensure that SAS troops were not wrongfully employed.

tasks, might stay there much longer than had been anticipated, and might require variations in equipment. In general operational planning would be done on the basis of resources immediately available. It was soon clear that these 'resources' would need to be expanded rapidly. Furthermore a separate base organisation for the SAS had to be arranged, and air supply be co-ordinated with 1 Airborne HQ, Special Forces HQ, and 38 Group RAF. There was a considerable problem in the fact that the portable radios used in the field were of low-power, and therefore had to work to high-power, highly sensitive apparatus at the base; the latter was installed by the BBC at 1 Airborne HQ. Here, as in the desert, enormous responsibility was placed on the Signals personnel, who met every demand made on them. A vital factor was the GHQ Liaison Regiment, better known as 'Phantom'. This had been founded by Lieutenant Colonel (later Major General) G.F. Hopkinson, who commanded it.

The broad task for Phantom (who wore a white P as a shoulder flash) was to find out what was happening in forward areas and radio the information straight back to GHQ – not the Paschendaele spirit at all! It was an envied unit for its members received Intelligence pay and, in view of the responsibility of their task, tended to be promoted quickly. Among the members of this unit were John Hislop (of racing fame), J.J. Astor, Hugh Fraser (later Minister for Air), Maurice Macmillan (son of Harold Macmillan), David Niven (the actor), Sir Richard Keane and Michael Oakeshott (later to be Head of the London School of Economics).

The SAS had one squadron, F, attached to it. Although Phantom had a different mission from SAS there were considerable similarities between the two units; both were mobile, flexible, unorthodox, persistent and extremely fit. Colonel Hopkinson, who was later killed in Italy, insisted on the highest possible standards, and the unit therefore combined cavalry dash with the expertise of professional signalling. Phantom exploded two illusions: one was that cavalrymen and infantrymen could not be made into top-notch signallers; and the second was that Royal Signals personnel would not readily adapt to hazardous reconnaissance work.

The SAS had had a previous link with Phantom for Major (as he then was) Brian Franks had commanded H Squadron in the desert before being invalided home in the autumn of 1941. Subsequently he returned to the Commandos and later commanded 2 SAS.

The wartime story of Phantom was written by R.C.T. Hills in *Phantom Was There* and the full account given by Philip Warner in *Phantom*, published by Kimbers in 1982.

F Squadron had to begin by adding parachuting to their other accomplishments. Two patrols went to 1 SAS and two more to 2 SAS; the French and Belgian regiments had their own signals who also worked back to F Squadron HQ. All were Phantom trained. Patrols carried the Jedburgh set which did not require batteries and could be carried by two men. Midget receivers were also used for picking up BBC messages. The BBC was of course constantly giving messages, sometimes in code and sometimes – if personal – in clear. It was possible to listen to an ordinary BBC programme and be quite unaware that a simple entertainment carried eagerly awaited information to a host of overseas agents.

There were of course, problems. There were the inevitable language difficulties which occur in mixed units, and there was occasional friction of the type which ensues when specialists feel their toes are being trodden on. But friction was eased and difficulties overcome.

Pigeons were used with great success, although occasionally one would decide the homeward journey was not worth it and would decide to stay abroad. They were particularly valuable for indicating bombing targets for they could carry small maps and diagrams.

F Squadron was commanded by Major the Hon. J.J. Astor. One of the patrols which was sent to 2 SAS was commanded by Captain John Hislop. He wrote a book about his experiences with Phantom, with F Squadron and the SAS, entitled *Anything but a Soldier*. It was a modest title, for his abilities as a soldier were second only to his abilities on the

140

Turf where his reputation was international. Hislop mentions that Astor was one of the best W/T operators in the regiment.

According to Hislop the Airborne planners used to think up uses for SAS troops which – if put into effect – would have rapidly killed off all the personnel in the regiment. One of them, apparently, was to drop a few SAS and a large number of dummies into the Calais area immediately before D Day in order to give the Germans a false idea of where the invasion would take place. Hislop also mentioned that the SAS was something of a 'Foreign Legion' and that although the system worked well enough on active service it became rather difficult in England as some of its members were not officially enlisted in the British Army. Although not easily surprised, Hislop noted that the SAS was even more individualistic than Phantom; although capable of walking for hundreds of miles, on one occasion they held up a train merely because they wanted a lift.

Hislop's first operation was 'Loyton' in the Vosges, which will be described more fully later. Even for people with steady nerves and battle experience the feeling of being behind enemy lines – particularly when the enemy are actively looking for them – can be somewhat wearing. Hislop and his companions had a fairly narrow escape on arrival and then settled down to a few quieter days.

The respite of those few days was a halcyon calm [Hislop wrote] after the stormy passage of our encounter and escape, which I welcomed. It emphasised, once again, the extraordinary contrasts found in the complex pattern of war ... Here was beauty and tranquillity, the hours revolving round us softly and smoothly ... My thoughts strayed down corridors of the past and pondered what lay beyond the door of the future. I repeated in my mind favourite pieces of poetry and memorised others copied into a pocket book which, happily, was in one of my pockets. It was to prove a solace both to me and to some of my companions throughout the operation, becoming known as The Anthology.

A further mental stand-by were the many lines of Milton learnt at Wellington for the School Certificate, and later in life, through having developed a delight in the beauty of language. In times of stress it is the resources of the mind rather than those of the body which enable the individual to face the issue.

There were certainly issues to be faced. He goes on to say:

By now the Germans were very much alive to our presence, and began to move troops into the area. We had to keep on the move continually. Every now and then the Germans would find our camp and move in to attack, but always we got away. The forests of the area were a great boon, since they made it difficult for the Germans to find us and, having done so, to pin us down. They did not seem anxious to stray far from the tracks and never ventured into the woods after dark.

When it rained fires could be lit with safety, as the mist made the smoke invisible. Except for the cold at nights, the chronic diarrhoea produced by the unaccustomed diet, to which the French were immune, and the sudden periodical appearance of the Germans, life was tolerable, if uncomfortable and somewhat nerve-racking.

When we moved camp, unless surprised by the Germans, we always travelled by night. A Maquis guide would lead the way, sometimes in impenetrable darkness and through thick woods, when we would follow holding on to each other's belts so as not to lose contact.

Life brightened up considerably with the arrival of Brian Franks and twenty SAS.

I found Brian, whom I had known slightly before the war, an excellent commander. In build tall, lean and athletic, he was by nature cheerful, understanding, full of initiative and brave, appreciated the exigencies of the circumstances in which we were operating, and left us to get on with working the wireless without interference.

Parties of the SAS would go out on operations, such as mining roads, reconnoitring concentration of enemy armour and noting the map reference, which we would send back on the wireless enabling the RAF to come over and bomb them, and ambushing unsuspecting German troops. Every now and then we would be supplied, when all of us assembled at the DZ to receive the drops. It was hard work, since the place had to be cleared by first light and everything had to be carried to whichever camp we were occupying, these always being high up a mountain.

142

To Hislop, at the time, 'Loyton' seemed an expensive failure. Of the ninety-two men who took part thirty-one were killed, twenty-eight of them being executed by the Gestapo after capture. But as he says:

It was not until later that the discovery was made of the disruption and alarm to which our presence gave rise among the Germans. The troops in the area were kept in a state of permanent tension, never knowing when they were likely to be ambushed, or blown up by a mine laid on the road, or the strength of our force and how to pin it down.

Instead of being able to contain the district with a few sparsely scattered units of mediocre calibre they had to divert an increasing number of first-class fighting troops from the American front until, finally, an entire SS Division was withdrawn for the sole purpose of destroying us. This threw a very different light on the operation, for it showed that the comparatively little material damage we inflicted was more than counterbalanced by the number and quality of the German troops which our presence tied down.

Hislop gave considerable thought to the problems involved in this type of soldiering:

In straightforward warfare a man in the line who breaks down or proves wanting can be sent back. But if he does so on an operation behind the enemy lines he is a menace to himself, to his companions and to the whole project and there are no means of getting him out of the way. Nor is it easy to pick the right men for the task. Those without experience of warfare of this nature are largely unknown quantities, while some who have distinguished themselves in this sphere have lost their nerve as a result, which may not be discernible to them or to the selectors of the force until the operation is in progress; then it is too late.

When small successful private armies, such as the SAS in its early stages, came into being, two tendencies in particular emerge: they expand beyond their capacity to keep up the necessary standard of personnel; and the Army, which has never viewed unorthodox forces with favour, takes a closer hold on it.

In the first case the private armies become less effective, and in the second their flair is liable to be ham-strung by red-tape.

143

After 'Loyton' Hislop took part in further operations on the Dutch-German border. He noted that most units were taking things easily, allowing bombing and shelling to kill resistance before they moved in. It was not so with the SAS who continued to fight with the daring and enterprise with which they had made their name. He quoted Mayne who came upon a machine-gun post which was holding up a unit's advance. Mayne drove up casually in a heavily-armed jeep and when very close opened fire; the post was destroyed.

Mayne's approach was matched by that of Brigadier M.M. Calvert, who took over the SAS Brigade after Brigadier R.W. McLeod in March 1945. 'Mike' Calvert came with an outstanding record from the Chindits in Burma. Hislop relates one story:

Shortly after VE day he [Calvert] was chatting to Jakie [J.J. Astor] and me when he announced enthusiastically: 'Now for the Far East and a bit of action! I remember one splendid scrap we had when I was in Wingate's crowd; we ran into a bunch of Japs in a clearing in the jungle and there we were, hacking at each other with knives, swords, bayonets and the lot, just like an old-time battle'.

We have followed up the part which Phantom played in the SAS although what is written here is by no means the full story, as the SAS would be the first to acknowledge. It is now time to return to the SAS in Scotland in 1943.

As may be imagined there was more than one doubt about the wisdom of placing the SAS under the command of Airborne and brickbats have occasionally been bestowed where bouquets would have been more suitable. It has, for instance, been thought that Airborne took over SAS because it was jealous of the latter's free and easy way of success; in fact Lieutenant General Browning was so appreciative of the efforts of the SAS that he went to great trouble to get them into the Order of Battle for the invasion of Europe. It might be remembered that neither 21 Army Group nor SHAEF – the Supreme Headquarters Allied Expeditionary Force – were prepared to take the SAS under direct command, and in

144

fact Airborne was the only Headquarters with the transport, knowledge, and experience for the job. Subsequently however the SAS did work directly for SHAEF and 21 Army Group on certain occasions by arrangement with 1 Airborne.

Experience soon showed that for any operations behind the enemy lines it was vital that the special forces should have their own tri-service base at GHQ and that there must be as few intermediaries as possible between the top command and the people employed on the job.

Initially the SAS rôle in Europe seemed somewhat limited. 21st Army Group was firm that nothing could be allowed to begin in France before the invasion took place and that when it did the SAS job would be to prevent German reserves reaching the front line. Approximately half the SAS were held in reserve in England for later use. A restricting factor was that all troop-carrying aircraft would be fully booked till after the invasion and that the SAS would have to wait its turn for air-drop transport. Fortunately the idea of using the SAS immediately behind the invasion area had to be abandoned for lack of aircraft.

However, it was possible to get off reconnaissance parties for four vital operations known by the code names of 'Houndsworth', 'Samwest', 'Dingson' and 'Bulbasket'. These were strategic operations covering an area not less than fifty miles ahead of the Allied armies. The plan was to co-operate with resistance and other agents in the area, and to cause the maximum harm and dismay to enemy communications. If the enemy was thus persuaded to use large numbers of troops to hunt small groups of SAS this would be very satisfactory.

The situation with these and other operations now becomes complicated, detailed and confusing. As it is clearly impossible – without filling many volumes – to give a full account of all the operations and their ramifications a few have been selected, either because they were large or because they brought points of unusual interest.

There were of course administrative problems on a heroic scale. Airborne HQ could achieve miracles in the way of

| WALLACE | Jeep Patrol |
|---|---|
| 1 | 1 SAS Regiment |
| 2 | 2 SAS Regiment |
| 3 | 3 French Para Battalion |
| 4 | 4 " " " |
| B | Belgian Para Company |
| 5 | Phantom SAS Signal Section |

0  10  20  30   50        100
Scale of Miles

Boulg

Cherbourg

D

Ro

DEFOE     Caen     TRUEFORM
                    2 & B

TITANIC 1

Brest    DERRY 3                         HAFT 702    BUNY
         SAM WEST 4          St.Malo
              St.Brieuc
                    COONEY 4
                                Mayenne
         GROG 4    Pontivy        F        R        Le Mans   A
                                                              CHA
           Lorient                                 SHAKESPEARE B
              COONEY 4      DUNHILL 2
                    St.Nazaire       Angers     Blois
                         Loire                  Loire
    Bay    of       Nantes    DICKENS 3
                                              Indre
                                                    Chateaur
    Biscay                    MOSES 3              Chateaur

                                                    MOSES 3
              La Rochelle                           Lim
                 Rochefort
                              SAMSON 3
                         Angoulême          MARSI

GOBBO (PORTIA) B
FABIAN (REGAN) B
CALIBAN B
BRUSSELS
BELGIUM Liège
Mons Namur BERGBANG B
Arras BRUTUS B GERMANY
eville Amiens NOAH B
St. Quentin LUXEMBOURG
SEY 5 Aisne Rheims Verdun
BENSON B
PARIS Marne Chalons-s-Marne
St. Dizier
RUPERT 2
N Troyes C E
N 1 LOYTON 2
rans Auxerre HARDY (LAUREL) 2 Vesoul
KIPLING
WALLACE
SPENSER Dijon
AGGARD 1 Nevers HOUNDSWORTH 1 ABEL 3
NEWTON
Le Creusot
BARKER
HARRODS 3
Montlucon JOCKWORTH 3 Lyons
Clermont-Ferrand L. Geneva

E.G. Morton

delivering personnel and supplies but they could scarcely be expected to handle problems of evacuation by land or sea. Many of the administrators at brigade HQ had no previous experience of the type of work they now found themselves engaged in.

The French were first-class at parachuting, but lacked administrators and were very light on SAS experience; and add to this the fact that every separate component of the SAS brigade was extremely independent in outlook.

The need for secrecy in fast changing situations meant that planning was usually done at top speed with a number of factors unknown. Yet it worked. The answer to many of the problems was found in the establishment of bases behind the enemy lines in occupied territory. This was not an entirely new development in SAS thinking but it was certainly a new dimension. In Europe it required the close co-operation and advice of local resistance forces, and others. From this base other expeditions could be launched. There are obvious problems connected with establishing a base in enemy held territory, however remote, wooded or mountainous.

Supply was always a problem but there were some notable triumphs. One was the case of the request from the middle of France for a pair of size eight medium boots. They were delivered by air from England exactly four and a half hours later.

There were forty-three operations carried out in the four months after D Day and this figure was soon stepped up. Eventually one night in April 1945 some 700 men from 3 and 4 French Parachute Battalions were dropped in 50 small parties in north-east Holland to harass German communications.

Two methods were employed to get them in. The first was to work in conjunction with 'Jedburgh' teams which consisted of guides provided by Special Forces Headquarters. These would organize the local forces, supply them with arms, arrange Dropping Zones and so on.

The other method was to drop blind in a selected area. When this method was used it was clearly an advantage if there was an SAS base within reachable distance; however, even when the bases were far away and movement difficult this method was often surprisingly successful. It was used in the later stages when there was a good chance of working back to our own lines.

No one in the SAS at that time will have forgotten the part played by the RAF, mainly 33 Group, sometimes 46 Group, and also RAF Tempsford. The sort of achievement which they treated as routine is illustrated by operations on the 4th/5th August 1944 when 38 Group sent 42 aircraft from five airfields to 22 DZs with a total cargo of 150 troops, 4 jeeps and 700 containers of miscellaneous stores. Even with long preparation, no enemy opposition and perfect weather this would have been no light task. Meanwhile 11 gliders, 45 troops, and 11 jeeps were landed behind the enemy positions in Brittany.

'Houndsworth', near Dijon, was a highly successful beginning to SAS operations in France. It began on 6th June, and continued till 6th September, during which time the party of 18 officers and 126 soldiers from 1 SAS blew up the railway lines Lyons-Châlon-sur-Saône-Dijon-Paris and Le Creusot-Nevers twenty-two times. It also took 132 prisoners, killed or wounded 220 Germans, and reported 30 bombing targets to the RAF.

On the same night 'Bulbasket' was launched for the area south of Châteauroux. This was 1 SAS and 3 Patrol Phantom – a total of 56. They attacked the railway lines Limoges-Vierzon-Poitiers-Tours, cut the railway twelve times, and inflicted 20 enemy casualties besides sending vital information to the RAF, but had heavy losses themselves through treachery. After losing 36 out of the original total it was decided that the remainder would be evacuated by air; this was done at the beginning of August by Hudsons and Dakotas.

'Gain' ran from 14th June 1944 – 19th August 1944, and consisted of 9 officers and 49 soldiers from 1 SAS. It set out to cut German rail communication between Rambouillet-Provins-Gien-Orléans-Chartres. Ten SAS men were killed, including the commander Major Ian Fenwick.*

'Gain' discovered just how much can be done if men are alert, flexible, and impudently brave. They drove their jeeps around quite openly, taking them up to the railway lines they were going to demolish. When they observed that the Germans used their headlights they proceeded to do the same. They had a merry time destroying railroads because the repairers could not hope to cope with the rapidity and diversity of the attack. Their jeeps were used for purposes other than transport and with their Vickers Ks they destroyed transporters, trucks, petrol carriers and trains. There were hair-raising moments as when they found themselves mixed up with German convoys of troop-carrying vehicles and Tiger tanks. The odds were usually heavily against them – once three detachments were encircled by six hundred Germans, but usually speed, the French Resistance, or the ruggedness of the country, enabled them to slip through the enemy lines. On this and other occasions there were times when a jeep cruising merrily along a road would turn a corner and see a large, heavily-armed, German convoy approaching. The jeep would promptly do a right-angle turn and endeavour to crash through the nearest woodland. The Germans were never slow to react and infantry would soon pour out of the trucks and begin a search operation. If the jeep had to be abandoned, the ensuing moments could be tricky.

Operation 'Samwest' was also launched on the night of 5th/6th June. It totalled 145 including thirty locally recruited French Resistance fighters. As originally conceived it was a disaster, for the local recruits turned out to belong to different groups who hated each other nearly as much as they hated the Germans. Furthermore, some of the SAS personnel were a little too slap-happy and started having meals in local restaurants. Eventually the Germans put in a full-scale attack, and inflicted 32 casualties, but they paid a heavy price, for their own casualties amounted to 155. These disparities in

* He was an artist of exceptional promise.

casualty rates tend to flatter the SAS but are accounted for by such factors as vastly superior fire power and experience, better-quality soldiers, and first-class local knowledge. The result of a German patrol discovering an SAS hide-out could well be the extinction of the German patrol. However, although 'Samwest' as originally conceived had to be abandoned the ultimate results were good, for 30 SAS members stayed with the local resistance and organised them into a most effective unit. Other survivors of 'Samwest' linked up with 'Dingson'.

'Dingson' had been established near Vannes, and was on a much larger scale. The SAS party from 4 French Para battalion numbered 150 and was joined by a local resistance group of nearly 3,000. The Germans attacked the base on the 18th June and, although 'Dingson' gave a good account of itself, it was clear that this was not its right use and it could not engage in continuous action of this nature or scale. The Resistance therefore dispersed and the SAS broke up into small groups to operate in the north-west. It cut all rail, telephone and other links in the Morbihan area, in southern Brittany.

A different type of action had also been launched on June 7th. This was Operation 'Cooney'. It consisted of eighteen parties varying in number between three and six men, all of whom were dropped 'blind' in the area between St Malo and Vannes. They destroyed their allotted objectives, and a few more besides, then dispersed and linked up with the larger groups.

Once the invasion force was established and the Germans began to withdraw, the SAS had a different task. A series of harassing operations were undertaken, as for example 'Dunhill', just north of Nantes between 3rd and 24th August. This was conducted by 10 officers and 44 soldiers from 2 SAS. The Belgians had considerable success west of Paris and north-east of Paris, and a mixed force of the Belgians, 40 members of 2 SAS and 5 of 1 SAS was 'blind-dropped' south of Rouen in two groups. These managed to get very close to German troops and inflicted much damage without being counter-attacked; the Germans had too much on their plates to spend much time looking for them.

'Haggard' and 'Moses', the former east of Vierzon and the latter north of Limoges, inflicted considerable damage on enemy personnel and material, the former accounting for 233 Germans. 'Haggard' took place from 10th August to 23rd September with 79 members of 1 SAS. 'Moses' ran from 3rd August to 5th October with 46 members of 3 French Para battalion; its main target was railways.

Operations designed to make life difficult or impossible for the enemy in southern France were 'Barker', 'Harrods', 'Jockworth', 'Samson', 'Marshall' and 'Snelgrove'. All came from 3 French Para, all were successful, and the two last acquired a reputation for near-suicidal recklessness in attacks.

Not least of the problems of World War II was the choice of code-names which were memorable, secure, whimsical, but not easily confused with other code names.

A more important task was to disrupt communications between Germany and France but this posed considerable problems. Among them were the shortness of the hours of darkness in July/August, and the amount of enemy reaction that would be aroused. 'Rupert', north of Dijon, which was carried out by 58 members of 2 SAS, had a number of setbacks, including casualties from aircraft which were shot down, but 'Loyton', in the Vosges was more successful. A base was established by Lieutenant Colonel Brian Franks with 89 other members of 2 SAS. In theory 'Loyton' – which lasted some $2\frac{1}{2}$ months – should have had much help from French Resistance forces in the area but the amount of co-operation proved disappointing, as the latter were not well-organised. Hislop's account of this operation has already been recorded. As will be seen later, some of its members were murdered by the Gestapo.

There was a certain amount of frustration as SAS activities were frequently delayed by two factors; one was that the presence of SAS troops in the area would give away the next move of Allied strategy, the other was that they might bring down brutal measures on the local population in order to terrorise them into betraying the SAS. Consequently, many SAS operations were only launched when a number of potential opportunities had been lost. However the first operation in Belgium, 'Noah', conducted by 41 members of the Belgian Company between late August and early September produced a handsome dividend in the way of information and the infliction of casualties. Their 'bag' was 138 Germans and a quantity of transport. Their own casualties numbered only 4. A typical incident is recounted in one of the reports:

Luckier this time in a night ambush and caught big game using a string of 75 grenades and 4 tyre-bursters reinforced with 1 pound of plastic. Engaged one of the small convoys protected by armour. A leading wheeled armoured car was blown up and engaged with LMG, 36 grenades and heavy Gammon bombs (5-pound types) and turret blown off. One 2-ton and one 3-ton lorry smashed and personnel mown down. One very large Reichsbahn lorry filled to the brim with arms and explosives hit squarely by the Gammon. Twenty-one men killed and ten wounded, all SS. No casualties on our part. 4th September 1944.

2 SAS had considerable success on 'Hardy', during August 1944, although numbering only 50. Among its other activities was an engagement with 300 Germans who had a heavy tank, two light tanks, six armoured-cars and two half-tracks. The half-tracks were captured and twelve civilian hostages, who had been taken by the Germans from a local village were released.

'Hardy' was eventually joined with 'Wallace'. The latter had begun on 19th August with 60 members of 2 SAS and 20 jeeps. It was commanded by Major Roy Farran. Forty members of 1 SAS plus 20 jeeps set off at the same time to join the others in the Morvan mountains. 'Wallace' drove 200 miles behind the enemy lines having various interesting encounters on the way. 'Wallace' lost 11 jeeps and was reduced in numbers to 32 but killed at least 50 Germans, apart from inflicting considerable material damage. Once the combined 'Hardy/Wallace' force was in operation it took on a wide assortment of tasks and in the course of them ravaged an area some seventy miles wide.

'Newton', south-east of Orléans, and 'Spencer', north-east of Vierzon, were carried out in late August and early September by members of the French parachute battalions. They created considerable devastation along the German line of communication and with 'Haggard' and 'Moses' forced 18,000 Germans to surrender. Having no means of administering large quantities of prisoners they made contact with the nearest Americans and made an officer a present of 18,000 captured enemy personnel; he was probably the most surprised man in the war.

As the German forces were pushed back SAS attention was concentrated on Belgium and Holland, and finally on Germany. There was however, considerable activity in northern Italy as will be mentioned later. The quantity and quality of SAS work in Belgium and Holland was greatly influenced by the ability and effort of the local resistance groups.

The problem with all operations behind the lines in occupied territory is whether your activities will bring down reprisals on the people who have helped you. This is what happened in the Vosges on 'Loyton'. HQ was near Moussey, whose people gave every possible form of help to 2 SAS. Unfortunately the operation which was expected to take ten days took nearly nine weeks. The part played by the inhabitants of Moussey and the reprisals on them by the Nazis are described later.

As the Germans fell back through Belgium it was clearly necessary to give maximum help to the Belgium resistance. 'Noah' (see above) had already begun this assistance and 'Brutus' continued it. 'Brutus' opened south-east of Namur, 'Bergbang' south-east of Liège. Both these operations were conducted by the Belgian Company and were accompanied by the supply of considerable quantities of arms to the Belgian resistance.

'Fabian' was a six-month long operation conducted by the

Belgian unit, commanded by Lieutenant G.S. Kirschen.* It began on 19th September 1944. He describes this and previous operations – 'Benson', 'Bunyan' and 'Shakespeare' – in his book *Friends Arrive Tonight*, which was published in French and Dutch in 1946 and in English in 1949. On 'Benson' they acquired information of great value by a somewhat unusual route. Having sustained a crop of minor injuries in the descent the parachutists needed medical attention. The local Resistance leader offered to call in the local doctor who, he said, was friendly and could be trusted. When this doctor arrived he completed his surgical tasks swiftly and expertly, and then mentioned that the previous day he had paused to watch a German major directing military traffic at the nearby St Just-en-Chaussée crossroads. The major had checked every vehicle personally and directed the driver. When the major went off to a nearby café to have a drink the doctor followed him in. The German laid his map on the table and, quickly and unobtrusively, the doctor made a sketch of it. 'This is it,' he said. 'And now I must leave you for I have other patients to see.'

The SAS looked at the sketch. It showed every German division on the Somme, their numbers, those in the line, those in reserve, even the position of Army Headquarters. It was a quite simple map – but of exceptional value.

It was vital to get this important information back as soon as possible but as they began to transmit back to GHQ there was an interruption. They were working in a barn with a door which would not close. Apart from the roof over their heads they were as obvious as if they had been in the open air. At this vital moment a German self-propelled gun, with half a dozen Germans on the carriage, clanked up and stopped three yards from the open door. The SAS promptly opened fire, to which the Germans replied with incendiary bullets. As the barn caught fire the German gun suddenly reversed and took up a position on the other side of the barn. The SAS took

* Kirschen's father, who was a barrister, had defended Nurse Cavell in a German military court in World War I.

advantage of the lull and dashed out behind the screen of smoke. One man was shot through the arm but described it as 'nothing much'; they found cover under rain-soaked cornstacks in a nearby field. The Germans were clearly confused about the direction they had taken and the parachutists lay there till dark listening to a patrol shouting orders as they searched. Cold, wet and hungry though they were the fugitives had one overriding priority – to get back to the vicinity of the barn, collect the parts of the set from where they had been hastily hidden in a nearby bush, and send the rest of the message. The set had not been improved by its recent rough treatment, and the signal it sent out was weak. Power came from a hand-cranked generator. As they transmitted they could see German transport going along a road five hundred yards away. Eventually the message, with repeats, was sent.

It was, of course, vital information, and one of the great scoops of the war. There was a lot of luck in it – bad as well as good. But the episode may be seen as the justification for this type of mobile, resilient, fighting unit which could obtain information from local sources and get it away. It is not, of course, impossible that other organisations might have achieved the same results but it seems unlikely. This, though a notable achievement, was only one of many pieces of valuable and reliable information produced at this time. Later, Kirschen's detachment helped members of 1 Airborne to rejoin their unit when the main body had already crossed the Rhine. Kirschen lived in a hen-house at this time; he says it was a very comfortable hen-house and, in comparison with some of the other shelters he lived in, perhaps it was.

Between December 1944 and April 1945 there was considerably less requirement in Europe for the SAS. During the winter there would be much reduced activity on the European front, but there was a suitable strategic task to hand in Italy.

To understand the need and task for the SAS in Italy it is necessary to take a brief look at the Italian campaign which we saw begin with the invasion of Sicily in July 1943. In the ensuing months the Germans, under Field Marshal Kesselring, had put up an ingenious and stubborn resistance. The Allies had complete air superiority but to some extent this was vitiated by the ruggedness of the country and the exceptionally bad winter weather conditions. Although suffering somewhat from being regarded as a sideshow the Italian campaign demonstrated the fighting qualities of both sides at their best: the Germans were resolved on stopping the Allies from advancing too fast or far on the southern front, and the Allies were equally intent on tying down the maximum number of German divisions in Italy, thus preventing them from reinforcing their positions in France. A measure of the Allied success was that after the battle for Rome the Germans withdrew divisions from France, Belgium, the Balkans and Denmark, and used them to bolster their forces in Italy. The fighting in Italy affected many more units than those on the mainland and it is affirmed that during 1944 as many as 55 German divisions were contained in the Mediterranean area.

However, during the autumn and winter of 1944, the Allies were themselves hard pressed. Their own divisions were starved of replacements, and short of ammunition (at one point they were down to 25 shells a day for field guns and 15 for medium and heavy).* Bologna was still in enemy hands – it was not taken until 21st April 1945 – and the Germans were still capable of fierce counter-attacks. At this delicate stage in the war it was known that there were an estimated 50,000 Partisans operating behind the German lines. They were mainly in small groups and without any clear aim except preserving their independence and inflicting minor damage on any neighbouring German units. These small isolated groups were usually unaware of the presence of potential allies in their area. In one was Charles West, whose account of his aircraft's part in the Gazala raid is given earlier in this book. By now he had escaped from a prison camp and joined a group of partisans in the mountains. He was completely

---

* *World War 1939–45*, Brigadier Peter Young, DSO, MC.

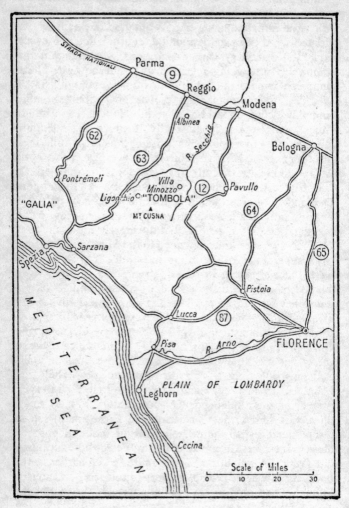

**GALIA AND TOMBOLA AREAS**

In December 1944, 3 Squadron of 2 SAS was despatched to Italy under the command of Major Roy Farran. Initially they were looked after by SOE at Bari. SOE was the body responsible for helping to organise and co-ordinate partisan resistance in occupied countries. Farran had a new squadron which, though inexperienced, had been thoroughly and properly trained.

The first operation in northern Italy was 'Galia' in which a troop of 33 men under the command of Major R. Walker-Brown operated inland from Spezia. In that area roads were few but vital to the enemy. 'Galia' lasted from 27th December till 15th February when the force walked through the German lines and linked up with Allied forces at Leghorn. It was a highly successful operation in that the unit killed more than four times their own number of Germans and destroyed a quantity of enemy transport. The operation was historically notable in that the weapons employed were now heavier, especially the 3-inch mortars and medium machine-guns. Mules supplied some of the porterage but, as every soldier knows, no amount or variety of transport saves him from doing a lot of kit-humping himself. The 3-inch mortar contributed considerably to the success of the expedition by virtue of its greater range but in the opinion of those present the principal reason for success was the leadership of Walker-Brown. Conditions were appalling, with Arctic weather which not only made life most unpleasant but also prevented adequate resupply. The Germans were so harassed by the SAS activities that they used 6,000 troops to sweep the area, and included a ski battalion in their number.

Unfortunately, a later expedition in the same area was much less successful and sustained heavy casualties. Another disaster was the attempt to block the Brenner Pass by creating a landslide. It was known, appropriately as Operation 'Cold Comfort' for it operated in near-impossible conditions. Captain Ross Littlejohn and Corporal Crowley were executed by the Gestapo after capture. Nearly two years before Pinckney had been executed for an attempt to blow up the railway tunnel. The executions were a war crime and the perpetrators were appropriately dealt with later. Unfortunately one of the greatest dangers faced by those who work deep behind enemy lines is the panicky, sadistic action of an underling who kills a prisoner in cold blood. War crimes trials have been criticized by the stupid or inexperienced, but those who in future fall into enemy hands may perhaps come to look on the word 'Nuremberg' with gratitude, whatever their nationality.

In January 1944 an important railway bridge near Rimini was destroyed by a party which landed in West-African paddle dories from two destroyers. Other small parties operated along the Adriatic coast, destroying communications and releasing prisoners of war.

In February 1944 a small group of parachutists was dropped near Perugia. They swam the Tiber and destroyed 11 aircraft on the aerodrome.

Others were not so fortunate. Some were captured; others found the enemy lines too tight and installations too well guarded.

'Tombola', which began on March 4th 1945, was commanded by Major Roy Farran. He had been ordered not to accompany the expedition himself but had, it was thought, managed to trip and fall out of the aircraft by accident. The story is an oversimplification. He had been refused permission to go by 15 Army Group, but felt that in the circumstances he must accompany his men; in the event he was proved right.

Farran paid a tribute to the Americans, which deserves inclusion:

I felt a surge of gratitude for the American squadron leader, the lean colonel who commanded the Dakotas from Leghorn, for he had already done much for us. I remembered how, when Walker-Brown's men were scattered by the Germans in the mountains north of Spezia and were sick to death with dysentery and scabies, he personally flew in Jock Milnes, our doctor, through fog-clouded mountains in a lone, unarmed Dakota, dropping him accurately in an isolated valley.

'Tombola' operated approximately midway between Spezia

and Bologna. Its centre was a rough valley, south of the River Secchia and north of Mount Curna; on all sides were steep slopes. It was an excellent area to use as a base for attacking the German supply lines to the south of the Po valley.

The force which would operate from this area was – to say the least – mixed. It included Communists, Christian Democrats, escaped Russian prisoners, German deserters and Italians. These, like other Partisan forces, had been under German pressure for some time, mainly by ski battalions. Although the Germans had failed in their objective of breaking them up they had caused the Partisans to become cautious and less aggressive than was desirable. Eventually this had settled down to a situation where the Partisans did much as they wanted, unmolested, even to the extent of receiving parachuted supplies in broad daylight. On the other hand, if the Partisans became active the Germans would launch a drive against them, although this would soon be called off as the Germans had too few troops to spare any for long operations of this sort.

The Partisans also possessed other familiar and unfamiliar qualities. They were burning with a desire to liberate their country but were liable to be high-spirited, reckless and unpredictable.

Farran's book *Operation Tombola* gives an illuminating account of his thoughts on reaching the village of Secchio. Although only thirty miles behind the front line the area was apparently peaceful. Partisans in bizarre and colourful costumes sauntered around unconcernedly. For the moment most of them were doing little or nothing, but in the past they had fought strenuous actions with great courage. The arrival of the SAS, which would stir up the Germans into retaliatory action was greeted by them with mixed feelings, as they were by no means certain they would not all be wiped out in the process.

Some of the Partisans had a peculiar and involved history. Modena, a young Russian lieutenant, had escaped from a prison camp in Austria and built up a team of Russian partisans. Some of his men were genuine escaped prisoners but most were double-deserters who had gone from the

Russian army to the Germans when the Germans were apparently winning and then to the Partisans when the tide seemed to be turning. However there were still plenty of Mongolian and Ukrainian troops in German battalions in the area so the Partisans might very well find themselves fighting their own countrymen, or equally well be in close alliance with nationals of enemy countries. Apparently many of the Russians fighting with the Germans were primitive peasants who hardly knew, still less cared, who they were fighting for provided they were fed and paid.

Farran totalled the numbers at his disposal and found they amounted to three hundred. The immediate need was to give them arms and train them in their use.

I drafted out a signal to Walker-Brown. In the next drop I wanted a piper complete with kilt and bagpipes; khaki berets and distinctive hackles for the Italians; three more officers to instruct both the Russians and the Italians; an Italian interpreter; a seventy-five millimetre howitzer, heavy mortars and heavy machine-guns; Lieutenant Stephens who could speak German to Modena, and Karl Nurk, the White Russian, as soon as he could be found; and a long list of other supplies for the new force.

To most the order would have been impossible. Hidebound staff officers would have regarded a request for a piper, for feathered hackles and for a specific officer from outside the Italian theatre as too fantastic to contemplate. But to Walker-Brown everything was possible. And I knew that Jackie Profumo* would provide him with the aircraft for there is nothing like a co-operative politician for cutting through red-tape. I sensed that colour was the tonic to inspire these Italian partisans. They were already playing a game, imagining themselves successors to Garibaldi and we could do no better than encourage them.

Colour seems to have been a feature of these activities; one of the Partisan groups was called the 'Green Flames' another the 'Black Bats'.

Looking at his troops when he paraded them for inspection Farran had some misgivings:

* Later the Right Hon. J.D. Profumo, CBE, Secretary of State for War.

Approximately half were armed with ancient rifles, rusty shotguns or pistols, but from their condition I doubted if they would fire. If they did, the chances were at least equal that they would harm the firers more than the enemy.

The men themselves were young and small. Many had physical defects – one eye, a withered hand or a lame foot – and from the blank look on their faces I had the feeling that here we were scraping the bottom of Italian manhood. The strange angles at which they held their weapons showed that few had ever experienced military training, either having avoided service because of age or because they were physically unfit. Now, in danger of recruitment for forced labour on German defence lines, they had fled to the hills. Some were no more than boys.

Farran spoke to them:

After remarking on the fine body of men they were, I said I felt proud to have them under my command. They would receive shoes and uniform and good food and arms. Through their efforts glorious Italy would be reborn to live again. Soon Italy would be liberated from the German tyrant. Soon they would have the opportunity to strike a blow, to fight for Italy their motherland.

The round, stubble-shadowed faces gazed blankly up at me. I could detect no emotion whatsoever until the translator talked of fighting. Then I sensed that a ripple of discomfort, a shuffling of feet and averting of eyes ran through the mob. Long live Italy, I concluded, and called for three cheers. A weak half-hearted cheer floated back.

This was hardly a promising start but the next two weeks of intensive training soon saw a difference. The value of training and discipline have been appreciated since Roman times, if not before: their principles were set out by Vegetius in the 3rd century AD with such classic statements as 'Men are seldom born brave but they acquire courage through training and discipline – a handful of men inured to war proceed to certain victory; while on the contrary numerous armies of raw and undisciplined troops are but multitudes of men dragged to the slaughter.'

Farran's observations on his experiences at this time are of considerable interest in the light of later events. Since 1945 there have been all too many examples of primitive peoples learning how to handle modern sophisticated weapons in a brief space of time; rather more amazing is the fact that Governments and 'higher authority' seem to have an endless capacity for being surprised by this phenomenon. And it is not only 'higher authority' which remains blinkered as Farran points out:

Orthodox soldiers will shudder at the idea that a simple peasant can be taught to fire and to maintain a three-inch mortar in little over two weeks. But all the Partisans, and especially the Russians, proved quick pupils. One demonstration was enough for Modena's men. And their imitative ability was so great that the Russians would place the various gun parts on exactly the same corner of the groundsheet as had the instructor during the demonstration. The Italians were also eager to learn. Just as the British army proved in remote corners of the world from India to the Sudan that it was not necessary for the instructors to be linguists, somehow the Italians and Russians were able to follow instructions constantly reiterated in a mixture of pidgin-Italian and English until they were able to assemble and dismantle the guns as well as the instructors themselves. Our only disadvantage was that through the shortage of ammunition, and the need to preserve secrecy from the Germans on the other side of the mountain, practice in live shooting had to be kept to a minimum.

Farran, although himself a regular soldier, found the orthodoxy of some of his fellow regulars exasperating. They knew as well as he did that the British army is second to none in training local forces to a high degree of efficiency. Being, however, somewhat of a perfectionist in these matters the British instructor will usually claim that he requires ten times as much time as he believes is strictly necessary.

Not least of the remarkable characters encountered by Farran on 'Tombola' was Louis, an Italian sailor, whose English had been acquired on the Brooklyn waterfront. He had attached himself to Walker-Brown when the latter had been operating north of Spezia, and had guided him through the mountains in conditions of immense difficulty.

Though he was over sixty, Louis could outmarch any of us. He knew the northern Appenines thoroughly, and was as useful as a guide as he was as an interpreter. He had the heart of a lion.

Louis belonged to no organization and received no pay.

Prior to Farran's arrival with 3 Squadron, British contact with the Partisans had been in the hands of Captain Mike Lees, a determined officer who had worked out a number of plans for distressing the Germans. Among them was an attack on the German Corps headquarters at Albinea, a village in the Po valley. Lees had acquired a thorough knowledge of the headquarters from the 'Staffetas'. These were Italian girl partisans who were able to bicycle through German positions without attracting any more attention than a few wolf-whistles. '*Staffeta*' means messenger in Italian; these were under the command of an Italian named Kiss.

Even Farran himself was a little concerned at the audacity of the plan. In the past he had taken part in almost every form of demolition and sabotage but had never attempted as big a target as a corps headquarters. It was to be a twenty minute raid with the object of killing the maximum number of German officers and setting fire to the buildings. As experience told them that the Germans would be likely to react quickly, Farran ensured that the damage would be done in minimum time, and then withdrawal must be prompt. At the critical moment, when the SAS was already on the move, a message was received by wireless from 15 Army Group to say that the attack should be postponed for ten days. Realising that the senders had no idea of the necessity for using the Partisans once their morale was high and resolve firm, Farran decided to pretend the signal had failed to reach him in time. The German HQ was distributed between the Villa Rossi and the Villa Calvi.

The approach march, although nerve-racking, was un-eventful. The attack was a different story ...

The silence was broken by a tremendous burst of fire from Villa Calvi above. It sounded like a whole Bren magazine fired without pause and, as much as if it were a signal for which both Germans and ourselves had been waiting, it triggered automatic fire from every

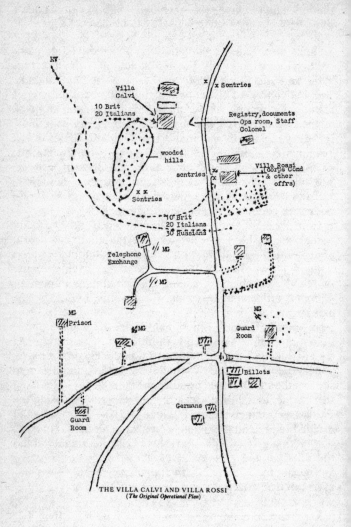

N

Villa
Calvi
10 Brit
20 Italians

x  x Sontries

Registry, documents
Ops room, Staff
Colonel

wooded
hills

sentries  x
x
x

Villa Rossi
(Corps Comd
& other
offrs)

x  x
Sontries

10 Brit
20 Italians
30 Russians

MG

Telephone
Exchange

MG

MG
Prison

MG

MG

Guard
Room

MG

Guard
Room

Billots

Germans

THE VILLA CALVI AND VILLA ROSSI
(*The Original Operational Plan*)

were firing back. Bullets whistled over our heads, as if the Germans could see us, which was impossible. Even mortars added their thuds to the general racket and, between the rattle of small-arms fire at Villa Calvi above, I heard the thump of a bazooka.

At the Villa Calvi a party of 10 British and 20 Italians had managed to creep close to the villa without being observed. There were four German sentries standing outside the villa, and these were mown down in the opening burst from a Bren. The party charged, shot in the front door with a bazooka, and got to hand-to-hand fighting. Some of the Germans managed to retreat up the stairs where they could fire across the landing without being seen. Several attempts were made to rush the stairs but the fire was too brisk. Then the Germans countered by rolling grenades down the stairs. This new stalemate was consuming time which could ill be spared so the British made a bonfire of maps, papers, files and furniture in the middle of the operations room. With the aid of a bottle of petrol and some explosives an excellent fire was started; while it gained a good hold the Germans who had retreated to the upper floors were kept in position by swift bursts of fire up the stairs and through the windows.

Events at Rossi were not dissimilar, although here the attackers lacked the advantage of surprise. Nevertheless a number of enemy were killed on the ground floor before the remainder established themselves firmly in the upper storey. Time and again the British tried to rush up the spiral staircase but on every occasion were held by concentrated fire across the landing. Lees and the Italian leader of the Black Bats were both severely wounded, several others were killed outright.

Much cheered by repulsing these attacks the Germans then attempted to regain the ground floor. Their optimism proved premature for they made a perfect target as they descended the staircase. As there was little to be gained by exchanging fire in this way the raiders made a bonfire in the kitchen and withdrew with their wounded.

Although Lees and Bruno, the leader of the Black Bats, were being carried, neither arrived at the rendezvous by the time Farran felt he must withdraw unless his whole party was to be killed or captured. In the event both were carried for four days on ladders and escaped capture, although hundreds of Germans were methodically combing the area for stragglers.

The main party had a gruelling enough time. Climbing the hills on paths made slippery by rain, encumbered by the wounded they were carrying and too exhausted to be able to do more than plod, they felt remarkably unlike the survivors of a successful raid:

> We marched mechanically now, tramping wearily in step with our heads down. If we had encountered any Germans, resistance would have been impossible. Our weapons were caked with mud and we were so tired that we were incapable of anything more than this monotonous trudging along the track. We marched without scouts for no one had enough energy to climb to higher ground ...
>
> I remembered that Mark Antony had made his soldierly reputation not so much from feats of arms as from his endurance while retreating from Modena through this very country ...
>
> We had marched for twenty-two hours without pause and, excluding the eight-hour halt at Casa del Lupo, had been awake for more than two days.

Total casualties on the raid were three killed (all British), three British, three Italian and two Russians wounded, and six Russians captured. Its main gain was not merely to kill the German chief of staff and a number of other Germans, and destroy the headquarters, but to create apprehension in all German headquarters so that troops would in future be immobilised in quite unnecessary garrison duties. It has been described here in some detail – though by no means completely – because it shows how skill in this type of expedition had developed since the days of the Tragino aqueduct and the Keyes raid. It brought out the points of SAS philosophy and training; a few men, preferably multi-national, the ability to cross difficult country, mostly at night, surprise, but no death-or-glory attacks, and, finally a return by a forced march which could not be managed by any but hardened troops. It was, in fact, not only the ability to get in but also the endurance to get out once the fighting had been broken off.

This raid is sometimes compared, somewhat unfairly, with the Keyes raid on Rommel's HQ in the dark days of 1941. But the earlier raid had taught many useful lessons and in the following three and a half years the technique of this type of raid had been brought to perfection. The SAS arrived at their objective without being observed and knew exactly what their task was on arrival. Surprise was lost as soon as the first gun fired. Germans in surrounding areas reacted very quickly with their Spandaus, but however quickly the enemy reacted on this type of raid the damage the SAS set out to do would be done before they could be effectively checked. In this case 60 people, including the Chief of Staff, had been killed, and maps, operation orders and vital reports burnt, in a key Corps headquarters. This was, in fact, 51 Corps HQ and it controlled the whole enemy front from Bologna to the sea. The total strength of the Corps HQ was 300.

(It was the sort of raid which the SBS had frequently made on a smaller scale in the Aegean, but on this occasion it was made by a party from 2 SAS whose previous experience had been mainly on jeep-raiding in operation 'Wallace' in France; this too had been very successful, but was quite different.)

Immediately after the raid the Germans moved round the 'Tombola' area with a security battalion. Its companies were under strength but it totalled four hundred and it was well-equipped with mortars. As this approached the valley it came to a place called Gatta. As Gatta was the point where the rivers Secchia and Sechiello met, the high ground over-looking the junction was obviously of considerable importance. Here Lieutenant Mike Eld had established himself with ten British soldiers, one 3-inch mortar, one water-cooled Vickers machine gun and a selection of Brens. On his flank he had trenches occupied by Italian partisans. As the German battalion moved up to the river junction Eld watched them critically. He had personally reconnoitred the area and as the Germans began to dig trenches in positions he had taped to a yard he gave them a brisk welcome with his mortars. His knowledge of the enemy ground enabled him to do some effective night shoots. Eld enjoyed himself. He posted signs denoting minefields where there were no minefields and exploded heavy charges of dynamite at intervals. The Germans, unaware that they were being held up by less than a dozen men, paused for a week. The Partisans, who would normally have faded away in the face of so large a German force, gained in morale each day. Eld's only worry was shortage of ammunition.

The Vickers proved a useful weapon for the occasion and was regarded with an almost sentimental affection.

Skilled gunners [Farran recounted] could do things with it that were impossible for light machine-guns with a flatter trajectory. The technique of indirect fire with a machine-gun, perfected by the Australians at Gaza in the First World War, is beyond the scope of more modern weapons. And here, at Gatta, the very inaccuracy of the Vickers was an asset.

Eventually, as might have been expected, the Germans worked round to the south of Eld's position and crossed the Secchia at a point where the Partisans were supposed to be guarding it. This could have been disastrous but a swift counter-attack sent the Germans back and the whole of Partisan morale soaring.

From then on supplies began to build up to formidable proportions and included jeeps which were dropped with a parachute at each corner. In consequence the SAS was able to extend its area of operations. They were able to lay ambushes on, or shell, vital roads. They made every effort to create so much trouble in the immediate rear of the German front line that the Germans would be bound to mount retaliatory attacks. The howitzer proved its value beyond all expectations. Troops in rear areas may be upset by small-arms fire but in time will realise that the attacks signify no change in the general position. However once a few heavier shells land in rear areas the assumption is often made that the enemy has broken through the front line and is driving forward in a full-scale attack. The only handicap to extending this impression was the shortage of shells.

How valuable guerilla warfare of this nature actually is makes a subject of eternal military controversy. Does it eventually have any effect on winning the war? Is it worth the possible reprisals which local people – often innocent – may suffer? In the Western Desert the gain was obvious for the damage to enemy aircraft had a significant effect on Axis strike-power. In France, the Aegean and Italy the gains were more difficult to measure, except on the few occasions when they were startlingly obvious, as when a goods train carrying 100,000 gallons of petrol was destroyed in France. Even some SAS men, particularly if they have been brought up in infantry battalions, are inclined to doubt the value of their own marauding, much though they have enjoyed taking part in it. Farran, who had experienced all forms of warfare, had this to say of SAS activities in Italy:

Judging from my own experience in two desert withdrawals and from the fiasco of Crete, the psychological effect of our attacks was far greater than any material damage inflicted. Whether the outcome of a battle is victory or defeat depends on far more than the casualty roll. And we knew, in the Special Air Service, that we played a part in that time-honoured aim of military tactics – making the enemy feel so insecure that he leaves the field. That, after all, is the object of all military manoeuvres whether they are attempts to outflank or direct frontal attacks. Sometimes soldiers and generals kid themselves with arguments about wars of attrition, that the basic principle of war is to destroy the enemy. But of course they are wrong, for it is when a feeling of insecurity corrodes the morale of the enemy that the battle is almost won. And towards this important objective we felt we did our bit.

When I fired shells at enemy convoys I remembered how quickly panic spread among our columns retreating from Agedabia in 1941. I remembered the false rumours that German armoured columns had mixed into our ranks. I recalled the dreadful insecurity we knew on Crete when the sounds of battle came from behind us. And I felt that the Germans, tough though they were, must surely have felt the same. Rumours of shelling and raids deep in their rear areas must

171

have been more than unnerving for infantry locked in the death struggle of the last big battle around Bologna. And when at last they began to retreat, attempting an orderly withdrawal to a new line on the River Po, we must have shaken a wavering morale by bombarding from such a radically new direction as to give the impression that the front had already been broken.

The traditional Special Air Service technique was to attack with machine-guns from ambush or with explosive by stealth, but in Operation 'Tombola' we did not confine ourselves to this. Walker-Brown, an Infantry officer by both inclination and training, pioneered bombardment by mortar in his operation north of Spezia, and having proved its effectiveness himself, strove to supply us with even heavier mortars and ample ammunition. It was his idea to drop a seventy-five millimetre howitzer in pieces, it was his invention by which shells were dropped in wicker-baskets and, therefore, it was Walker-Brown who, from our base in Florence, ensured our success. It did not need military genius to see that surprise bombardment with high-explosive shells caused more confusion among the Germans than the ambush of a few trucks by night. With our jeep-drawn artillery we could mount an attack almost anywhere, fire a few shells or mortar bombs and leave in comfort long before the enemy could recover from his surprise.

I, who served with Jock Campbell in the desert columns, took a special delight in the justification of the idea so long after their heyday. Montgomery, the great general of the set piece battle, was right to criticise Jock columns when they meant a frittering away of strength like the Indian columns at Knightsbridge, but wrong when he dismissed them altogether, for surprise attacks on this soft underbelly of an enemy's supply lines contribute far more to the enemy's defeat than many generals who regard battles as 'killing grounds' seem to realise. Of course, the war of Gott and Campbell was not the war of the big battalions that came later. And Montgomery himself frequently used light forces against German rear areas – the Special Air Service under David Stirling, the Royals after Alamein and the scouts that led the way to outflanking the Mareth line. Probably it is presumptuous for a junior officer to say so, but the great general must be the general who is sold neither on the slugging infantry battle – on massed guns, tanks and men – nor on the cavalryman's dream of a war of movement. He is the general who shrewdly combines the two, who is both Patton and Montgomery rolled into one.

However, as Farran well knew, there were people in

authority who would not merely refuse to share this view but would be hostile to anyone who held it. After 'Tombola' he was lucky not to be court-martialled, first for parachuting himself behind the lines, and secondly for carrying on with the Albinea HQ attack after receiving counter-orders. He was fortunate in receiving the support of Colonel Riepi the US officer at 15th Army Group in charge of special operations.

There was one other notable feature about 'Tombola' which must be mentioned. British junior NCOs and private soldiers were put in charge of detachments of partisans and, given the responsibility, displayed high quality leadership, responsibility and modesty.

It was extraordinary how successful the British common soldiers were as detachment commanders [Roy Farran recorded]. They reacted to their sudden responsibility magnificently. Very few of them were non-commissioned officers or had ever had responsibility before. Parachutist Murphy commanded a section of ten Russians with a heavy Browning machine gun and two Brens at Civago, which was the remotest and most dangerous outpost. He became the benevolent despot of this little village within three days. On one occasion when a Partisan drank too much in the local café, Murphy promptly put the place out of bounds. The intelligence about the enemy, which he sent back by runner, was most valuable.

It would, of course, have been difficult not to have been at one's best. The Partisan girls who cooked, served and generally looked after the troops could march better than any man in the company, and their morale was high in spite of the fact that they lived in the same filthy conditions as the men.

One girl in particular will always live in my memory. Her name was Noris and she was a tall, raven-haired girl with Irish blue eyes. She was as brave and dangerous as a tigress, and was completely devoted to the British company. When she was not dressed in her finery for a reconnaissance, she wore a red beret, a battledress blouse and a thick grey square made from an army blanket. The pistol in her waist-band was a sign that she was more than capable of taking care of herself. John Stott, the Liaison officer from Modena valley, used to say she had all the devils of the world in those eyes. Noris was worth ten male Partisans.

The last throw of 'Tombola' was perhaps the most effective of all. On 13th April 1945 they were ordered by 15 Army Group to attack the main German withdrawal route, which was also carrying supplies. This task was carried out with such vigour that four German divisions were thrown into a state of confusion and near panic; the withdrawal was held up for many hours and the effect on German plans for the next phase may readily be seen.

# CHAPTER VI

# The End of the War in Sight

As the Allied armies approached the German homeland the opportunities for the SAS seemed to become more limited. At that time it was thought that for the SAS to operate behind enemy lines the area must be either friendly or very lightly populated. As neither of these factors were going to apply, a new employment had to be devised. Inevitably this would use less men. Consequently 1 and 2 SAS were allocated to jeep reconnaissance, while 3 and 4, plus the Belgian squadron, were used partly in this way. Those members of the French and Belgian units who were not employed on reconnaissance were given further training for airborne employment.

In March 1945 Brigadier R.W. McLeod was posted to India as Director of Military Operations, GHQ New Delhi. As mentioned, his successor was J.M. Calvert, who had already won great fame in Burma, where he had earned the nickname 'Mad Mike'. The fact that he is alive to-day bears out the point that what may be suicide and madness for one man may merely be a dangerous enterprise for another with quicker reactions and more battle experience. Like the other members of the SAS Calvert believed in the virtue of severe training and careful preparation. As he put it: 'One advantage of exceptionally hard training is that it proves to a man what he can do and suffer. If you have marched thirty miles in a day, you can take twenty-five miles in your stride.' He had always been interested in guerilla warfare and in 1940 had written a paper entitled *The Operations of Small Forces behind the Enemy Lines*. In the dark days of 1940 he had worked with Peter Fleming organizing guerilla defence in Great Britain.

Peter Fleming was a very well-known traveller and author

in the 1930s, as may be followed in such books as *Brazilian Adventure* and *Travels in Tartary*. Many years later his brother, Ian Fleming, became widely known as the creator of James Bond and his reputation overshadowed that of Peter Fleming who had had almost as many adventures as James Bond, though somewhat more credible ones.

Calvert, like Stirling, Jellicoe, Mayne, Woodhouse and others was a creative military planner and thinker. This is obvious from his book *Prisoners of Hope* describing his activities in Burma, and also from his later activities with the SAS, as described in this book.

On April 6th 1945 the SAS mounted what was to be their last traditional operation in the European theatre during the Second World War. The Germans were retreating stubbornly through Holland, pressed back by the 1st Canadian Army. The SAS was under the command of the 2nd Canadian Corps. Their task was to harry the retreating Germans to the point at which it would be impossible to adopt an adequate defence line against the oncoming Canadians. The SAS brief was broad; it included preserving a vital airfield, Steenwijk, from destruction, preventing the demolition of some eighteen bridges, reconnaissance of all available advance routes, and the supply of intelligence. Whenever possible they would co-operate with local resistance forces in these tasks. This was Operation 'Amherst'. In so far as it involved sabotage or impeding the enemy behind his own lines it was a typical SAS task; in so far as it was a matter of blind-dropping close behind the enemy positions it was a task for which they were neither suited nor equipped. However, at this stage in the war the SAS was not likely to demur at any task it was allotted; if it was going to survive the war it had to be in at the finish, with a record of adaptability to current circumstances. If at this stage the regiment had drifted into disuse, in the great post-war rundown it would be disbanded with all the other special forces which had done an excellent job at some stage in the war but whose creation and continuance had stemmed from very special circumstances. Once the special circumstances ceased to apply – as would happen in peace-time – so the new unit would cease to exist. There would, in any case, be enough log-rolling to preserve older, more orthodox formations, without considering the newcomers. In the event this desperate attempt to be in at the finish did not achieve its long-term objectives and when the SAS was recreated and found a new rôle it was due to its earlier history rather than its later activities. This end-of-the-war period has been criticized by some of the SAS as reckless and not over-intelligent; however, opinions vary.

'Amherst' was a large group; it totalled 700, of whom 86 were officers. The numbers were divided equally between British and French. They were dropped in nineteen different areas and split up to make 50 small parties. The drop took place at 1,400 feet through 10/10ths cloud – that is no visibility at all – yet the margin of error was very small. 38 Group RAF provided the 47 Stirlings and pilots required for the drop. The drop represented a remarkable achievement, for the parachutists could well have been dropped many miles away from their appointed zones, and aircraft could well have been lost under these exacting conditions. Unfortunately the plan to drop jeeps had to be abandoned as the lack of visibility would have made it impossible to place them in the required area.

The operation was scheduled to last 72 hours only but a lot of work was packed into the time. The Canadians were well-pleased by the chaos and disruption caused to the high-grade German troops facing them. The French appear to have enjoyed themselves enormously, as did the Dutch resistance who worked in conjunction with them. SAS losses totalled 29 killed, 35 wounded and 29 missing. Enemy losses could not be ascertained exactly but were believed to be 270 killed, 220 wounded and 187 taken prisoner. But the main gain of the enterprise was not the damage to humans but the destruction of transport and plans.

Another operation which took place in the same area (north-east Holland) was less satisfactory. This was 'Howard', using one and a half squadrons of 1 SAS, a total of 180. Their mission was to recce the area ahead of 4th Canadian

Armoured Division, for which task they had 40 jeeps. In reasonably open country an armoured jeep may be used very successfully in this type of operation for it is too small, manoeuvrable and fast moving to make anything but a most difficult target. However the Dutch countryside, although open, is too cut up by canals and dykes for this type of jeep use. Furthermore there were numerous minefields and strongly-held prepared positions. 1 SAS, commanded with great vigour, dash, and resource, by Lieutenant Colonel 'Paddy' Mayne, inflicted a certain amount of damage but sustained heavy casualties.

'Larkswood' by 300 Belgian members of the SAS with 45 jeeps paid heavily for its successes. This began with 2 Canadian Corps on 5th April 1945 but later operated with the Polish Armoured Division, on both occasions in a reconnaissance rôle. One of their more notable exploits was the capture of von Ribbentrop, who was about to commit suicide. Ribbentrop was one of the better known of the Nazi hierarchy as he had been a pre-war Ambassador.

'Archway' which followed was a mixed force in that it consisted of forces from both 1 and 2 SAS, making in all a total of 430. It had 75 jeeps, and a few three-tonners and 15cwt trucks for supply. The Commander, Lieutenant Colonel Brian Franks, had a variety of tasks and missions. Initially the force was engaged on reconnaissance – first with 6th Airborne, then with 11th Armoured Division, and then with 15th (Scottish) Division. They were the first British troops to enter Kiel. Later they were occupied in counter-intelligence work, and captured a number of Nazi war criminals. It might be thought that with Allied troops on German soil and the war clearly lost that the Germans would have put up mere token resistance. This was not so. In the closing stages the Germans fought with fanatical courage and determination. In consequence casualties among Allied troops were high and there was no question of an easy ride home.

The final score in France, Belgium, Holland and Germany was as follows: out of the 2,000 engaged, 330 became

David Stirling

Italy: 2 SAS at Castino, 1945

One of the original jeeps.
Note the Condensor at the front, the .50 Browning
and the Vickers Ks

SAS in Malaya, 1956.
Iban tracker on left of picture

Kiwi patrol, Malaya ▶

Outpost in Aden

Boat training in a Gemini.
Note frogman in the centre

The SAS parachutist of today

casualties. For this they had killed or seriously wounded 7,733 enemy and captured 4,784 prisoners. The total of prisoners would be increased by 18,000 if the Division which had been cut off at Issoudun was included. This had surrendered to the SAS after finding it was completely cut off from the rest of the German army; it had tried to slip away from the Atlantic coast and withdraw through a rapidly closing gap between General Patton's Third Army and General Patch's Seventh Army, which was advancing from the south, but its progress had been delayed by demolitions and harassment by SAS and Maquis. Approximately 700 motor vehicles were captured or destroyed. Seven trains were destroyed, as well as 29 locomotives and 89 individual trucks; 33 trains were derailed and railway lines cut 164 times. In addition numerous bombing targets were reported to the RAF. These were tangible gains. Less easy, but not necessarily less important, was the effect SAS presence had on morale. For the resistance fighter it was of the highest value to know that he was in touch with larger forces, could receive help, would be properly armed, supplied and assisted; for the enemy it was a constant drain to have a well-armed, elusive and deadly enemy at work in his rear areas. Experience taught that these parties should not be too large, and should be used – if the best advantage was to be obtained – well behind the enemy front lines.

Twenty-five or thirty years later, the life of an SAS man behind the lines may seem one long, glorious adventure. To some perhaps it was, but to others it was like any other part of the war – long periods of discomfort and boredom interspersed with brief periods of intense excitement. Danger was always present. You might be betrayed, captured by chance, or run into more firepower than you had bargained for. In 1944 the BDS (Befehlshaber der Sicherheitspolizei – Chief of the Security Police) issued a secret order that all parachutists captured behind the lines were to be shot. The fact that they would be wearing uniform would make no difference. These orders led to the murder of members of 2 SAS who took part in 'Loyton' and 'Pistol' in the summer and autumn of 1944. Three senior Gestapo officers were hanged for this crime two years later.

On 'Loyton' there were various small actions immediately after the drop and three men were captured by the Germans. On the second drop three more were carried away from the DZ by the wind and one broke his thigh. They too were captured. Another eight, who had become separated, were captured as the result of an action by a French informer. In all 31 were made prisoners, of whom only one escaped. The lesson from this was that there were a number of informers in the French Maquis, and small isolated detachments were liable to be betrayed to the SS or Gestapo who were concentrated in that area. East of the Vosges ridge the Alsace population felt some affinity with the Germans and the area was thick with collaborationists and informers. West of the Vosges it was an entirely different story.

A second Operation 'Pistol' dropped on 15th/16th September took note of the danger of co-operating operationally with the local maquis and dropped to pre-arranged DZs without local reception or lights. No information was passed to the local population and no contact made. However, some men were dropped away from their zones and were captured. Of the parachutists captured from 'Pistol' one only was shot, and this after some erratic treatment, some of which had been good and had included special medicines. The 'Loyton' parachutists were shot by the Gestapo, as were four American airmen who had been brought down by anti-aircraft fire. In spite of being interrogated under the threat of execution by shot or bayonet they gave away nothing, as Gestapo papers record.*

An account of the deaths of eleven SAS men came from Mademoiselle Geneviève Devie, who was imprisoned in an adjoining cell. The prison had been bombed, making cracks in the wall. These had been plastered up but Mademoiselle Devie discovered there was a crack low down where her bed

* 31 men from 1 SAS had already been massacred by the Germans on 7th July, 1944. They are buried in Rome.

had been pushed against the wall. Through this she could see what was going on in the next cell but talking was very difficult – she did not understand English well enough to grasp the correct names – but she learnt they were SAS and watched their methodical murder.

The executioners started with No.1 [she said] leading to a slow death at the end of three weeks. All knew themselves to be condemned. Everyone counted the days and all suffered from hunger and cold and lack of news from the outside world. But not one raised a murmur or lost his smile.

Near the DZ was the town of Moussey. The full story of the fall of this town was given in the SAS magazine *Mars and Minerva* for December 1961. It was written by Christopher Sykes, who was one of the members of 'Loyton'. As few people will have the chance to read this article, extracts are given here.

Every member of the SAS ought to know the name of Moussey. It is a small town situated in a valley of the Vosges mountains of Eastern France. It lies about 40 miles south-east of Nancy and about 10 miles north of St Dié. Any SAS man who finds himself in eastern France ought to go there. He will not be disappointed by what he finds. Like all the Vosges villages and towns, Moussey is spread along its valley, being over a mile from end to end though never more than a few hundred yards across.

In September 1944 the Commanding Officer of No.2 SAS Regiment, Lieutenant Colonel B.M. Franks, DSO, MC, led the last of our parachute operations on French soil. The original drop was near Baccarat to the north and after many adventures we migrated to the woods near Moussey, where we made a headquarters. The operation occurred at a time when General Patton's advance to Nancy was held up by a supply breakdown in the Army Group to which he belonged. That meant that our mission, designed to last about ten days, was protracted to about six weeks. During most of that time we depended on the people of Moussey for many of the necessities of life, and for help of every kind. They gave us everything we asked for, and more. They were the staunchest of Allies and in manifestly bad times, for with the hold-up of the

181

American army, and continued German reinforcement along the River Meurthe a few miles to the west, our difficulties increased daily. It was a nightmare time, but throughout it the civilian population was in far greater danger than we were. We could move rapidly from place to place, but, except for a few of the men, the civilians could not, and if they did, they perforce left hostages behind.

At length at the end of September, the Germans became exasperated at the help that they knew the people of Moussey were giving us, and they took their revenge. It was a terrible revenge, another hideous blot on the hideously sullied German record. They rounded up as many as they could find of the population and interrogated them with accustomed Nazi brutality. When no one gave us away notwithstanding, the Germans removed the men to concentration camps. The number taken to those horrible prisons was two hundred and ten. Only seventy came back, and some of the survivors died soon after their return as the result of what they had been through. By this disaster Moussey lost a tenth of its entire population. There is no evidence that even under torture and ill treatment any one of them at any time gave us away. Our Headquarters in the woods were never discovered by the Germans. I visited them after the war and found many relics of ourselves and no trace of our enemies having been there.

We ourselves suffered thirty-two casualties during the whole operation, most of them in other places, but ten of our men fell in the neighbourhood of Moussey. After the war, it was decided, at the suggestion of the parish priest, the Abbé Gassman, to make a little SAS cemetery at Moussey in the graveyard by the church. In the late summer of 1945 the whole Moussey population and that of the villages adjoining came to the funeral of our ten. Since those to be buried were of different religions, the parish priest organised a bi-denominational service. A Requiem Mass was said in the church by the Abbé Gassman, followed by the Anglican service for the dead conducted in the church by the Regimental Chaplain, the Reverend John Kent, at present Vicar of Selby. At the gravesides the same order was followed; Abbé Gassman performed the Catholic rites, Captain Kent the Anglican ones. The neighbouring clergy, both Catholic and Protestant, attended. Sometimes to-day, when talk turns to Church union, and the great difficulties in its way, I remember that beautiful ceremony at which I was privileged to command the guard of honour.

Sykes went on to say that a few years after the war the

Imperial War Graves Commission decided, quite reasonably, that the SAS should be re-interred in an official cemetery. This was bitterly resented by the inhabitants of Moussey who felt that the SAS graves were a part of Moussey. The War Graves Commission very sensibly appreciated the strong feelings and ties involved and designated the Moussey graveyard as an official war cemetery. Every year flowers are laid on the graves and on the 1919 and 1946 memorial. SAS men who visit Moussey feel a kinship with this town and its inhabitants; they are not foreigners or visitors but are a part of Moussey history.

The Abbé Gassman was 'the tower of strength round which the resistance in Moussey was so firmly and valiantly built'. Not only that, he was also full of compassion, and after liberation did 'all he could to ensure humane treatment for Germans captured by the Maquis and decent burial for the German dead'.

It can be imagined [Christopher Sykes records] how great is the anti-German feeling in a place which had suffered as severely as Moussey. The feeling persists to this day, and to this day the Abbé Gassman risks his popularity by insisting that, great as is the iniquity of many Germans, to condemn a whole nation is a folly.

What then is one to make of the story of Moussey. I find it very strange and awe-inspiring. The first thing to realise is that, had there been no SAS operation there, then, in all probability, the storm of war would have passed over this town. To a large extent it was on our unworthy account that so much was endured; a humbling and disturbing thought. When I first went back there after the liberation I was in some dread as to how I would be received. By what right had we taken such a cruel advantage of the innate courage and loyalty of the people? What could I say in reply if they blamed us for the loss of half their young men. But my fears were utterly groundless. As I have said, SAS men are members of the Moussey family, and it has been so from the beginning. Why has it been so? I can only guess.

The people of Lorraine are soldierly and direct in character and, as befits the inhabitants of St Joan's country, ardently patriotic. Strange as it may seem, I think that many people in Moussey feel positive gratitude that our presence enabled them to take an active part in the war against Nazism. I know that may seem extravagant but I can see no other explanation of the warmth of affection given to our regiment and to the chance visitor from among us. I think that what I have suggested may explain also the veneration accorded to our dead. When France was defeated in 1940 she fell from a great height. We who have not suffered comparable disasters are slow to imagine how fearful was the wound to French pride, and how deeply that wound was felt and is still felt by individual Frenchmen. The patriotism of France is a fiery and indeed terrifying force. If our operation did nothing else in 1944, it did open a way for that force to help in some sort to put right a great wrong.

Two messages in 1944 recognised the effect SAS activity was having. One was in the form of a letter from General Eisenhower to Brigadier McLeod:

Dear McLeod,
I wish to send my congratulations to all ranks of the Special Air Service Brigade on the contribution which they have made to the success of the Allied Expeditionary Force.

The ruthlessness with which the enemy have attacked Special Air Service troops has been an indication of the injury which you were able to cause to the German armed forces both by your own efforts and by the information which you gave of German disposition and movements.

Many Special Air Service troops are still behind enemy lines; others are being reformed for new tasks. To all of them I say, 'Well done, and good luck!'

Yours sincerely<br>Dwight D. Eisenhower

8 Oct 1944

The other was a broadcast by Lieutenant General F.A.M. Browning, KB, DSO, to SAS troops behind the German lines.

1900 hours 8th September 1944.
Now that the story of your operations and exploits since D Day is becoming known and confirmed, I am speaking to you this evening in order to tell you what Field Marshal Montgomery and the Commanders in the field feel about your activities.

I saw the Commander-in-Chief yesterday and told him I would be speaking to you to-day. He proposes to send you a personal message,

184

and in the meantime, I am going to tell you what views are held about your efforts.

It is considered that the operations you have carried out have had more effect in hastening the disintegration of the German Seventh and Fifth Armies than any other single effort in the Army. Considering the numbers involved, you have done a job of work which has had a most telling effect on the enemy and which, I fully believe, no other troops in the world could have done.

I know the strain has been great because operating as you do entails the most constant vigilance and cunning which no other troops are called upon to display.

I personally have kept in the closest touch with all your activities and have attempted to direct them as a result of the information the Armies and you have supplied so that, firstly, you were given fair, reasonable, but vital tasks, and at the same time those tasks were designed to have the most effect against the German armies as a whole.

To say that you have done your job well is to put it mildly. You have done magnificently. There is still a lot of clearing up to be done, and in this you are pulling more than your full weight.

You will get Field Marshal Montgomery's message shortly but in the meantime I want you to know how we and the rest of the Army feel about you. In this short talk I hope I have made that abundantly clear to you all.

Good fortune and good hunting.

With the SAS in France was the Reverend J. Fraser McLuskey who wrote a book entitled *Parachute Padre* describing his experiences. Although he did not carry arms he accompanied the SAS on many of their expeditions, exposed to all the risks without being able to defend himself. In quieter moments he conducted services and even held confirmation classes. Of his life there he wrote:

All the members of the troop were experienced campaigners and were as a rule more concerned by a plague of wasps which made cooking and eating a nightmare than by the proximity of the enemy. Two of the most highly skilled among them were Captain Johnny Cooper* and Sergeant-Major Jack Terry. Johnny and Jack, both

---

* Now Lieutenant Colonel J.M. Cooper, DCM.

veterans of the Middle East campaign, were inseparable companions, and I enjoyed sharing their patrols. Like most of our men, they had both graduated in the Commando School, and had learned the lesson of silent and speedy movement – the first lesson for the life we were leading. When we meet at reunions in Euston or Waterloo, both are wearing civilian clothes, and even yet, to my eye, looking a little odd out of uniform. I see them still, when a night alarm had been given, moving with quiet and unhurried step to their vantage-points, knives at the ready and tommy-guns unslung. Johnny Cooper has tried his fortunes now overseas. Jack is a police-constable in Sheffield. I fancy that upon occasion he wishes its good citizens were a trifle less law-abiding. And on those who break the law, so clumsily and ineptly, he must sometimes cast a pitying eye.

McLuskey was popular with the SAS because they realised that if he had not been in Holy Orders he would have made as good an SAS soldier as any. There are, of course, numerous examples of padres exposing themselves to greater dangers than the troops they ministered to, but usually the period of strain is much shorter. His comment on the feelings of the group merits inclusion here:

We did not worship in France solely because we were afraid. We lived continually 'at the ready' but we did not live in constant fear. Worship had meaning and reality for us because we lived together. We were at one in worship partly, at least, because we were at one in work. We shared life together; we ate and lived together; we shared the same night vigils, the same expeditions and the same chances, the same hopes, the same fears. The ground on which we cooked and ate and slept, was the ground on which at any moment we might find ourselves defending our possessions and our lives, was the ground on which we worshipped. Common ground was sacred ground.

Earlier, the jeep has been described as 'the greatest invention of the war'. This may not be strictly true but it is not surprising that the jeep was to the SAS what the horse has been to cavalry men; they believed their steed enjoyed the encounter as much as they did. Possibly the SAS attributed the same *berserkgangr** to their jeeps.

* Old Norse: 'joy in battle', an attribute of the Vikings and Normans.

Between seventy and eighty jeeps were landed by parachute. They varied a little in equipment according to what use was envisaged for them. When equipped with extra petrol tanks they had a range of up to 700 miles, but in situations where a certain amount of armour plating was advisable their scope was obviously less. Standard equipment was the twin Vickers .303 mounted front and rear but sometimes a .50 Browning replaced the Vickers at the rear. Frequently they also carried Bren MGs and a 3-inch mortar in every third vehicle. The value of the Vickers K has already been described. Within a range of 25 yards it was accurate and devastating; beyond that distance it was decidedly erratic because the build up of recoil and vibration caused it to shake widely. Properly mounted – as it had been when used on aircraft – its accurate range was greater but in the jeep it could only be mounted on its base. Jeeps towed the .75 Howitzers and 6-pounders. On certain occasions 4.2 mortars were also carried in jeeps. A jeep on operations, crammed with petrol, ammunition and time bombs, was a fairly hot seat, and about one third were lost on operations in Europe; happily though, even when a jeep was knocked out, its personnel were usually able to get away.

There is, of course, a vast amount more that could be said – if there were space and time enough – about these operations. Much of it has gone unrecorded and has faded from the memories of those concerned. Now and again a fragment of a report gives an illuminating insight into the conditions and debonair attitude of those concerned. For example Lieutenant Marx – on 'Loyton' – reported: *At 2200 our party moved into the cellar of a burning house to keep warm*. This, some might say, is taking adaptability too far.

In the operations in north-west Europe a number of men distinguished themselves by their coolness, daring, and efficiency, but none more so than 'Paddy' – Lieutenant Colonel R.B. Mayne – who commanded 1 SAS. Mayne's activities were recognised by the award of a DSO and three bars, but next to David Stirling he was probably the most under-decorated man of the war in relation to his activities.

Mayne was not only big, but was immensely strong and

187

quick. He was highly intelligent and a good organiser. He was also compassionate. These qualities alone would not, of course, have made him the great fighter and leader that he was. Mayne probably owed much of his success to methodical, careful planning. If he had to venture into the unknown he would go without hesitation, but if there was any possibility of preliminary reconnaissance he would carry this out meticulously. An example was when he parachuted into France on several occasions before the French operations started. He had heard conflicting reports about the reliability of the French forces, and wished to meet British agents on the ground to hear their views personally. In an apparent crisis both Mayne and Lassen would sometimes display a surprising lack of concern, rather like Drake finishing his game of bowls before the Armada. The reason was that they knew the exact time and place to hit the enemy where it would hurt most.

On occasion Mayne seemed to bear a charmed life, as when he won a third bar to his DSO. He was near Oldenburg at the time; a squadron commander – Major Bond – had been killed, and the drive forward had been halted. Mayne moved around in the open with complete disregard for heavy enemy fire, and cleared two enemy-held houses personally. He then rescued the wounded under heavy fire.

The end of the war in Germany was not quite the end of the war for the SAS. In Norway there were still 300,000 German soldiers. The task of disarming this vast army was given to 1 and 2 SAS who were agreeably surprised to find that the Germans were quite happy to lay down their arms without giving any trouble. Their motivation was due to the fact that the SAS arrived swiftly – and probably had an awesome reputation. The Germans could have caused endless trouble by destroying factories, fighting to the death and so on, but did not.

At the end of the war Mayne had no desire to stay on in a peacetime army so he returned to his former profession as a solicitor. He was appointed Secretary of the Incorporated Law Society of Northern Ireland. In 1955 he was killed in a car accident in Newtownards, near Belfast, the town where he had been born forty years before.

Although the war in Europe was over on 8th May 1945, out in the Far East the fighting was still as bitter as ever. In Burma, Rangoon had just been captured but this was by no means the end of the campaign. There were still large Japanese forces under arms – possibly a total of 60,000. The number involved was less important than their fanatical determination, and the ruggedness of the country. There was also a large Japanese army in Malaya. Had the latter country been invaded before the Japanese surrender the Allied casualty rate would have been enormous, for the Japanese had made detailed preparations for resistance in the best Samurai tradition. In the Pacific American forces had captured Iwo Jima, an island $4\frac{1}{2}$ miles long by $2\frac{1}{2}$ wide which lay roughly half way between the Mariana Islands and Tokyo. Of the 20,000 Japanese garrison only 216 were taken prisoner. The battle for Okinawa, which had begun on 1st April 1945 and which would continue till June 20th, was of equal toughness. On the Japanese mainland, old men, women and children were being given rudimentary military training and could be seen at the end of a long working day lunging away with bayonets. If Japan had to be invaded there could be no doubt that – as estimated – Allied casualties could amount to a million, not including those surviving prisoners of war who would be prudently disposed of by machine-gun fire as had been done in the Philippines. Europe might be settled but there was a lot of work still to be got through in the Far East.

David Stirling, who had now been freed from Colditz, was – as might be expected – already planning fresh tasks for the SAS. Foremost among them was an extensive guerrilla operation along the railway line running from Manchuria. However, before this could be put into operation the atomic bombs on Hiroshima and Nagasaki ended the Far East war on 15th August 1945.

With the end of all fighting it was clear that there was no further use for the SAS. In August 1945, 1 and 2 SAS returned from Norway. On 21st September 1945 the Belgian regiment was formally handed over to the Belgian army, which retained it. On 1st October 1945 the French regiments were handed over to the French army and were retained. These units were presented with flags and medals by Brigadier J.M. Calvert. On 8th October 1945 HQ SAS and 1 and 2 regiments SAS were disbanded. It was all over. A regimental association was formed not so much to revive old memories as to give a hand to any former members of the regiment who might need it. And that was that.

But while the regiment was in abeyance there were several former members who, though they themselves were now demobilised, could envisage a continuing use for a force such as the SAS. If there were ever to be an atomic war the sort of soldier likely to survive it would be the SAS man, but what was vastly more important was the fact that if he was trained in the right way he might help to prevent it beginning or, if it had begun, to play a substantial part in winning it. The key to the future would be the vital artery, the nodal point, or, perhaps, the ability to inhibit altogether. Whatever the task, it would probably be more specialised and complex than anything previously attempted. And, in any task, there could be no doubt that the traditional SAS qualities, initiative, endurance and intelligence, would be essential.

# CHAPTER VII

# 21 SAS (Artists)
# The Rebirth

In a regimental history such as this it is essential to identify significant changes and the reason for them. The policy-makers of the period 1941–45 are easily singled out, and their contribution has been described already; the figures who enabled the SAS to be reborn are less easily brought to light. As may be expected, enquiries tend to meet with modest disclaimers from those concerned. But among the many to whom credit is due three names stand out. They were Brigadier J.M. Calvert, Lieutenant Colonel B.M.F. Franks, and Major L.E.O.T. Hart.

During 1946 the War Office conducted an enquiry into the use of Special Air Service troops. This gave a very full analysis of the part played by the SAS during the past war and reached the following conclusions:

1. There was unlikely ever again to be a war with static front lines, except perhaps for short periods.
2. Small parties of *well-trained* and *thoroughly disciplined* troops operating behind the enemy lines achieve results out of all proportion to the numbers involved.
3. Their operations are, and should be quite distinct from non-regular groups such as Special Operations Executive, or Secret Service.
4. The full potential of such units is not yet fully known but there is clearly scope for tremendous development.
5. The rôle of SAS troops should never be confused with the normal rôle of the infantry. The SAS task is more specialised. The SAS does not necessarily drain the infantry of its best men but will often take a person who is no better than average in his ordinary tasks and

transform him into a specialist. A man of great individuality may not fit into an orthodox unit as well as he does to a specialist force. In wartime the best leaders were independent, well-travelled men who were often good linguists; university men, who had made full use of their brains at and after the university and were mature, were often successful.

With these broad guidelines it was obvious that the fund of SAS experience should not be relegated to limbo but should be used and developed. Ideally this would be in a regular unit with a supplementary reserve. However this was not conceivable in the prevailing conditions so instead a Territorial unit was approved. This was 21 SAS.

The numbering of Army units is always somewhat of a mystery, even to those serving inside them. As 1 and 2 SAS had gone before, the new TA unit should presumably be 3 SAS. However, there had already been a 3 SAS (the French regiment) and also a 4 SAS (French) and what virtually amounted to a 5 and 6 SAS in the form of the Belgian regiment (originally a squadron but a regiment in 1945) and F Squadron Phantom. Perhaps the new regiment should be 7 SAS. On the other hand the two strictly British units were 1 and 2 SAS so perhaps it should be called 12 SAS. This was sound except for the fact that there was originally in existence a unit called 12 Airborne (TA) Battalion. The solution was surprisingly easy. The numbers were reversed and the unit designated 21 SAS. Those who did not understand the sudden numerical leap ahead philosophically put it down to a well-meant attempt to confuse friends and enemies alike. Once the new numbering had begun it continued in a logical sequence and 22 and 23 SAS followed naturally.

The regiment was reborn in 1947 with Lieutenant Colonel B.M.F. Franks, DSO, MC, TD, as its first commanding officer. Second in Command was Major L.E.O.T. Hart, OBE. Major Hart had come to the SAS from the Rifle Brigade and had been Brigade Major in SAS HQ during 1944 and 1945.

The new unit looked around for a Regular parent body to which it might be affiliated. Several possibilities were considered and eventually it was attached to the Rifle Brigade. In the event there turned out to be a certain historical basis for this affinity, for the Artists Rifles, with whom the SAS shortly became merged, had a long-standing affiliation with the Greenjackets. The Rifle Brigade (originally the 95th Rifles) had been raised in January 1800 by Colonel Coote Manningham to exploit the possibilities of the new Baker rifle. Dressed in dark green with black buttons they soon acquired a reputation for tough fighting combined with novelty in tactics. They saw more fighting than any other unit in the Army at the time. Their success was due not only to the camouflage effect produced by their uniforms but to the fact that they insisted that every individual soldier must be a master of his craft and be able to operate alone and without orders.

The merger with the Artists Rifles was also singularly appropriate. The Artists Rifles had come into existence in 1859 when the formation of volunteer corps had been approved. The background to this movement of far-reaching importance was that England was almost at war with her recent (Crimean) ally France, and as a safeguard against sudden invasion the Conservative Government approved the Volunteer movement. 12,000 men enrolled in 1859 and although the French invasion scare was soon forgotten the force remained in being. Among those stirred by patriotic feelings was Edward Sterling – a curious coincidence that the two famous regiments were founded by men of the same name, apart from a minor difference in spelling – who was at that time a student at Cary's School of Art. The conception of an artist in those days was still of the Elizabethan variety, a vigorous man of action who could nevertheless turn his hand to painting, poetry, music or sculpture, with impressive results. Among the regiment's first members were such distinguished names as G.F. Watts, Lord Leighton, Holman Hunt, J.E. Millais and William Morris.

In accordance with normal practice the 38th Middlesex (Artists) Rifle Volunteers designed their own uniform and made up their own badge. They also paid for their own uniform and basic equipment. On the first day of enrolment 10th May 1860 119 men were attested, and eventually paraded in light grey tunic and trousers, black gaiters and a shako. Their badge depicted Mars and Minerva, and was designed by Private J.W. Wyon, engraver to the signet. Like all regimental badges and mottoes it was the subject of a good deal of irreverent comment but greatly cherished for all that. To-day the regimental magazine is entitled *Mars and Minerva*.

The new regiment was soon up to its establishment of four companies but this number was doubled by 1877. Initially they were equipped with muzzle-loading Enfields but these were replaced by Sniders in 1871. In 1900 the regiment's establishment was increased to twelve companies of which one was a machine-gun company and another cyclists and signallers. The first machine guns were a privately purchased gift from two brothers – they were Vickers-Maxims; subsequently the Vickers Ks were a form of private armament so throughout its history the SAS (Artists) has had a tradition of unorthodox initiative in the way of acquiring weapons. Another traditional similarity was in the wearing of beards. Mayne's red beard was well-known to the SAS and others, and although there were plenty among the early members of the SAS who liked to be clean-shaven there were plenty who didn't. In the original Artists it was twenty-three years before they had a CO without a beard, and even then his moustache and whiskers were a distinction of no uncommon sort.*

Although after 1863 the volunteers became an official part of the British army, which meant that commissions would be granted by the Sovereign on the recommendation of the Lord Lieutenant, they did not give up their practice of insisting that all officers should first serve in the ranks and subsequently be elected by the entire battalion. Subsequently the practice of battalion election fell into disuse but the tradition of officers all having to serve in the ranks continued until 1933. To-day most of the officers of 21 and 23 SAS have

* Beards are regarded with disfavour today.

served in the ranks; it is not obligatory to have done so, but it is customary.

The regiment was mobilised on 3rd August 1914. By the end of the First World War 15,022 men had been members of the Artists. They had won 8 VCs, 56 DSOs, 891 MCs, 20 DFCs, 15 AFCs, 6 DCMs, 15 MMs and 14 MSMs. In addition 564 were Mentioned in Despatches.

During the Second World War the Artists became an Officer Cadet Training Unit. Nevertheless they did not lose their excellent premises at 17 Duke's Road, Euston and these were extremely useful when the Artists was reformed in conjunction with the SAS.

In 1945 in the general demobilization the Artists Rifles disappeared like many another unit. In 1946 there was nothing, as its former members watched the politicians of the day repeat many – though fortunately not all – of the mistakes made by previous politicians after past wars. But in November 1946 the War Office came to the conclusion there was a place for a Territorial Army in the radiantly peaceful future and the announcement was made that it would be reconstituted on January 1st 1947.

Of the next stage, when the Artists was reborn in conjunction with 21 SAS, we have already spoken. Recruiting for 21 SAS (Artists) was started in September 1947. Once again the volunteers flowed in, many of them with experience in the other services. Again large numbers had to be rejected as not being up to the tremendously high physical standard required; again the principle of every recruit serving first in the ranks, whatever his previous commission or service, was implemented.

The new unit had certain advantages not normally possessed by TA units. Its type of work was properly known only to those who had taken part in it but the importance of that work was fully appreciated in the War Office. In consequence if the officers of the SAS said something about their work or requirements there was no one qualified to say otherwise. While Colonel Franks commanded 21 SAS it became a Corps of the Army, ranking next in seniority after the infantry; 21 SAS was the senior regiment in the Corps (see Appendix).

The blend of the two units has proved a happy one. Often when two highly individualistic units are merged one becomes a casualty and its history and tradition is regarded as a curiosity, not particularly interesting and certainly obsolete. The exact reverse applies with 21 SAS. As described earlier the SAS has considerable difficulty in sloughing off the false idea that they are a mysterious cloak and dagger unit, and the fact that they are also the Artists Rifles brings questioners back to reality. It is also highly beneficial to the TA to have units with a specialized function which makes them invaluable and indispensable to a war effort. Traditional functions of the Artists are still continued, and 21 SAS (Artists) mount guard at the opening of the Royal Academy Summer Exhibition. Another small guard is provided at the annual dinner of the Worshipful Company of Glovers for, in the tradition of City Companies, the Glovers 'adopted' the regiment in 1955.

The establishment of a TA unit is never easy and 21 (Artists) TA was hardly likely to be an exception. That it succeeded and prospered was due to the efforts of many, but notably to the Commanding Officers, Colonel J.N. Lapraik, Colonel D.G. Sutherland and Colonel J. Johnson. Commanding a TA unit successfully demands a rare blend of qualities which are sometimes found in an ex-Regular soldier, sometimes not. Sometimes civilians possess the right quality, sometimes not. With the right commanding officer a TA regiment may be able to put up a better performance than a regular unit – and sometimes does. Badly commanded, a TA unit is usually a disaster, whereas a regular unit may struggle along to better times.

21 had a good sprinkling of wartime experience of high quality, and this gave it a good start. Lapraik was the pioneer of overseas training, which has now become a regular feature for the Army. But it was not merely COs who solved the early problems; they were resolved by Warrant Officers, NCOs and troopers. A vital but often overlooked part of any unit is

196

the Q side – which can easily become chaotic in a TA unit. The task of organising the Q side of 21 with its ever-changing problems caused by its unusual assignments fell to Lieutenant Colonel Pinnock. Quartermasters are sometimes mentioned in military reminiscences but seldom with enthusiasm; here was one who was.

Of 21, and the later creation 23, their activities and training, we shall say more later. The next chapter deals with the reasons behind the creation of 22 SAS.

# CHAPTER VIII

# 22 SAS

In 1948 when the world was still recovering from the devastation of the Second World War a sinister portent of a troubled future was suddenly revealed. In Europe the Russians launched the 'Berlin blockade' by which they denied all road or rail access to the city, which lay in the Russian-administered zone of Germany, although the city itself was under four-power Allied government – England, France, America and Russia. The published reason for the denial of land access was to safeguard their zone against the effects of the new reformed currency which the other Allies had recently introduced in their zones, but it was clear that it was neither for this nor for any other reason advanced at the time that the blockade had been imposed, but merely to test the Allied resolve to stay in Berlin. The blockade had in fact been broken by a massive airlift which transported every form of food and fuel into the beleaguered city.

When the Berlin blockade was going on there was considerable communist pressure on other governments in other parts of the world. Subsequently it transpired that a directive had been issued for all Communist Parties to make a bid for power at the same time as Mao-Tse-Tung launched his campaign to take over the government of China. Suddenly – and usually unexpectedly – one country after another found itself struck by a minor revolution. India suffered less than some because she was in the throes of independence and the creation of India and Pakistan, but elsewhere, in Burma, Thailand, Indo-China, Malaya, Indonesia and the Philippines, the situation was all too clear. At the time of writing – 1970 – it would appear that all these movements with the exception of Indo-China (Viet Nam) have petered out, but it would be rash to assume that what does not show is not there.

One of the major prizes in 1948 was Malaya, which produces one-third of the world's supply of natural rubber and over half its supply of tin. At the foot of the peninsula was the great harbour and base of Singapore and, as had been shown in the Second World War, troops in control of the mainland would have no difficulty in acquiring Singapore.

The technique of revolution was quite simple, and Malaya was particularly vulnerable to it. Terrorist gangs would live in the jungle, emerge to destroy stocks or machinery, and fade back into the unknown taking with them food they had extorted from the villagers. As time went on they extended their activities to ambushing road convoys and trains, slashing rubber trees, murdering Chinese and others who were asked for protection money but were unwilling to pay, and generally bringing production virtually to a standstill. As time went on the terrorists gradually became more daring and as they had built up a huge intelligence organisation, were able to intimidate people in the towns, and even assassinate the High Commissioner. Orthodox military units which went out to do battle with the terrorists found the experience frustrating. The hard core of terrorists – and their leader Chin Peng* – had lived in the jungle with British troops in Force 136, a force to train and arm Chinese guerillas so that they would attack Japanese communications before and after we invaded the country. They were well aware of British methods, assets and liabilities. Furthermore they had been given many weapons by the Japanese after the surrender. The Communists had coerced or terrified the aborigines into co-operating and, therefore, long before a patrol could come on to one of the Communist Terrorist camps, the latter would have advance warning of the approach; they would therefore either disappear or have an ambush ready. The CT technique of ambushing was very highly developed, and they had a disconcerting habit of catching units as they emerged from

* He was awarded an OBE for his work!

the jungle after a long, wearying patrol with little in their minds except the thought of a cold shower and a long drink. CT numbers were not precisely known but were thought to be 5,000 in the jungle; subsequently it was realised that nearly twice this number was concerned. Last but not least they were hard core fanatics who would endure extreme privation, take any risk, and had no scruples whatever. The jungle in which they operated was in places very thick, and unmapped. About three-quarters of Malaya is still covered by jungle. Rubber plantations have been established in cleared areas and most of them had patches of jungle on the fringe. Tin mines were often in remote areas and had a long history of disaffected Chinese labour of Communist persuasion. The first necessity was to protect law abiding workers, such as rubber-tappers whose job was to empty the latex cups but who were often informed by the Terrorists that they would be nailed to the trees if they tried to continue. Against all this, orthodox units made some headway, but not enough. There were problems of acclimatisation, disease, jungle sores from cuts and scratches, heat, humidity, insects, finding one's way, and acute discomfort and boredom. Furthermore, once in the jungle it was often difficult to know who was the hunter and who the hunted.

However, it was not the unsatisfactory nature of the first phase of the Malayan campaign which brought the SAS to Malaya but an entirely different conflict – the Korean War.

The Korean War, it will be remembered, had begun on 25th June 1950 when North Korean troops crossed the 38th Parallel. The 38th Parallel was a demarcation line arranged by the local commanders when the Japanese war ended and American and Russian troops moved in to occupy this former Japanese colony. It was not a proper defensive position but merely a convenient line of latitude, and this fact seems to have encouraged the Communist North Korean government to think a quick push would take them south before the South Koreans could organise any adequate defence against a surprise attack. The calculation went wrong immediately, for on the day of attack the United Nations passed a resolution condemning North Korean aggression and authorizing support for South Korea. Even so the South Korean forces were pushed back to the outskirts of Pusan before effective help could materialize. On 15th September US Marines landed at Inchon and before long the South Koreans and their United Nations supporters were sweeping up to the Manchurian border. In November the Chinese intervened and the conflict see-sawed back.

As soon as the fighting began it was clear to 21 SAS that here was a war which lent itself readily to SAS type operations behind the lines. Accordingly M Squadron, a force made up of volunteers mostly with war-time experience and from the Z Reserve, was organised under Major Anthony Greville-Bell. Before they could embark for Korea the situation had changed dramatically, first through the UN successes and then the Chinese intervention, and there was no longer any scope for SAS activity in the area.* It seemed a pity to waste the effort that had gone into organising and equipping this force, so with Korea out of the question they were sent to Singapore. Here they were able to link up with the Malayan Scouts and, in January 1951, became the joint founders of a Regular regiment – an event which had never happened to a' TA unit before and is unlikely ever to happen again.

The Malayan Scouts, referred to in the previous paragraph, were the creation of Major J.M. Calvert – at the end of the war, with the reduction in establishment he had reverted from Brigadier to Major; the Regular army at this time was full of people who had held much higher ranks in wartime. Calvert was in Hong Kong in 1950, when he was sent for by General Sir John Harding, the Commander-in-Chief, Far Eastern Land Forces, who asked him whether in view of his experience of fighting Japanese in the Burma jungle he had any ideas on fighting Chinese in the Malayan jungle. Calvert had plenty of ideas, and the result was that he

---

* General MacArthur had specifically asked for an SAS force but then decided to use Marines instead. In M Force was Anthony Royle, MP, who was suddenly crippled by polio but made a miraculous recovery – by determination.

returned to Hong Kong with the authority to recruit a force to fight the Communist Terrorists in the Malayan jungle – Hong Kong was full of under-employed troops in 1950. The garrison had been built up to 30,000 when the Communist Revolution in China was in full spate and it seemed likely that a few probes might be made towards the Colony to test its resolution. When the Communists appeared to have no immediate aspirations in Hong Kong there were too many troops doing too little in the Colony, and many were prepared to volunteer for anything out of sheer boredom.

As we have seen, Calvert was already a legend. A Cambridge double-blue, a man who had resigned his regular commission to fight in Finland as a volunteer – he rejoined the British Army as a private – and founder member of the Commandos, an expert on jungle-fighting, holder of 13 decorations, Calvert was undoubtedly a man to follow. He was also an idealist who believed in the Commonwealth as a means of spreading justice, faith and honesty. He was chivalrous almost to the point of folly, and would never agree to brutal methods of acquiring information. Furthermore he was absolutely loyal to his own staff. Unfortunately a number of those who followed him into the Malayan Scouts were not of the same dedicated stamp. They were virtually useless in the jungle, but owing to the problem of finding replacements it took years to eliminate them from the force. This, as much as anything, reinforced the SAS conviction that a rigorous selection technique must be applied before training even began.

However, if the Malayan Scouts contained a number of losers it also produced some winners. Among them was J.M. Woodhouse. He is described by those who fought with him – of all ranks – as the best squadron commander the regiment ever had and one of the finest COs a regiment could hope for. He came from Dorset and had joined the Army as a private on leaving his public school in 1941. He had had a varied experience and, having spent two years learning Russian, had worked as an interpreter with the Russians. Calvert recruited him as an Intelligence Officer and it was only later when

Woodhouse rejoined the SAS as a regimental officer under Colonel Lea* that Woodhouse's † remarkable talent for leading men, finding his way, and fighting in the jungle was fully realised. Men who served with Woodhouse admired and were greatly attached to him but regarded him with cautious respect bordering on fear. With Woodhouse someone said: 'You just had to be on top of your job. God knows what would have happened if you weren't because nobody ever took a chance on it.' Yet no one meeting and knowing Woodhouse could miss the fact that relentlessly efficient though he was, here also was a man of great compassion and understanding. You would also note that he had a sense of humour, an enquiring mind, was extremely modest, and was a professional soldier to his finger-tips.

Woodhouse was briefed by Calvert who had sized up the Malayan situation; his assessment would be proved right. Calvert, who was not merely a great guerilla fighter but a creative thinker as well, had seized on the two main requirements for success as far as his own unit was concerned. He did not, of course, think they could win the war on their own but he did think they could have a very considerable influence on it. The first was to win over the Aborigines; a preliminary step would be to cease to refer to them as 'Sakai' which was a derogatory Malay word meaning slaves; the second was to protect the isolated Chinese and therefore stop the Communists extracting food and money from them. Calvert's views on this latter point were sent to Lieutenant General Sir Harold Briggs, the Director of Operations, and formed the basis of the famous and successful 'Briggs Plan' by which thousands of villagers were moved to fresh villages or 'Kampongs' or in safe areas where they could be protected. Eventually many of them became so attached to their new homes that they did not wish to move back to their old ones

* Now Lieutenant General G.H. Lea, CB, DSO, MBE.
† When a man let off his rifle by accident, Woodhouse took it off him and substituted a grenade – with the pin out. 'Carry that for a week' he said, 'til you've learnt to handle a rifle'.

when the Emergency was over. Meanwhile the Army, in close co-operation with the police and intelligence sources, would ambush the Communists when and where they emerged from the jungle. As areas of the country were gradually stabilized the scouts would send in deep-probing units which would live in the jungle for months on end and hunt the terrorists on their own home ground. Calvert, it was clear, was not a mere tactician but had a brain which thought strategically, deducing the weaknesses of the apparently unconquerable enemy. Above all he was suspicious of preconceived ideas. Most of the previous ideas about settling the Malayan emergency had come from people who had never seen the jungle and were not aware that an enemy could lie unnoticed within a few yards of the hot, harassed and often bewildered men looking for him.

Training for jungle warfare is always arduous but had to be especially so for the type of operations now envisaged. Calvert's schedule was nothing if not realistic. There was no grenade range to practise on so they ran between monsoon drains – narrow concrete channels four or five feet deep; on the order they would all leap for cover and one man would throw the grenade. Leaping into a concrete drain can be a painful process but no one hesitated. Stalking was taught with similar realism. Two men armed with airguns, and wearing fencing masks, would crawl towards the centre of a piece of scrub about one hundred yards long. The aim was to shoot one's opponent before being shot by him and there was every inducement to do so for an air gun pellet can be very painful on bare flesh.

A vital requirement in the jungle was the ability to find one's way. Visibility would probably be up to twenty yards – or less. Densely packed foliage overhead would blot out the stars and prevent a night check. There were no landmarks. If you went wrong you went very wrong indeed; you carried your own food and if you did not arrive at your destination on time you could be very hungry, if not actually starving. Confrontation with the enemy, when it occurred, would be so quick that a man would kill or be killed in a second, and a missed shot would mean an enemy lost for weeks and a long patrol wasted. Preconceptions were thrown overboard, particularly the one that men could not patrol for longer than three weeks at a time in the jungle. Other points were discovered less quickly. At first they carried too much ammunition and would use it wastefully, later they carried much less but used it to much greater effect; this was because they were less exhausted and therefore more alert. Men never messed together, but would cook singly or in twos and threes, usually choosing curry and rice. Occasionally there would be fresh vegetables, and a rum ration.

All this did not, of course, come at once. The Malayan Scouts, SAS, arrived in Malaya in 1950 and the regiment spent nine years perfecting jungle fighting. Subsequently their ideas were still further improved in Borneo.

Calvert was invalided home in 1951; after he left, the unit was taken out of the jungle and used as infantry at the edges. Woodhouse continued to train it but was himself returned to England in 1952 where he initiated a new selection system for recruits. Woodhouse returned to Malaya in 1955 and although he found the regiment fit and capable he was sorry to see that Calvert's ideas were no longer considered. During the next two years he himself implemented them.

Not least of the problems of Malaya was signalling. Conditions for wireless communication were appallingly bad owing to hills, trees and atmospherics. In the monsoons Malaya usually gets at least one first-class thunderstorm every day with almost continuous thunder and lightning. It might last an hour. Apart from the difficulties of reception there was the eternal problem of carrying a set large enough to do the task required. In the early days these weighed 30 pounds and each required a dozen 9-pound batteries to keep them going. Anyone who has not carried a 30-pound wireless on a slippery track should give himself the experience.

The SAS, which had never overlooked the fact that feet are probably the most reliable form of multi-purpose transport, was once more confirmed in its belief. Outside the jungle they used three-tonners – these trucks which must have the longest service record of any vehicle surely deserve an anthem – and the inevitable jeep. The RAF supplied Valettas known as 'the flying pigs' and helicopters when required. Helicopters were invaluable for evacuating casualties. Later in the campaign Beverleys were introduced.

It was an existence of contrasts. Outside the jungle they could sample the comfort and the luxury so easily provided in the tropics. Back on an operation they lived a life closely resembling that of mesolithic man, certainly as far as the basha was concerned. A basha was a shelter consisting of a crossbar six feet long tied to two uprights four feet high. A few more sticks, about seven feet long, were laid sloping from the crossbar to the ground. Ponchos were laid on the ground and on top. The only difference between this and pit-dwellings 10,000 years ago appears to be that in the absence of ponchos branches were used and the floor was hollowed out to give extra snugness.* The SAS man carried a pullover, PT shorts, socks, and a strip of parachute material to use as nightwear. Clothes were always soaking with rain or sweat. He carried a field dressing, maps, a compass, a rifle, grenades, a heavy sharp machete 18 inches long and a water-bottle. His top speed would be about one mile an hour but this pace would be discouraged as it might mean overlooking vital clues to the passage of others. The slow cautious, quiet, observant movement of primitive men was what was needed, and produced.

Rations had a little more variety than had been seen in the early days in the desert. Desert rations had included oatmeal which had been parched, browned in the oven and then rubbed into a coarse flour. A man could eat about three dessertspoons of it with a little water or sugar added. If he became thirsty he was given an onion to chew. In the jungle constant sweating made him thirsty but water was always available. Oatmeal appeared again in the shape of a breakfast

---

* Some bashas were made entirely of branches and leaves. British soldiers soon pick up native skills, and are often better at local craftsmanship than the 'locals'.

biscuit which could be eaten with a 4-ounce tin of ham and egg, and another biscuit and jam. Dinner was more substantial, usually being 4 ounces of steak and kidney pie, mixed veg, a pudding and cheese biscuits. There were variations in some packs such as beans, bacon or corned beef. Tea accompanied everything.

Experience gained at this time led to the development of the SAS 7–14 day ration, which became the forerunner of the British battle ration. The SAS ration pack was one of the outcomes of Lieutenant Colonel Oliver Brooke's study periods, and owed a great deal to the experience of Major Hugh Mercer. Colonel Brooke also emphasised the importance of what later became known as the 'Hearts and Minds' campaign, by which it was thought that the SAS might win over the aborigines by helping them and proving that it was in both the long and the short run better to support the British than the Communist Terrorists. The help would include medical aid but it was made absolutely clear from the start that help and friendship would be absolutely sincere and not just a means to an end. A consequence of this was that the SAS felt that they were leaving friends behind and were by no means happy about doing so when withdrawn from certain areas where the aborigines were vulnerable.

On the opposite side rations were also a problem. Rice is bulky and heavy, and it is not easily grown in jungle areas. The jungle produces wild bananas and other fruits – if you are lucky enough to find them – tapioca, and bamboo shoots and there are plenty of animals and fish, but the presence of traps for fish or pigs would give away enemy presence. When the SAS came upon these traps they would usually booby trap them or lay an ambush nearby.* Food from outside was supplied by the Min Yuen which was an organisation of civilian sympathisers; their exact number was probably quite large when the Communists appeared to be winning. Food was so important that there were severe penalties for stealing – death by strangulation.

* A turtle was once booby-trapped so that its unfortunate discoverer would be blown to pieces.

Wild animals were not as difficult as might be thought. Perhaps the most intense moment was that experienced by Sergeant Turnbull's patrol. They heard noises and took up ambush positions. Into the ambush walked a huge bull elephant, a little too large for the grenades they were holding with the pins out. The patrol scattered smartly and fortunately the elephant also decided to change direction. Tigers, with which Malaya abounds, usually took evasive action although on several occasions a patrol met a tiger face to face. Only old tigers became man-eaters, but the SAS were in no position to guess a tiger's age when they turned a corner and met one; usually the tiger disappeared before it could be questioned. Most dangerous of all animals was the seladang – or water buffalo – for it would circle and then charge without warning.

Snakes were rather more of a problem because they were plentiful and live in the sort of places which one might use for hasty concealment, as would scorpions. A snake will usually move swiftly away, but occasionally one would decide on a confrontation and had to be shot. The krait was particularly deadly and would sometimes rear up in the middle of a track.

Leeches were a frequent problem and there was no apparent answer to them. A big leech such as a lanchen could take half a pint of blood before being detected and removed. One man was seen to have 74 small leeches around his ankles. Removing them was difficult and required salt or a lighted cigarette. Leeches had extraordinary penetrative powers and could get in through the eyelet holes in a boot. They would come not only from damp ground but also from tree branches. If a patrol was in an area infested with leeches it was philosophically accepted that some – perhaps many – would get on to them. They were painless and therefore would not be detected for a while, although they might become painful later. The leech clearly had some anti-coagulant in its mouth for the bites would ooze blood for some fifteen minutes after its removal. Woodhouse's first experience of leeches was when he stripped down one night and found seventeen inside his trouser waistband; the blood ran to his ankles as he removed them. Fortunately leeches were not encountered in swamps, except when they dropped off trees. The worst area for leeches was the Kerbau valley, where they advanced towards the intruder like jerky little inverted Vs. Fortunately it was possible to avoid them at night for they would not venture on to a dry surface such as a poncho.

The two most dangerous insects were hornets and mosquitos. Hornets, which were of the thickness of the forefinger, had a powerful sting and were easily disturbed; mosquitos were everywhere and, of course, apart from the irritation of their bites, carried malaria.

There were a host of minor irritations such as ants and ticks, and skin infections which are inevitable in a hot, wet, climate. Prickly heat – a rash which can irritate until a man wishes to tear the skin off his body – tineas of various descriptions, such as footrot, were almost too familiar to deserve comment. The SAS were wryly amused when a police officer's wife was horrified to see aborigine women wearing nothing but a loincloth. She hastily provided them with bras – and in consequence tinea.\* Although the SAS were by no means immune to the charm of women when on leave, aborigine women were sacrosanct. Major Dare Newell had laid down: 'When dealing with guerillas ignore their women folk like poison; the women might not appreciate it but the men will.'

'Jungle' covered a wide variety of conditions. There was forest which consisted of large trees up to 200 feet high with their branches interlaced at the top, and there was bamboo which grew in clumps and fell in all directions, some of it being full of spiky thorns. Bamboo could be one of the most difficult types of jungle. Then there would be lalang, tall grass up to 12 feet high, probably rich in snakes. This would reflect the sun and be extremely hot. And of course there was thick scrub where everything had grown into a tangled mass.

The governing features of Malaya were a high temperature,

---

\* The first missionaries in the Pacific had done precisely the same in the 19th century.

high rainfall, and high humidity. This meant that vegetables grew with great speed; you can plant a pumpkin seed and ten weeks later eat the pumpkin which has grown from it. The country, including the mountainous area, is therefore covered with a thick coating of vegetation and under that cover the land may be reasonably dry or may be swamp. Swamp is not, of course, all of one type but in general is about thigh deep. Some swamp is caused by heavy rainfall and dries out in the dry season, other swamp is permanent. The water is full of trees and their entwined roots, mud and leaves. It is usually reddish, like the soil. Passage through swamps was by wading and was inevitably slow; sometimes it entailed clambering over tree roots or hacking through tangled branches.

In the spring of 1958 an extraordinary operation took place near Telok Anson, about 30 miles north-west of Kuala Lumpur in a swamp measuring approximately 10 by 18 miles. D Squadron under Major H. Thompson – who had been invalided home with chest trouble in 1955 but had recovered – knew there were Communist Terrorists living in the swamp and decided to winkle them out. The squadron had already considerable experience of living and operating in swamps. Their objective was two groups of CTs who had lived in the swamp many years under the leadership of Ah Hoi, nicknamed the 'Baby-killer'. They had a tremendous nuisance value over a very wide area and large numbers of troops had to be allocated to protective work because the CTs could not be tracked and eliminated. D Squadron parachuted in about 3 miles from the western edge, and gradually tracked the Communist Terrorists down. The squadron adapted itself to swamp life, and apparently found it pleasanter than many other areas they had been in. Not everyone would agree about swamp life being preferable to life elsewhere. Swamps in certain areas were up to twenty feet deep, extremely hot and infested with snakes. Men slept in hammocks and got out every morning into water – in which they stayed all day. This, as they put it, was 'less enjoyable than walking along the tops of mountain ridges, when with a little imagination you could think you were going for a Sunday afternoon stroll'. The

| | |
|---|---|
| | Jungle |
| | Tin |
| | Rubber |
| | Swamp |
| | Mountains |

0          40          80
Scale of Miles

THAILAND

PERLIS

Alor Star
KEDAH
S. Patani
PENANG
6105
PROVINCE
WELLESLEY

Kota Bahru

6194

KELANTAN

Kuala
Trengganu

TRENGGANU

R. Trengganu

South
China
Sea

PERAK
7110
Ipoh
CAMERON
HIGHLANDS
4794

R. Perak
6993
Kuala
Lipis
Fraser's
Hill
PAHANG
4958
Kuantan
R. Kuantan

R. Pahang

SELANGOR

Kuala
Lumpur

R. Langat
NEGRI
SEMBILAN
KUALA
LANGAT

MALACCA
4187

JOHORE

Malacca
Kluang

Strait
of
Malacca
R. Muar
Johore
Bahru

SINGAPORE

SUMATRA

Em

MALAYA

swamp was warmer than the hills at night and the sickness rate was low. They attributed the fact that swamp life was comparatively healthy to the iron in the water. It could of course have been otherwise, for some water in Malaya, and elsewhere, is contaminated with leptospirosis, a germ passed in rat's urine which enters the body through scratches or drinking. Leptospirosis takes about ten days to develop and is usually fatal. The bigger trees grew on a cupola of roots and this enabled both the SAS and CTs to build secure and comfortable bashas between the buttresses. By digging down between these roots they could also obtain clear water. Such hideouts were particularly advantageous for the Communists for it was extremely difficult to approach through the water without making some noise.

It is not, unfortunately, possible to give a detailed account of this operation here, but it ended in the complete elimination of the terrorists from the area. A considerable factor in its success was the skill shown in tracking. It is well-known that Ibans were imported from Borneo to assist in tracking but it is probably less well-known that British soldiers also developed an extraordinary skill in this art – and in not leaving tracks themselves – in every area. In the swamps they could follow from a piece of dislodged bark, a twisted leaf and so on. Notable among British trackers was Sergeant Turnbull who was better than the Ibans and more consistent. Turnbull was a Yorkshireman who had joined the Royal Artillery 'in order to see a bit of the world'. He joined the SAS and showed an exceptional ability to learn. He learnt three things exceptionally quickly and well; one was the ability to shoot fast but under perfect control, the second was fluent Malay so that he could talk to aborigines and Ibans as if it was a first language, and, as mentioned, tracking. On this operation he tracked the Communists for some 14 weeks, including a ten-mile stretch in the last week. Tracking, whether in swamp or otherwise, is an exhausting activity because it requires constant, non-stop, concentrated observation, and, of course, can be frustrating. Turnbull missed nothing, and could move with the speed and agility of a cat.

He carried a repeater shot gun – as many did – and this would fill a man with holes like a Gruyère cheese.

On one occasion just when his patrol was moving off south-east of Legap they spotted a terrorist some 20 yards away. Major Cartwright, who was then a new subaltern, said that Turnbull fired with such speed that the first three shots made an almost continuous bang. By the time the echoes died away Turnbull was standing over the terrorist to make sure he did not need a fourth. The terrorist on this occasion was the famous Ah Tuck, an important Communist organiser who had a great influence on the aborigines. Other expert trackers were Sergeant McFarland, an ex-Seaforth Highlander, Sergeant Hawkins and Sergeant Creighton. Tracking in Malaya was complicated by the fact that rain might destroy traces and the terrorists, once alerted, would move very fast indeed, faster, in fact, than British troops.

By the end of 1958 a massive anti-terrorist organisation had been built up in Malaya, and the SAS were only a small part of it. Some 6,398 terrorists had been killed and another 3,000 had been captured or had surrendered. The terrorists seemed to attract a flow of recruits although many of these became bored by the indoctrination. However, once a terrorist, you would be unlikely to give up easily – you might be disposed of if you appeared to waver and therefore endangered the group. However, many surrendered and were induced to persuade others. On our side 3,000 civilians and 2,000 of the security forces had been killed. Planters had displayed remarkable courage throughout the entire emergency although many were killed. The biggest factor in causing CT surrenders were the loss of leaders and the cutting off of food supplies.

The SAS contribution to the number killed was 108. It might reasonably be asked: what did the SAS do, if anything, which other troops could not do.

There were, of course, a number of regiments which performed extremely well against the terrorists. Perhaps the outstanding ones were the Suffolks and the Gurkhas, but there were others who did almost as well. Those which came later derived considerable benefit from the experiences of the earlier regiments. In 1950 the situation in Malaya was very bad indeed. Even the main Singapore railway and road were not secure; the train would probably be shot up every night. The Communists were very well led and organised by Chin Peng (mentioned above) a product of Singapore University who had been with Force 136 where Major Dare Newell, now Regimental Adjutant at the Duke of York's Headquarters, Chelsea, met him. Newell returned to the SAS in 1952 and was able to impart many of the lessons he had learnt about jungle-warfare in 1945.

The SAS, mainly from Calvert's inspiration, realised that superb physical fitness and alertness were necessary. Calvert also envisaged the deep probes which would kill Terrorist leaders in their 'safe' areas and create a feeling of insecurity over the whole region. After he returned, a number of people contributed ideas and influence. Initially it was a slow battle. Many of the aborigines had never seen a white man before, and needed some persuading before they trusted them. Part of the battle was won by medical orderlies, privates, corporals, sergeants, who not only looked after their own casualties but also found time and energy to treat the TB, malaria, and other ills to which the aborigines were particularly susceptible. 'Medics' enjoy, or perhaps endure, a mixed reputation in the Army, purely because low grade personnel in wartime were often shunted into the RAMC and did as badly there as they would have done anywhere else. However, every soldier knows that there are 'medics' for whom nothing is too much trouble, and they combine skill and careful nursing in a way which better qualified men are unable to match. Furthermore a 'medic' NCO or private can frequently get through to a primitive tribesman far better than can a qualified doctor, even though the latter may speak the language fluently. Out of this experience in Malaya, and, of course, much Second World War experience, has come the knowledge that one of the most vital soldierly characteristics is the ability to tend your own casualties and have something to spare for the people you are living among. In the SAS every soldier is expected to have some medical skill.

214

The SAS were well aware that they were only a part of a large effort. Calvert had originally said: 'Be under no illusions about this business. We in this unit are not going to win the war. All we can do is to play a particular part in it which other Army units are not trained for or suited for.'

Although in the Kuala Selangor swamp the SAS managed with minimal outside supply, for the most part they relied heavily on the RAF and its auxiliaries. Malaya is bad country for aircraft, and particularly unsuitable for helicopters, yet both spared no effort to achieve the impossible. Malaya was the birthplace of the helicopter – as far as the British were concerned – as a military vehicle. The S51 was the pioneer, mainly due to Flight Lieutenant 'Chips' Fry who would fly anywhere in support of the SAS. Helicopters often took appalling risks. Perhaps the most highly esteemed of all the troops who supported the SAS was the 55 Company RASC. They lost over a hundred men in aircraft crashes during the campaign but never lacked volunteers. It was a point of honour to them and the RAF that supplies should always be delivered however dangerous the flying weather. Even the SAS messages that they could wait a day or two longer did not deflect them from their schedule knowing, as they did, that all their tasks were essential. Emergency supplies might include anything from air photos to presents for aborigines. The value of helicopters in evacuating casualties was enormous, although some of them nearly became casualties themselves in the process.

Once on operations if a man could possibly continue he would have to carry on. If he collapsed through heat exhaustion he would be revived but would have to carry on at the same pace or find his way out as best he could. Exhaustion was always a possibility to be reckoned with, and was probably a greater hazard than insects, disease, animals or the enemy. As the terrorists moved swiftly it was always necessary to press on, and to go deeper and deeper into the jungle. Anyone who encountered an SAS patrol might think they were an unhealthy-looking lot – dirty, scratched and pallid; life under the trees gives much the same complexion as life in a cellar. Monotonous food, lack of success, the absence of diversion all tended to build up a state of exhaustion much more rapidly than hard work would do in better conditions.

Deep in the remote jungle the Communists had established communities where they grew their food in jungle gardens, and made plans for the future. One of their Headquarters was at Belum, a valley near the Thai border, and the most isolated spot in Malaya. There were Malay settlements at each end of the valley and these had no option but to keep the Communists supplied with food they did not grow themselves. The Communists paid a fair price for their supplies.

There were a hundred terrorists in the valley and they were removed by the SAS, a troop of Royal Marine Commandos and a Police Field force. This was an early operation, taking place in February 1952. The approach was up a long steep mountain track. They marched from 7.30 am till 5.30 pm with very short halts. Inevitably on marches of this sort the steep descents which occur periodically are even more gruelling than the upward climbs for they destroy the rhythm and seem to knock the energy out of the body. On the second day they were walking up the bed of a nearly dry mountain stream, getting sand into their boots and losing skin through chafing. On Woodhouse's patrol there was a Lance Corporal named Moseley. At the end of the second day Moseley showed his feet to Woodhouse who was concerned to see the man's socks were wet with blood and as he took them off a lot of skin came too. Woodhouse told him to make his way back with two others, who were also in a bad way. The rest of the party went on for another three days, climbing muddy slopes, occasionally marching in open country in the full glare of the sun, sometimes crossing rivers on hastily made bamboo rafts. Eventually they arrived at the valley but the Communists had moved and the journey was in vain. When Woodhouse stopped on the fifth night he was astonished to see Moseley – with the two others in scarcely better shape – limp up. Woodhouse could scarcely believe his eyes – or his ears – when he was told that Moseley and the other two had followed in their tracks. Moseley had been unable to take his boots off again, but when they were cut off disclosed that he had been walking on suppurating flesh which in parts had decayed to the bone. He was evacuated by helicopter, recovered quickly and soldiered on.

It was this sort of mental toughness which the SAS was constantly looking for in the screening tests. Such qualities were not, of course, only to be found in the SAS but they were more in demand there than anywhere else. The order of priorities was intelligence, mental toughness, physical toughness. Without intelligence the other two qualities would not enable a man to survive and be useful, without mental toughness he would never reach the peak of his performance. Probably the biggest contribution the SAS made to the Malayan campaign was the proof that a patrol – if properly selected and trained – could stay in the jungle for months at a time. Previously it had been thought that three weeks was the outside limit of human endurance under those conditions; experience proved otherwise, but only for the carefully selected few.

Although the Belum operation was inconclusive it produced a discovery which had far-reaching effects. A party was dropped in a very small DZ, when flying conditions and visibility were bad. Anticipating that some might land in the trees they had been each given 100 feet of rope. Most of them in fact did land in trees, but only three out of 54 were injured and these were only minor hurts. It was immediately clear that parachuting into trees was a possibility and probably no more dangerous than landing in the open. With this knowledge further experiments were conducted and, in consequence, parachuting into trees has become a normal SAS accomplishment. A large contribution to tree parachuting was made by Major Hugh Mercer, ex-Indian Army, ex-Jap POW, ex-East Surrey, and at the time Second in Command, 22 SAS, but the initial experimental work was done by two famous wartime SAS, John Cooper, 1 SAS, and Alastair MacGregor, 2 SAS.

In 1955 a new squadron was raised from the Parachute

Regiment, which at that time had three battalions in England.

The introduction of a Para squadron into the SAS did nothing but good. Once it settled in and was trained to jungle warfare it gave a very good account of itself indeed. A mutual respect and friendship stemmed from this time and has not diminished. The Para squadron was commanded by Major Dudley Coventry. The same year New Zealand sent another squadron so that by 1956 the SAS had five squadrons, about 560 men, just over half the strength of an infantry battalion. The New Zealanders, all superbly fit men of good physique, tended to have a higher sickness rate than their British counterparts. The same had been noticed in the Rhodesian squadron which Calvert had personally flown to Rhodesia to recruit in the early days. Both parties practised first-class hygiene and the explanation offered was that their better living conditions had robbed them of some of their immunity to disease.

Up till 1957 the SAS carried Brens and found them effective enough (see Appendix), but after that date they were replaced by the 7.62 self-loading rifle which is now standard equipment for NATO troops.

There were very few of the original SAS now with the regiment but those who were included 'Bob' Lilley MM and 'Bob' Bennet MM, who had both been with L Detachment in the early days. The presence of veterans such as this gave the regiment a sense of continuity which might otherwise have been lacking; it was also a sharp reminder that the early founders of the regiment were as good as they were reputed to be. They were a good deal older now and had seen a lot of action, but they were still as fresh and keen as ever. Most striking was their readiness to learn, and their modesty about their own achievements.

The Malayan campaign was of great importance to the regiment as it provided the experience on which the post-war SAS was built. Although conditions varied enormously in Borneo, Oman and Aden, the basic principles established in Malaya held good. Had there been no Malaya there could have been no Oman operation. Malaya established the need for certain types of selection, tactics, equipment, training, mental attitudes and so on. The full list is long. By their freedom – and need – to experiment to find the possible equipment and method, the regiment was able to make discoveries which would soon be used widely in the Army. Some of the results of these experiments were seen at their best in other theatres – such as the belt-pack in the Oman.

One of the most effective devices used in Malaya was the jungle fort. These were fortified camps, enclosing areas which might be up to two square miles, where aborigines could live in safety without their way of life being disturbed. They were situated several miles inside the deep jungle. They bore a striking resemblance to the prehistoric hill-forts – although not necessarily on hills – but differed from their ancient counterparts in that instead of being mere refuges they were also forward bases, cunningly sited strategically.

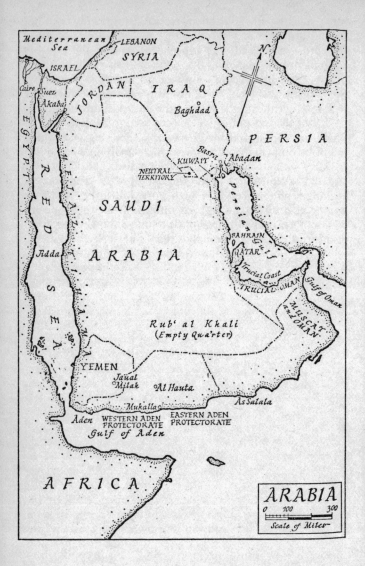

ARABIA

0    100    300

Scale of Miles

# CHAPTER IX

# The Oman

As the Malayan operations drew towards their close the SAS once more began to ponder about its future. It was, of course, a corps, but official standing alone would not enable it to continue if the Army was further reduced. In 1958 the Army Council had stated that there was a long-term future for the SAS in Army planning but there was no knowing – yet – how large, or small, a force was envisaged. In 1958 Lieutenant Colonel A.J. Deane-Drummond, DSO, MC, Royal Signals had been appointed commander of 22 SAS, and found them 'real professional soldiers by any standard. They could take the rough with the smooth and joke about it.' Deane-Drummond was in fact a newcomer to the SAS, although, of course, he had taken part in the pre-SAS, deceptively named 11 SAS, raid carried out in Italy, in February 1941. He had made a number of remarkable escapes during World War II, one of which had involved his standing in a cupboard for thirteen days in a house occupied by Germans*. He held the British Glider record. Deane-Drummond came to the SAS with an open mind and similar experience; if he found the SAS good, they were good.

He was soon able to put his impressions to the test. Within a short period of his appointment he was sent on a reconnaissance to the Oman with a view to the SAS going on operations in that area.

'The Oman' is the Sultanate and independent state of Muscat and Oman which lies on the south-east of the Arabian peninsula. On the south-west of the peninsula lies Aden and

* See *Return Ticket*, A.J. Deane-Drummond, London, 1953.

immediately to the north of Aden lies the Yemen. The Oman has a coastline nearly 1,000 miles long and extends inland to the South-Eastern Arabian Desert which is appropriately known as the 'Empty Quarter'. The Oman consists of coastal plain, a plateau and mountains. The coastal plain varies in width from 10 miles to a few yards. A mountain range – The Hajr – runs approximately south-east to north-west, in the broadest part of the state which is in the north-west. The highest point is the Jebel Akhdar, about 10,000 feet, which is called the 'Green Mountain' because parts of the area, unlike the other mountain regions which are sterile, is heavily cultivated. Portions of the coastal plain are fertile and thus prosperous; others are barren and are not. The Oman supports a total population of 550,000 in an area which is believed to be 82,000 square miles. Thus an area equivalent to England and Scotland has a total population rather less than half that of Birmingham. Most of the inhabitants are Arabs, but Muscat with 6,000 inhabitants, and Matrah, almost adjoining, with 14,000, have few Arabs and the numbers are made up of immigrants from Baluchistan (Pakistan) and Zanzibar (East Africa). Dates and sugar are grown with considerable success, but there is no important industry* and the country lacks good ports. The tribes of the interior breed excellent camels which are much in demand elsewhere. Roads are virtually non-existent and the tracks are unsuited to motor transport. In a country of this nature most of the figures quoted, whether of population, distance or area, tend to be approximate. Confusion extends to the designation as the area is really the Oman and the word Muscat only appears in the title to indicate the importance of the capital city in the country. The word 'Oman' is thought to mean 'peace' but if so is not a particularly appropriate term. The country lies at the entrance to the Persian Gulf, and is obviously well situated to be of considerable interest to the oil producers of that area and their potential opponents. Control of Oman by a hostile power would affect such vital places as Kuwait,

* Oil soon will be: present output is worth about £35 million per annum.

Bahrein, Basra (Iraq) and Bushire (Persia) to name but a few.

Long before the possibilities of oil were thought of Britain had been forced to take action against pirates from the Oman coast as they preyed, if unchecked, on the trading ships of the East India Company. The first move had in fact been made in the 17th century. Over the years the ties between Britain and the Sultanate had strengthened, and in 1951 a new treaty of friendship, to last for 15 years, was signed between the United Kingdom and the Oman. The history of the Oman might appear to be a fairly uneventful one from the above summary but in fact has been one of battle, murder, massacre, piracy, treachery, slavery, rape and cruelty that at times seems scarcely credible.

Whatever stability the Oman has had in this century has been mainly due to the Muscat Infantry. This was set up in 1914 under an Iraqui officer, but in 1922 a British commanding officer was appointed and ran the regiment with the help of Indian Army officers. There was a short interval of no British officers between 1933 and 1936. It should be noted that this was not a British force under the British Government but an Omani army staffed as the Sultan thought best. Subsequently, arrangements were made, at the Sultan's request, to second British Army officers to the Omani army for a period of up to three years.

The key to understanding the background of events in 1959 is the position of the Imam. In the very early days of Omani history in the year 751 the Oman Ibhadis elected an Imam – a leader who was the head of both church and state. His reign did not last long for he was killed four years later by an invader from Baghdad, named Abu al-Abbas, nicknamed, with good reason, 'The Bloodshedder'. Although fairly fully occupied with slaughtering and orgiastic feasting the Bloodshedder managed to find time to sleep with each of his four thousand concubines. With such a high standard to emulate it is not surprising that his successors lived spectacularly and died violent deaths – all nineteen of them. However, before the Bloodshedder's dynasty was extinct the Omanis had managed to elect a second Imam in a small corner of the country. Thenceforward, although there were good Imams there were also a considerable number of others, 'such as "The Upright Ibadhi" in whose twenty-six-year reign (1620–46) no Omani, whatever his rank or position, died a natural death' (allowing for some exaggerations the statement probably gives a fair picture for the old, women, and children would often die in regular massacres). However, the Oman is not by any means the only country in the world to have had unpredictable and tyrannical rulers, and in common with other countries has modified its habits considerably in more recent times. For approximately the last two hundred years the Sultan has been the ruler of the country and the Imam was elected as the most suitable person to be the spiritual head of the country – a man of great goodness, learning and humility. If not already poor he would be required to divest himself of his worldly goods. It was not always possible to find a man worthy of the office and there were breaks in the succession, which was never hereditary. These breaks were sometimes caused by other reasons than the lack of a suitable candidate. There was a break between 1871 and 1913 because the Sultan had killed the Imam in 1871 and it was forty-two years before there was enough religious feeling – and power – to elect a successor.

A considerable factor in events since the 1880s has been the arms traffic. In the late nineteenth century the Oman was receiving arms to the extent of a quarter of its entire imports, and Muscat soon established itself as a flourishing centre of the arms trade. Apart from official import/export there was a vast illegal traffic. The Imam's supporters felt that it was entirely wrong of the Sultan to control and restrict this profitable activity. The Sultan may well have shared their views but was probably subject to other influences. The new Imam remained in running conflict with the Sultan until 1920 when he was assassinated by one of his discontented supporters. Although his successor was scarcely more friendly, a settlement was reached – negotiated by the British Consul at Muscat – and, in return for a general amnesty by the Sultan, the rebel demands were withdrawn or modified.

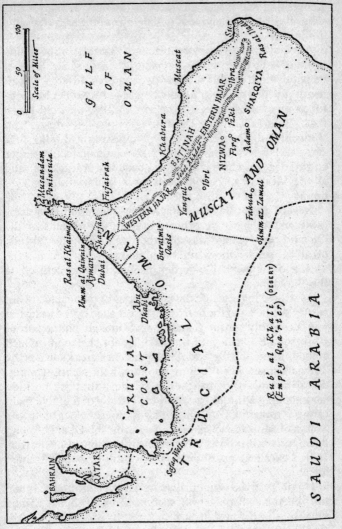

In 1921 the Sultan signed the International Arms Traffic Convention and it seemed – though possibly wrongly – that some of the more dangerous possibilities of the area were now diminished.

Any optimistic views of chances of stability in the region could only be taken in the complete absence of knowledge of its population. There are about two hundred different tribes, many of which are traditionally hostile to each other for long-forgotten reasons, buried in the past, but active enough for all that. Inside the tribes there are plenty of jealousies and antagonisms. The hill Arabs despise the coastal dwellers. All carry arms of one sort or another, the common factor being a curved dagger, which is usually as beautiful as it is lethal, and is the ideal weapon for resolving a minor difference of opinion.

Nevertheless, ancient antagonisms, ambition, the arms trade and religion were not the entire ingredients of the Omani bomb. There was also the rivalry of other powers, great and small, who wanted to obtain more influence in the area, and the inevitable border dispute; this last centred on the Buraimi oasis.

As will be appreciated the boundaries of the Oman are not clearly defined and the outlying tribes ranged over a wide, but not necessarily constant, area. Approximately on the border between the Oman and the Abu Dhabi sheikdom, which belongs to the small group of independent states known as the Trucial Oman, lies the Buraimi oasis, with plentiful water, dates, bananas and mangoes, a valuable strategic position commanding a useful pass, and the intersection of five main caravan routes. Of its nine villages three belonged to the Sultan of Muscat and six to the Sultan of Abu Dhabi. Among its imports and exports was a substantial quota of small arms. It had excellent possibilities as a centre of Saudi Arabian intrigue.

Up till 1955 the Buraimi dispute did not concern the Imam but when he died he was succeeded by a Sheikh named Ghalib who did not appear to be very widely supported. Ghalib's brother Talib continued to wield the power and soon enlisted the help of Saudi Arabia to the cause of furthering Imam power. He was able to obtain money and arms from Egypt which was only too ready to reduce the influence of the pro-British Sultan of Muscat and thereby extend the area of Arab nationalism, as envisaged and controlled by the United Arab Republic. However his plans were disrupted by a swift military move in which the Sultan's forces captured the Imam's capital of Nizwa. Talib and Ghalib escaped and went on support-raising tours of Egypt and Saudi Arabia; from that they went on to train, collect and arm an Omani liberation army. In 1957 the Sultan of the Jebel Akhdar, who had long nursed secret ambitions to be independent of the Sultan, threw in his lot with Talib. Against this the Sultan had the Muscat Regiment's 120 men, who were normally employed on guard duties in Muscat, the Batinah Force of some 200 and the Oman Field Force of 300 untrained men whose function was to protect the oil company – this was subsequently named the Oman Regiment.

What happened next was clearly going to be of more than local interest. If the rebels succeeded, western strategic and economic interests would be severely disturbed, while Saudi Arabian and Egyptian ambitions, with their supporters from Eastern Europe, and possibly China, would be greatly assisted. At this point the Sultan turned to the British government for help.

The response was immediate. The First Battalion of the Cameronians sent three companies; three Royal Naval frigates began searching coastal shipping for arms; and the RAF made reconnaissance flights followed by attacks on forts after due warning.

The ground forces, which, as well as the units designated above, included troops from the 15/19th Hussars and the Trucial Oman Scouts,* had a series of successful engagements against the rebels but failed to prevent their

---

* A battalion raised in 1951 for internal security duties and frontier patrols. It contained 160 British officers and soldiers.

withdrawal to the Jebel Akhdar from which it was clearly going to be extremely difficult to dislodge them.

In September 1957 all British forces were withdrawn with the exception of small detachments from the Trucial Oman Scouts and the 15/19th Hussars – shortly afterwards relieved by the 13/18th Hussars and a reorganised and greatly reduced Sultan of Muscat's army. Attempts to penetrate the rebel fastness were unsuccessful as the enemy were well-armed and positioned and every approach road was heavily mined (with American mines which had been supplied to Saudi Arabia).

During the next few months a full survey of the situation was undertaken by Colonel D. de C. Smiley, MVO, OBE, MC, who had been made Chief of Staff to the Sultan. Smiley made an appreciation, based on his experience of mountain warfare, which caused him to request a brigade for the completion of the campaign. This was not available so he asked for two battalions, specifying that one should be a Royal Marine Commando, a Parachute Battalion or an SAS unit. His appreciation included the fact that an ordinary infantry battalion would not be acclimatised, would not be fit enough for mountain warfare without considerable and lengthy training, and would not possess the sort of experience required.

Eventually he was allocated D Squadron SAS, one squadron from the Life Guards, and a detachment of Royal Signals – invariably present on such occasions but rarely mentioned.

D Squadron SAS arrived on 18th November 1958. When Deane-Drummond had returned to Malaya at the end of October the squadron was 30 miles inside the jungle on the Thai border and had been on operations for six weeks. Within 48 hours the whole squadron was back in Kuala Lumpur, 250 miles away, having covered the distance by forced marches and hastily constructed river rafts. There was a considerable problem of re-equipping it and, to some extent, intensive retraining. In the jungle, as we have seen, SLRs and shotguns were the most favoured weapons, the ideal being something which would have adequate killing power over a short distance and would not be caught up in the tangled vegetation. Visibility was rarely more than 25 yards, and concealment was no problem at all.

In the Oman visibility was up to 30 miles, and potential opponents had the binocular-like vision which enables a hill tribesman to put a bullet neatly through any portion of a body which appears on the skyline. And just as the CTs had been adept at melting into the jungle so the Omani rebels could melt into the rocks – or seemed to. The enemy had a useful assortment of arms, which included light machine guns, 3-inch and 81-mm mortars, .50 Brownings, Berettas, .303 rifles, mines, grenades and adequate ammunition for them. Fortunately, there were only some 600 rebels involved in defending this last stronghold, for the remainder of the tribes showed no disposition to support the Imam and his brother. Had they done so, the picture would have been entirely different and the 'Green Mountain' might have justified its reputation for being impregnable, a reputation it had acquired 1,000 years before. The plateau at the top is 20 by 10 miles, and the base is not much wider. As much of the side is almost vertical, all the forty so-called paths at the top could have been made impossible; as it was the approach was so difficult that the rebels assumed they had nothing to fear from the attackers.

The nature of the country made ultra-fitness and ability at mountain warfare an absolute necessity. There are, of course, very few Army units trained for this type of work. As any daylight advance would immediately have been spotted by the rebels, all aggressive movement had to take place at night. This, of course, was in complete contrast to operations in Malaya which were very rarely in the dark. On more than one occasion the arrival of dawn was the signal for a fierce engagement with enemies who were fit, skilled and unperturbed by the hottest fire.

The first footing on the top was made by a night climb by two troops from D Squadron. A local Sheikh had mentioned that he knew a path on the north side and was promptly persuaded to lead the way. This was a climb of about seven thousand feet up a path with no cover and no scope for outflanking movements. The way to the summit on all sides was defended by 'sangars', small rock fortresses, the equivalent of slit trenches above ground. Many of these gave a field of fire down the path which would have enabled three men to hold up dozens indefinitely. The first thing the Sheikh did on reaching the top was to fall down in thankful prayer. However, this was merely a foothold and working further in was no simple problem. It was bitterly cold at night, so cold as almost to numb thought. Supply, which would have been done so effectively by 55 Troop was chaotic; 12 out of the first 17 parachutes sent down 'Roman candled' and the SAS had the dubious experience of being bombed by their own mortar bombs when the badly-packed containers broke open. Doubtless it was good experience for the aircrews who were doing the job for the first time but it was hard on the SAS sense of humour.

The SAS were pinned by a strong rebel force whose sniping was extremely accurate. Walker, the troop commander, and CSM Hawkins once had to deal with a sniper who was a mere fifteen yards away but impregnably sited. Walker threw a phosphorus grenade followed by two 36s. The second 36 caught on a lip of rock and rolled into the gulley where Walker and Hawkins lay. It rolled between them as they tried to press themselves into the solid rock. Then it went up; neither was hurt. Eventually in order to free the SAS for patrol activity, this base was manned by a dismounted troop of Life Guards, attached signallers and REME mechanics. The Life Guards had good cause to enjoy coming to close quarters with the rebels; every one of their Ferret scout cars had been mined at one time or another. (The Trucial Oman scouts had a similar experience.) They were using nine Browning machine guns from Ferrets which had been put out of action.

Being on top of the plateau in no way meant the end of the campaign. There was still an intact rebel force to be defeated and a large number of strategic and tactical points to be occupied. The SAS were not alone in taking offensive action; at night rebel forces used to come down the mountains and make life very lively indeed.

Tracks and paths had to be discovered by patrolling, as all potential guides had been impressed by the rebels. Possibly it was better that they should be because there was plenty of evidence of treachery in the so-called trustworthy allies – who might perhaps be exonerated on the grounds that they would be attempting to live in the area when British forces were withdrawn to other spheres; perhaps a few scores notched up in this campaign will still be being avenged in family feuds in 2159. Some managed to satisfy both sides – ostensibly. One 'friendly' tribal leader in charge of anti-mining operations on a mountain path was subsequently found to be mining the path himself.

Subsequently the 'flexible' attitude of the SAS helpers was successfully used against the rebels. Donkey columns had been organised to transport supplies to the forward base. It was difficult at times to know which was the more difficult, the donkey or his handler. Somali donkeys, owned by the army, required grain and were not used to mountains; Jebel donkeys lived on dates and were experienced mountain walkers, but they tended to be almost as obstinate and unreliable as their handlers. Of the latter it might be said the only reliable feature of them was their unreliability; they managed to 'lose' some of their loads, required frequent and varied food and payment, and were suspected of being in league with the enemy. This last point was exploited when before the final attack some of the donkey handlers were briefed on the route they would be taking the next day. They were warned that disclosure of the information would be rewarded by summary execution. As hoped, the 'confidential' information was promptly passed on to the rebels, who then concentrated in the wrong area.

The sequence of the final ascent was determined by the weather, enemy resistance and the ruggedness of the countryside. Although the SAS had obtained a foothold on the top, and could convert it into a base for further moves, the operation would be slow and might not be completed before the hot season began. December and January are the rainy season and bring storms, flood and temperatures of 25° below. February was liable to be the worst month of the year for it could bring high winds and a temperature which could range between 120° by day and 20° by night. In late December a rebel stronghold in front of the base at Aquabat had been attacked, killing 9 enemy without loss, but it was clear that the country was too rugged and their numbers too small to obtain more than a temporary success. Smiley therefore asked for a second SAS squadron; A Squadron was promptly posted in from Malaya, 4,000 miles away, given five days' intensive training and sent up to relieve D Squadron in front of the Aquabat position. Meanwhile the RAF were attending to the rebels with Venoms carrying SAP rockets and 20-mm cannon. Aerial reconnaissance played a vital part. Apart from the discovery of an unused, and apparently unknown, track they were able to confirm what ground patrols suspected – that certain obstacles might be impossible to outflank.

The first attack was made from the south; this being decided by the fact that it was short enough to be climbed in a night – provided you had a force capable of climbing 9,000 feet in the dark – and could therefore be supplied from the air at dawn. Diversionary attacks were made at Aquabat and Tanuf while the main body went up the special path to Kamah. (The Tanuf track was the one which had been mentioned – in the strictest confidence – to the donkey drivers.)

Donkeys were used to carry machine-guns and wireless sets. Although air supply meant that the use of donkeys would be restricted to the minimum, there was always the possibility that bad weather might make flying impossible and donkeys would have to be used much more. The assault involved 9½ hours of hard climbing plus the addition of two hours spent in crossing a high ridge involving the use of ropes.* Surprise was

* Everyone was carrying a load of at least 60 pounds, mainly of ammunition.

232

so complete that enemy-held villages promptly surrendered. The Sheikh of Jebel Akhdar just managed to slip away and escape but left behind a quantity of personal letters which disclosed who had been assisting him and how many of our supposed allies were, in fact, enemies. Success depended entirely on the surprise effected by this night climb, which made an interesting change from jungle warfare! Because of surprise much bloodshed was averted.

It was an interesting battle and a great achievement for the SAS, who were highly and widely praised. They themselves were only too ready to stress the achievements of other units, the Life Guards who had worked so closely with them, the 13/18th Hussars, the Royal Signals and the few but overworked administrators. The only helpers who did not earn praise from the SAS were the donkeys who, on occasion, not only refused to carry their loads but had to be carried themselves by members of the SAS and Life Guards, who had never imagined that military service would contain such exigencies.

The brisk but tough little campaign was over in two months, but only the most impractical optimist would assume that it was the prelude to an era of stability and prosperity. Subsequently the political positions have changed in the area although motives remain the same as ever. Britain is on friendly terms with Saudi Arabia; Egypt and Saudi Arabia are hostile to each other. The Egyptians switched their attention to the Yemen which seemed to offer great possibilities – although it eventually produced even greater frustrations – and the small states in the area continued to regard with suspicious apprehension all attempts by outside powers to involve them in grandiose schemes of whatever nature. It seems unlikely that the Oman will not one day become vastly richer through the development of oil or some other mineral resource. When this day arrives there will be many adjustments to be made, internally and externally.\*

\* In July 1970 the Sultan was deposed and replaced by his son, a man with progressive ideas.

The SAS learnt, as well as gave, some useful lessons in this campaign. Training on the Brecons in January is remarkably similar to conditions in the Jebel Akhdar at the same time of the year. If the Oman ever becomes a prosperous country the richest men will be the boot manufacturers, for a boot lasts five days on the shale. Other clothing too has a very high wastage rate. Water is the most valuable substance in the world – a fact which was probably overlooked in Malaya where the swamps were full of it, even if it does sometimes freeze solid in your bottle at night and reach near boiling point in the day. And although there's nothing an Arab can stand which a British soldier cannot, it is not a bad idea to take note of how they avoid heat exhaustion and conserve their energies for the big moment.

In 1960 A Squadron returned to the Oman for a training period. It was preceded by an intensive driving course at Bisley. Other units may have felt that it was not a driving course that the SAS needed but a full course on vehicle maintenance. Once in the Oman it was obvious that training was designed to remedy the deficiencies disclosed during the previous year. In spite of the scorn with which critics denounce the practice, there is a great deal to be said for training for the next war by re-fighting the last – at leisure. The Jebel gave ample opportunity for practising map-reading and navigation and, as had already been found in Malaya, a little medical attention to local people does more to establish friendly relationships than any number of displays of firepower.

Among the other lessons learnt was that flying in the heat of the Oman is one of the more uncomfortable activities, owing to turbulence; the camels – although not lovable – are very useful for patrolling; and that social relations – which involve consuming vast quantities of greasy mutton stews and rice using only the right hand – are exacting but essential.

Not least is the value of holding an exercise in former enemy-held territory, or even a potential one – in that the local people are able to judge you as you are, which may be very different from the picture painted by enemy propaganda.

234

Soldiers, for the most part, make good ambassadors. They have a rough kindliness that is appreciated but not mistaken for weakness. It is a far cry from the brutalized unfortunates of other centuries who were less to blame for their excesses than were the politicians who neglected them, starved them, under-equipped them and then took the credit for their military prowess. However, even to-day there are soldiers who do not always cut too pretty a figure and, as we have seen, the SAS has had its sample of them. The SAS attitude to local people is of watchful friendliness, bearing in mind that a careless remark might ruin an operation and cost lives at some future date. To captured prisoners, even spies, the attitude is humanitarian. This view was strongly reinforced by Calvert, and carried on by Woodhouse. Calvert had even treated captured Japanese leniently, which was remarkable in view of the way the Japanese treated their own captives, but the Calvert view was that if you are fighting a war for civilization you might as well be civilized about it; possibly, too, those former enemies might later become firm friends.

The 'Hearts and Minds' campaign, which is now widely practised throughout the Army, was given a boost in 1960 when the SAS saw the use the American Special Forces made of languages and medical skill. It may be that any foreigner can understand English provided it is shouted loudly enough, but the experiences of the last few years have shown that fluency in languages – several languages – and the medical skill to do minor operations in remote areas – pay a very handsome dividend. And, of course, the more people qualified and experienced in minor surgery the less the pressure on the overworked and probably exhausted doctor in time of battle.

The lesson which was all the time being hammered home was that the mental attitude was more important than the apparent physical aptitude. There were plenty of men who looked as if they could survive week after week in the jungle but in the event it was proved that only the carefully selected and highly trained could stand the isolation and loneliness. The SAS had what appeared to be a very useful collection of

235

tough soldiers in the early days of the Malaya emergency, but in 1953 over 50 were dispensed with from one squadron alone. Consequently there were less problems of adjustment later in the Oman, Borneo and Aden. Whenever the SAS has temporarily relaxed from requiring the highest standards and had to accept lesser quality to make up numbers, the experience has ultimately cost them dear. It is, of course, well known by every regiment that if the hard core is too greatly reduced subsequent expansion creates problems which take years to solve, and the SAS is hardly likely to be an exception to the rule.

# CHAPTER X

# Borneo and Aden

As Clausewitz so rightly said: 'War is the continuation of policy by other means.' This is probably truer now than ever. On the other hand:

> Theirs not to reason why
> Theirs but to do and die

has a hollow ring today when most soldiers like to know what they are doing, whether or not they are required to die in the process. The soldier tends to be a little less optimistic than the diplomat, because when the latter's careful construction for eternal peace and friendship crashes to the ground the soldier is often required to pick up some very jagged pieces.

On 31st August 1957, Malaya ceased to be a Crown Colony and instead became an independent country of the Commonwealth. Although there were still several thousand Communist Terrorists roaming around in the jungle at that time, the move was obviously appropriate. It is the custom for the British Government to grant independence, either within or without the Commonwealth, to its Colonies or Protectorates as soon as they are ready – or even before, in the eyes of some. And it was sound policy to give the inhabitants of Malaya a valid reason to fight for the unity of the country, to build it up, and to combat subversion. Of Malaya's 7 million people, $3\frac{1}{2}$ million were Malays, $2\frac{1}{2}$ million were Chinese, about $\frac{3}{4}$ million were Indian and Pakistanis and the remainder came from a variety of countries. The Chinese, although hardworking and often prosperous, had felt themselves underprivileged in relation to their efforts in the country and a number of them had worked off their feelings by becoming Communist Terrorists. The hard core of terrorists would not, of course, be impressed by independence but would now change their strategy to obtain control of the country through political infiltration.

Singapore, which is an island 26 miles by 14, became a self-governing state under British sovereignty in 1959. Its population of approximately $1\frac{3}{4}$ million included approximately $1\frac{1}{4}$ Chinese.

In September 1963 Malaya and Singapore joined with British North Borneo – known as Sabah – and Sarawak, to make the sovereign federal state of Malaysia. Brunei was invited to join but declined. Two years later Singapore withdrew from Malaysia at the request of the central government.

The establishment of the Federation of Malaysia was regarded with dismay and hostility by the government of Indonesia. Indonesia is a group of 10,000 islands with a population of one hundred million people; over half live in Java. These territories are close to Malaya, and are also within easy reach of Borneo; the population is very similar.

The two countries have, however, a somewhat different history. Both had been colonies, Malaya of course being British, and Indonesia Dutch. Both had been overrun and occupied by the Japanese in World War II. Subsequently, while Malaya was set on the road to independence, the Indonesians saw little prospect of that occurring unless they fought for it. The Dutch considered they had run, and could continue to run, the country very efficiently and prosperously, and saw no reason why Indonesian, or American, opinion should bounce them out of a rich colony which has been described as 'the tail which wagged the Dutch dog'. However after intermittent fighting and a lot of pressure on Holland the country became a sovereign independent state in 1949. One small pocket of land was however retained by the Dutch – West New Guinea, which then became better known as West Irian. This proved to be a 'bone of contention' between Dutch and Indonesians for many years, with the

238

United Nations involved. President Sukarno of Indonesia eventually decided to obtain the territory by force and, greatly assisted by arms and naval equipment, mainly from Russia but also from elsewhere, launched a joint airborne/naval invasion in the summer of 1962. Volunteers had been readily forthcoming for this invasion, and when on 15th August 1962 the Dutch were persuaded at the United Nations to hand over the territory to Indonesia there were large numbers of trained saboteurs, some being Malays from Malaya, who found themselves out of a job and somewhat frustrated. Two days after the agreement Sukarno launched a fresh confrontation – this time against Malaysia – which he branded as neo-colonialist. His view of the correct treatment for this neo-colonialism would be to incorporate Malaysia with Indonesia; this would not of course be colonialism or imperialism but a step forward in liberation.

The territories in Borneo, on which Sukarno now had his eye were Brunei, a former British protectorate with a good revenue from oil, north Borneo (Sabah), another former protectorate, and Sarawak, which had been ruled for a century by the Brooke family as hereditary Rajahs since Sir James Brooke had been appointed Rajah by the Sultan of Brunei (then its ruler) in 1842. The Brookes handed over Sarawak to the British government in 1946. There were good reasons for these former British territories now wanting to join the prosperous and well-ordered Malaysian federation.

The first sign of major trouble was a revolt, mainly in Brunei, in December 1962. The main rebellion was crushed in eight days but 1,000 of the rebel army disappeared into the jungle on the Brunei/Sarawak border, and took six months to remove. This rebellion was not at first the concern of Indonesia for it was the product of a young Brunei sheikh named Azahari who had launched it as a first step to creating a new state to be made up from Sabah, Brunei and Sarawak, and to be called North Kalimantan. He had appointed himself the first Prime Minister. The Indonesian Communists, although respecting neither the ambitions nor personality of Azahari, promptly realised that this was a

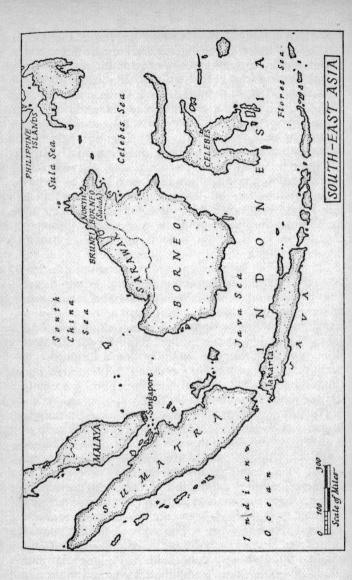

situation which could well be exploited for their own ends. Therefore just at the moment when the new Federation of Malaysia was launched there was a determined, trained and formidable army waiting on the borders with a mission to torpedo it. Raids over the border built up steadily in 1963, and it was soon clear that the only way these could be checked was before they had penetrated far. It was a typical jungle area, swamp, mountains, river and thorny scrub, as tough an area as anywhere in the world. In short, ideal SAS country.

Early in 1963 SAS patrols were already in position in the jungle. Twenty-one three-men patrols from A Squadron were watching the 700 miles of Indonesian frontier. Although these numbers might seem pitifully small in relation to the task, they were in fact reasonably adequate, as the places where the Indonesians could cross were limited by the terrain. Furthermore the SAS had established an excellent relationship with the border tribes who were only too happy to use their shotguns against potential invaders. Indonesia was not yet playing an active role.

D Squadron relieved A Squadron early in the summer. They had spent the previous months training for winter warfare in Germany and Norway so they had the interesting privilege of breaking new ground in rapid acclimatisation.

In the Borneo jungle the SAS lived closer to the natives than ever before. In order to understand possible intelligence information it was necessary to understand not only the language but even the dialects; in order to win friendship it was necessary to perform useful services, of which the most popular was routine medical treatment; in order to move around unobtrusively it was necessary to live off the land, catching fish and buying rice.

Towards the end of 1963 it became clear that the infiltrators were no longer irregular rebel forces but properly organised and trained units of the Indonesian army. Some of these groups numbered between 50 and 100. Even then the situation was not too difficult because the invaders had to travel a considerable distance before they could reach a suitable objective and by that time adequate warning would have been sent back to the SAS recce parties. In the autumn of 1963 the SAS were switched to a shorter but vital frontier on the invasion route to Brunei. Here they had several brisk engagements, including one in which 9 out of a party of 21 rebels were captured, and the remainder fled, leaving most of their weapons and ammunition behind.

In 1964 the 'confrontation' continued to develop. A number of large parties continued to cross the frontier and it soon became clear that they had a different attribute to the Communist Terrorists in Malaya or irregulars in Brunei. These Indonesian detachments, some of whom were paratroopers, were not terrorists whose aim was to kill a few civilians and fade away, but proper military forces which if intercepted would make a fight of it and only withdraw after setting ambushes.

As SAS resources were now being strung fairly thinly there was a move for an extra squadron to be recruited. Fortunately the value of SAS work was fully appreciated by the Higher Command and the task of obtaining reinforcements, although difficult, was not impossible. Senior officers were unstinting in their commendation of SAS performance although at times slightly irritated by the SAS facility of being able to short-circuit the 'usual channels' and state their views and needs directly to top level. The upshot of this was that the Guards Independent Parachute Company, which normally formed part of 16 Para Brigade, was allotted to SAS duties. It will be no surprise to anyone to know that they performed well on operations although were somewhat slow to acquire the necessary fluency in languages.

There were a number of reasons why eventually Indonesia decided that 'confrontation' was not worth pursuing and called it off. Among them there was world opinion and the state of her economy, but as considerable a factor as any was the conviction that this was a war she could not win. Many units had contributed to Indonesia's forming that opinion, particularly the Ghurkhas, and not least of them the SAS. For the latter it was a new scene and a variation of the Malaya role. On this occasion they were not so often seeking out the opposition as waiting for them to appear, and providing a suitable reception. It was not, any more than Malaya, the Oman or Aden had been, the classic SAS role of deep penetration and sabotage; instead it was an infantry role but one which no infantry unit could tackle without special selection and training on SAS lines; this being so it made a case for applying more recruits to the SAS rather than more SAS training to the Infantry.

By this time it was clear to most people both within and without the SAS that the regiment was now a specialist force just as Sappers, Signals and REME are specialised units. The complication of the SAS was that a man's best age was around 25, and it was desirable, for a number of reasons, that a tour of duty should be three years. There was no real conflict of interests between the SAS and other regiments, the SAS did not remove the best officers and men and thereby denude the regiments; what it did do was give the right man experience that would make them better soldiers when they eventually returned to their regiments. Meanwhile the SAS was learning that maintenance of equipment and efficient administration was just as important to the success of operations as the fighting qualities of its patrols – or at least that each was complementary to the other.

'Confrontation' came to an end in 1966 when an internal power struggle, and the dire state of the Indonesian economy took precedence in the minds of Indonesians.

Life in Borneo may be pictured from the following extracts from *Mars and Minerva*:

The parts of Borneo they have seen and got to know so intimately are as varied as nature and man's complexity could make them: swampland, deep forest, high mountains, barren hills, fertile valleys; up to twenty races and ethnic groups; as many languages and almost as many religions.

In the east of North Borneo the mangrove swamp lined waterways give access to the sea and the piracy-ridden coast of the East Coast Residency. These waterways form a labyrinthine maritime Hampton Court maze through which a brisk smuggling trade flourishes and

243

the likelihood of Indonesian infiltration persists. Patrols here are mainly waterborne and it was here that an SAS patrol report included the sighting of an Indonesian submarine.

From the mid reaches of the Serudong and Kalabakan rivers to the river Pagalluggan 154 miles westwards in the Interior Residency there stretches an area entirely uninhabited, uncharted and, until July this year, untraversed. This is an area of dense rain-forest (where rivers rise 20 feet in a night), broken ridges rising to beyond 4,000 feet, great waterfalls and in which game of all kinds is as prevalent as man is absent. In a 31-day journey an SAS patrol traversed and reconnoitred this area with complete success. The report produced was of permanent value. Air supply and a diet of monkeys and venison sustained the patrol throughout its journey.

Throughout the remainder of the Interior Residency of North Borneo, amongst the tough individualistic Muruts, patrols have ranged widely. Here, to the accompaniment of frequent pulls at the *tapai* (native rice-wine) jar and fingerfulls of rancid fish, a great delicacy, the tall tales of the Japanese occupation are still heard. Murut attacks on retreating Japanese columns of the war were effective and many a shrivelled head still nods from the eaves of the long house roof. Many of the Regiment will long remember 'Murutania' with affection and already the doings of the long-haired *Orang Puteh* [White men] are finding their way into the Murut folk-lore.

The oil state of Brunei saw us frequently but after the initial stages of the rebellion and the swift retribution that followed, our eyes were turned mainly outwards to the new threat on the borders of Sarawak beyond.

The Haunted House, one of the two headquarters – the squadron commander operated from two headquarters as far apart as from London to Edinburgh and with only air communication between the two – will long be remembered. Hidden away behind the Sultan's Palace it had just the right atmosphere of sinister seclusion. No one saw many of the snakes that were reputed to plague it and the ghost of the pale, fair-haired girl never materialised. New ghosts may now inhabit it: a spectral and unending game of volley-ball might be for us the most appropriate manifestation.

To Sarawak, and from the Ops Room amidst fairies at the bottom of Tom Harrison's garden to the Kelabit Highlands of Bario, Long Banga and Bakelallan, to Belaga and the upper reaches of the Rajang, to the Ulu Katibas and the SAS-reported gang now active there, to the Ulu Ai, to Sibu, Song, Simangang and to the Land Dyak country

244

of the First Division – these are a series of giant strides, of strides across the doodle of rivers that encompass Kuching, west along the sparkling coastline and past the Turtle Islands to Tanjong Datu, or south and east across thousands of square miles of jungle – barren, broken and spent by Iban cultivation in the lowest reaches of the 2nd and 3rd Divisions, or luxuriant and magnificent as elsewhere. Over the long muddy tongues of rivers, almost endless, tortuous and yet life-sustaining for the long-houses echeloned along their banks. To more than a score of patrol locations, past and present, where in each four men, living as members of the longhouse itself for months at a time, watch, listen, patrol and report. Where, day by day, the sick come for treatment, the women to bring presents of fruit and vegetables, the men to gossip and bring news, the children to watch silent-eyed and the leaders of the community to discuss their problems and to ask, and offer advice. The patrol slips as easily into the primitive rhythm of the day and season as the people themselves, soon the cycle of burning, planting, weeding and harvesting becomes a part of life itself and customs, rites and celebrations as familiar as the Cup Final or Bank Holidays at home.

Here or there we may find one of the ten or more training camps established for the Border Scouts we have raised and trained. Here a strong patrol of five or six men will train ten or twenty times that number of tribesmen in counter-terrorist warfare. In each camp a simple longhouse houses the Scouts; a similar, but smaller version, their instructors. The daily programme is long and arduous, though the syllabus is basic and directly related to the skills required to be taught. The patrol embraces all responsibilities for its charges; training, administration, discipline and morale. The language difficulty is ever present, even fluent Malay does not reach everyone, pantomime is popular and some are skilful exponents of the art: helicopter training without helicopters is a test-piece. Throwing live grenades presents other problems, but no pantomime is necessary.

The second extract is an account of a patrol action in the jungle. Although this happened in Borneo the reader will feel that – scenery excepted – it could have happened to any of the SAS units mentioned in this book. It was a reverse, and nearly a disaster, but its effects were alleviated because those concerned reacted in a very cool and professional manner.

On a recent February morning a small 22 SAS patrol was moving

245

down from a ridge on a jungle track towards an old Indonesian Border Terrorist camp. This camp had been found the day before and appeared as though it had not been used for some six months.

As the leading scout, Trooper Thomson, ducked under some bamboo across the track – there was a lot of it in the area – a movement attracted his attention. He looked up and saw an Indonesian soldier six yards away to his right, just as the latter fired a burst at him. Several other enemy opened fire simultaneously.

Thomson was hit in the left thigh, the bone being shattered, and was knocked off the track to the left. He landed in a clump of bamboo two yards away from another Indonesian soldier lying concealed there. As the latter fumbled for his rifle, Thomson picked up his own, which he had dropped as he fell, and shot him.

The second man in the patrol, the commander, Sergeant Lillico, was also hit by the initial bursts and had collapsed on the track, unable to use his legs. He was still able to use his rifle, however, and this he did, returning the fire. The remainder of the patrol had meanwhile taken cover.

Thomson, unable to walk, hopped back to where Sergeant Lillico was sitting and joined in the fire fight. As he had seen Thomson on his feet, Sergeant Lillico was under the misapprehension that he could walk and therefore sent him back up the track to bring the rest of the patrol forward and continued to fire at sounds of enemy movement.

As Thomson was unable to get to his feet he dragged himself along by his hands and, on arriving at the top of the ridge, fired several bursts in the direction of the IBT camp. Whether the enemy thought that this fire came from reinforcements moving into the area is not known, but about this time, some ten minutes after the initial contact, they apparently withdrew. During the remainder of the day Thomson continued to drag himself towards where he expected to find the remainder of the patrol. He had applied a tourniquet to his thigh, which he released from time to time, taken morphia, and bandaged his wound as best he could with a shell dressing.

After sounds of enemy movement had died down, Sergeant Lillico pulled himself into the cover of a clump of bamboo, took morphia, bandaged his wound, and passed out until mid-afternoon. He awoke to hear the sound of a helicopter overhead. Realising that it would never find him amongst the bamboo he decided, in the morning, to drag himself to the top of the ridge which was covered in low scrub.

The balance of the patrol had decided that the best course of action was to move to the nearest infantry post, close by, and lead back a stronger party to search the area. This they did, starting back towards the scene of the contact late the same day.

The following morning Thomson continued on his way and by evening had covered 1,000 yards, about half the total distance he had to cover. However, soon after he had stopped for the night, a short while before last light, he heard the search party and was found at 1800 hours.

An attempt was at once made to winch him out by a helicopter but this failed due to the height of the trees. The next day, therefore, he was carried to a larger clearing nearby and was successfully evacuated at 0930, 48 hours after the contact.

Meanwhile, Sergeant Lillico had dragged himself to the ridge as he had planned – a distance of 400 yards – and on arriving there at 1500 hours, had fired some signal shots to attract the attention of the search party which he expected to be looking for him. These were immediately answered by three bursts of automatic fire some few hundred yards distant. Not by the search party, however, which at that time was too far away to have heard him firing. He therefore hid in the scrub as best he could and was able both to hear and see the enemy looking for him. One man climbed a tree about forty yards away and remained there for about half-an-hour in full view as he looked around and about.

While this was going on, he heard a helicopter close by but because of the nearness of the enemy and the obvious risk to the aircraft decided to make no use of the means at his disposal to attract it towards him. Not until the observer climbed down from his tree was he able to drag himself further away from the enemy and out into the scrub.

The helicopter, continuing its search operation, returned in the early evening. This time he signalled to it and, without delay, it flew over, lowered the winch and lifted him out, 33 hours after the contact.

In all, a rescue operation reflecting great credit on both RAF and Infantry but most of all on Sergeant Lillico and Trooper Thomson for their courage and determination not to give in.


Helicopters were of great value in Malaya and Borneo. They could bring in supplies, and evacuate casualties. Much of the time their pilots took appalling risks, missing trees by inches. Conditions for flying are bad in Malaya and Borneo but this fact was never allowed to make any difference.

In May 1963 the regiment lost three greatly valued members in Major R.H.D. Norman, MBE, MC, Major H.A.I. Thompson, MC and Corporal M.P. Murphy, in a helicopter crash in Borneo. All nine occupants were killed. The weather was very bad at the time. Major Norman had fought behind the Japanese lines in World War II and Major Thompson had commanded the Kuala Selangor swamp action.

## ADEN

The last phase of SAS activity was again in an infantry role – but again with a difference. This time it was on the opposite corner of the Arabian peninsula to the Jebel Akhdar in Aden. The colony of Aden was small, being only 75 square miles in area, with a population of 200,000. Adjoining it to the west was the Aden Protectorate, with an area of over 100,000 square miles. To the north was the Yemen, which contains some of the most fertile land in Arabia. The Yemen has a population of about 4 million distributed over its 74,000 square miles. It had joined the United Arab Republic of Egypt and Syria in 1958 but had ceased to belong in 1961.

Aden had been a British colony since 1939 and over the years had grown into a thriving city. It was a free port, a trade centre, and was an important coal and oil bunkering station. If the Oman was important strategically at the entrance to the Persian Gulf, Aden was clearly no less – and probably more – important at the entrance to the Red Sea. At all events both Egypt and Russia appeared to think so.

Relations between Aden and the Yemen had seldom been calm but were exacerbated in 1963 when Egyptian and Yemeni agents were constantly crossing the Aden border with the aim of stirring up trouble.

There was considerable movement of arms and the mining of roads. The situation became even livelier when the inhabitants of the Radfan mountains in the Protectorate were bribed by the Egyptians and trained by the Yemenis to conduct guerrilla warfare against the British and their

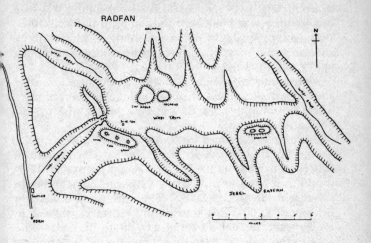

RADFAN

supporters. The Radfan guerillas were excellent fighters, good shots and tacticians, with plenty of guts. The country in which they lived was as wild as they were.

Britain was slow to take action, as her allies were quick to point out, and when she did move the action was not at first particularly effective. A combined force, of roughly brigade strength, was assembled to deal with the Radfan area. This was 'Radforce'. Unhappily, its component units were not experienced in the sort of mountain warfare entailed. Summer was approaching – it was April 1964 – and Radforce could look forward to day temperatures of 120°, night temperatures in the hills of below zero, a water shortage, and dust storms. All this of course, even without the attentions of the enemy, was bound to cause some wastage. Intelligence would be meagre, and probably unreliable if from local sources. A minimum period of seven days for acclimatization was prescribed for newly arrived troops although the SAS managed to get away with 48 hours.

One of the beauties of this operation which will not be unfamiliar to those who have served in other theatres at different times was that in Aden all accounting was on a peacetime basis and bills had to be sent to the Colonial Office. Fortunately Britain is not alone in these administrative anomalies and most of our opponents manage to get their lines equally twisted.

A Squadron SAS went into business gathering intelligence, and had an early success when they encountered forty enemy, who were promptly put at the receiving end of a brisk artillery bombardment.

The assault was timed for 30 April 1964. On 29th April, 3 Troop under Captain R. Edwards moved forward by helicopter to mark out the DZ for 3 Para to drop on to; 3 Para would then move to and occupy a strategic point known by the code name of 'Cap Badge'. The SAS force would fly by helicopter 5,000 yards into enemy territory, covered by artillery fire. As the DZ was thought to be under rebel observation and was certainly within reach of rebel fire, the artillery function was to keep the rebels unhappy while the helicopter approached, cease fire as it landed, but renew attentions after it had taken off. The landing was performed with classical expertise but during the night 3 Troop – numbering ten – was accidentally discovered and was surrounded by 50 enemy.

With daybreak the RAF joined in the battle. Numerous casualties were inflicted, both by the SAS and the RAF who managed to kill within 30 yards of the patrol – but the odds against the SAS lengthened as more tribesmen joined the attackers. By nightfall the troop was surrounded by nearly a hundred men who were cautiously closing in. The troop's radio operator Trooper J.N. Warburton* had been killed and the set damaged, so there was no further chance to direct the air firepower. As soon as darkness fell Captain Edwards ordered the patrol to make a dash for it. He himself was killed

---

* He was an ex-National Service Sapper, ever cheerful, invariably efficient.

outright, but the others managed to break out. They were pursued, but stopped to lay an ambush which killed one of their followers and discouraged the others. A further attempt to land by helicopter on the DZ was stopped when the helicopter was shot up, and the plan for a Para drop was then abandoned. Shortly afterwards Higher Authority decided that though Radforce had done very well the task set was beyond its limited resources, and thenceforward 39 Infantry Brigade would be used instead. This subsequently occupied the area.

The performance of 3 Troop in exacting circumstances won – as well it might – considerable praise. Unfortunately the occasion was remembered for a somewhat sordid incident which followed. As mentioned Captain Edwards* and the wireless operator Trooper Warburton had been killed. It was, of course, impossible to bring out the bodies. Subsequently they were decapitated and the heads displayed on stakes in Taiz, one of the twin capitals of the Yemen. This fact became known to the GOC – Major General J. Cubbon – and mentioned by him, after questions, in a Press Conference. Inexplicably, the American Embassy in Taiz denied that this was true, later the two headless bodies were discovered and identified. The worst aspect of this was that the Press published the story before the relatives of Captain Edwards and Trooper Warburton even knew they were dead.

It was not the first time that soldiers' bodies have been mutilated by an uncivilized enemy and it will not, probably, be the last. But it was felt that the Press should have kept quiet till the full facts were known and that Parliament should not have played party politics with the death of two very brave men.

The SAS part in the Radfan did not, of course, cease with

---

* Captain Edwards had contracted polio immediately after passing his selection course. This could well have been the end of his Army career, let alone with the SAS, but after a year – by sheer determination – he made himself fit enough to rejoin.

the end of Radforce. They continued in their rôle of reconnaissance, ambush and harassing attacks in the Protectorate and subsequently in an anti-terrorist rôle in the colony.

# CHAPTER XI

# The SAS Today

When 22 SAS returned to England – or rather went to England for the first time – it took up temporary quarters at Malvern. This was 1959; in 1960 it moved to its present quarters at Hereford. Hereford is, of course, very handy for training areas in Wales. Anyone visiting this old country town will immediately realise that the SAS like Hereford and Hereford likes the SAS. Hereford, being on the Welsh border, has seen a lot of warfare in its day and it appreciates a good fighting man when it sees him. Over the Welsh border – from which, in distant centuries, the raiders used to carve a path of destruction up to Hereford – the Welsh farmers also like the SAS. They do not like soldiers tramping over their land, and some of them are not too keen on the English, but their attitude to the SAS is full of friendliness and co-operation. Perhaps it is a feeling of affinity with people who will walk a mountain in all weathers, who can live hard and eat little, who are more interested in other people than themselves. The Welsh farmer is not indifferent to comfort but he can live without it, and he finds the SAS soldier a kindred spirit.

The SAS can be, and often is, useful. The local police like them because they work very closely together. SAS frogmen will search the beds of ponds and rivers for articles which the police think may be there. They usually are – but they take some finding in mud, or strong currents. Some of the local police go on SAS courses. Hereford is not a healthy place for criminals, although a few misguided people size it up as a dull rural area and decide to have a go. They only do it once.

As the Wye occasionally floods, 22 SAS is often asked to

rescue stranded cattle. And of course there are many other little services which the regiment performs and forgets about. Many towns are happy, and perhaps proud, to be the headquarters of a regiment but at times find it a bit of a nuisance, too involved in minor offences, and sometimes neither a credit to the town nor themselves when they work off surplus energy. The SAS manage to avoid this by the fortunate circumstance that they are often away on exercises. Any surplus energy is siphoned off in arduous tasks abroad. But even without this, internal discipline – by soldiers themselves – would keep the rash in check.

The best known aspect of Hereford is that it is the launching pad for the selection and training courses. These have unfortunately acquired the reputation of being rather more exacting than they are. They are, of course, testing but to most who take part they are satisfying and – although few like to acknowledge it – enjoyable. They are not exercises for supermen; they are physical and mental tests which a fit and alert person can pass. If the method and manner of these courses was known more widely there would undoubtedly be more volunteering for them, more passing, and consequently more people of the required type joining the regiment, whether Regular or TA.

The aim of the selection course is to find a man who has initiative, self-discipline, independence of mind, stamina, patience, a sense of humour, and the ability to work without supervision. These are all desirable military qualities in any unit. In addition to these he must be the sort of person who can endure loneliness without deteriorating. The particular loneliness may be experienced in complete isolation or as a member of a very small group. Some men are good when completely on their own but with one or two others lose their initiative and pull less than their weight. Yet in a larger group still they may be as good as ever. As an SAS man is likely to work in a group of very small numbers it is important that he should be neither a complete 'loner' nor yet a man who needs at least a platoon to give him moral support. These exercises are the same for officers as for men; if you pass, you at least know that those who work with you in the regiment are on the same footing.

Selection courses are usually preceded by a training course so that a man is reasonably well-prepared. They take place in the Brecon area. Each task takes about 36 hours and requires a man to find his way over moors and hills with only a map and a prismatic compass. There are no convenient signposts, nor landmarks, nor friendly natives to help. In an exercise he will have to visit at least four selected points and carry out certain tasks at each. A task might be to lay charges, or it might be to obtain information the intelligence officer would find useful. He will visit several check points; if he is a 'wide' boy who thinks he can beat the system this will soon be noted. Each check point may well be 30 miles from the last. En route he may encounter others also doing the course but as their tasks and route are different he will be unwise to waste time talking to them. He may find the physical side of the course a little beyond his untrained powers but this fact will not necessarily fail him. He can probably be brought up to standard physically but it might be impossible to develop the other required qualities if they are not sufficiently strong already. He is not told much. The qualities which are looked for tend to be care in recording information, ability to recall the exact sequence of events, a logical mind, and the presence to keep himself in trim physically no matter how exhausted he may become.

Although officers in the Regular battalion have probably not served in the ranks, TA officers usually have. However, the ranks of a TA battalion are – as we know – usually full of officer material. An officer in the SAS lives at very close quarters with his men, sharing the same basha, fending for himself. Once the detachment has moved out of civilization the trappings of rank mean little; the qualities which earned it mean much. If an officer is not up to this task both he and the others soon know.

Sometimes the selection committee is itself surprised. On one exercise men were sent into the Black Mountains when the fog was down to 500 feet. The task was arranged to take one day. However, on the second day one man had not reappeared. Nobody was unduly worried, the man had a rucksack and some rations. However, when he did not turn up on the fourth day they sent out search parties. On the sixth they were still searching and had been all night and had turned out every available man. Suddenly the missing man appeared. 'Where on earth have you been?' enquired the squadron commander, assuming the recruit had found a billet with a farmer and had waited for the fog to lift. 'I've been in the bog,' replied the man. He had. He had walked into one of those treacherous hill bogs which let you in up to your knees, and will take the lot of you if you struggle unduly. The man very wisely lay over his Bergen rucksack and, although he gradually sank to his chest, remained alert and kept shouting. Eventually a farmer heard him and pulled him out with a horse and a rope. He passed the course.

Although selection courses accustom a man gradually to his tasks the same cannot be said of re-training courses for the Regulars. The latter gave considerable attention to testing mental toughness, that is the ability to stand up to brain-washing. The accent is not so much on the physical as the mental side. Lack of sleep plays a large part in it, as does ceaseless interrogation. Re-training courses of this nature are not popular. However as with the selection course retraining courses are developed to build up rather than to test breaking points.

The relationship between the Regular Unit and its TA counterpart is maintained by posting experienced regular officers, NCOs and men to TA jobs. This promotes better understanding and co-ordinated training. 21 has never lacked experienced leaders but as the former wartime SAS retired there might have been a gap if there had been no one with operational experience to replace them.

In 1959 a new TA was added. This was 23 SAS, originally known as the Reserve Reconnaissance unit. Its function was to give practice in escape and evasion techniques. During World War II MI.9 had assisted many crashed airmen to return home from enemy-held territory. It was, of course, an enormous benefit if trained pilots could be brought home, and MI.9 was reasonably successful in that, and assisting other escapees. 23 SAS under the command of Lieutenant Colonel H.S. Gillies, MC was launched at Finsbury Barracks, London, in 1959. Soon afterwards it moved to Birmingham where it had 60 applicants on the first day that recruiting opened. 23 SAS now has two branches in Birmingham, one north, one south, and units at Doncaster, Leeds and Dundee. 21 has detachments at Hitchin (Hertfordshire) and Portsmouth. There are two other units which have not so far been mentioned. One is 63 (SAS) Signal Squadron (V) which has a headquarters at Portsmouth and detachments at Southampton and Bournemouth; the other is R Squadron, a reserve of regulars who could, if necessary, be called up for service with 22 SAS.

21 SAS is now established at the Duke of York's Headquarters, Kings Road, Chelsea, where Group HQ is in the centre block. As neighbours, 21 has 44 Para Brigade (TA) and the London Irish Rifles.

The only member of 1 SAS who is still serving is Captain (Quartermaster) J. Schofield. He is now with 22 SAS at Hereford.

Inevitably, much of SAS work, training, and methods today, must remain secret. And does. Now and again a little harmless but intriguing information is let out. In December 1969 a national paper disclosed that 200 SAS men were on the Malaya/Thai border dealing with infiltrators, at the request of the Malaysian government. It was rumoured that Chin Peng was active in that area. The SAS neither confirmed nor denied their presence in the area. 'It was possible,' they agreed. 'They have training exercises all over the world in convenient areas and that piece of jungle was an ideal place to use.'

In February 1970 another national newspaper came out with the information that a former commanding officer of 21 SAS had been concerned in an attempt to assist the Imam of Yemen in 1963. The fact that the 'news' was seven years old must have made newspaper history in every sense of the word. It was reported that the party had gone on a completely free-lance basis, without the knowledge of, and to the embarrassment of, the government. The Egyptians who were backing the republican revolt in the Yemen were extremely angry to find that a force of some 80 British and French guerrillas had established themselves in the area. They used thousands of men for several years to try to oust this force but without success, it seems.

Gradually the impression was gaining ground that as far as the Middle East and Far East were concerned the SAS was much more likely to preserve the status quo than to disturb it. Against the enemies of law and order, stability and freedom they would:

> Confound their politics
> Frustrate their knavish tricks

but only if invited to do so by the legal rulers.

With such high standards of physical fitness in the regiment it was inevitable that there would be attempts on endurance records of one sort or another. Most notable was undoubtedly the feat of Trooper T. McLean, who rowed across the Atlantic single-handed in 72 days. He landed at Blacksod, County Mayo, on 27th July 1969. His diet on the voyage was sardines, curry and tea. McLean, who was appropriately nicknamed 'Moby' had once been in the same troop as Captain J. Ridgeway and Sergeant C. Blyth who had previously rowed the Atlantic in 92 days.

McLean, who was 25 at the time of the 2,500-mile row, had been an orphan since the age of two, and, perhaps because of that, had developed a high standard of self-reliance. He certainly needed it for the weather was stormy all the way and once he woke up in the night in mid-Atlantic to find the boat swamped and sinking; he had another very narrow escape when he ran onto rocks off the coast of Ireland and took $1\frac{1}{2}$ hours to get off. As soon as he landed he sprinted 200 yards along the beach because he felt a bit stiff and wanted to get himself properly fit again.

258

In 1982 he established another world record by sailing the world's smallest vessel single-handed across the Atlantic. It was the 9ft 9inch *Giltspur*.

A later attempt by Lance Corporal A. Hornby to row the Pacific from Japan to Vancouver – a distance of 4,330 miles – in a nineteen-footer was unsuccessful but was a very worthy effort.

Not surprisingly the original British Free-Fall team all came from 22 SAS and also held the British High Altitude record. There are other events in which the SAS performs creditably – such as the Devizes–Westminister canoe race, which has been won by them on several occasions but, curiously enough, the only one of which they speak with unblushing pride is defeating the Fijian regiment at Rugby football in Malaya in the early 1950s.

Two rather different feats were those of Sergeant Michael Reeves and Major M. Walker. The former was instructing in parachuting 2,500 feet up over Staffordshire when a learner's parachute failed to open because the static line had entangled itself around the main parachute. Had he released the reserve parachute this would have caught the tail of the aircraft. It was impossible to drag the man back into the aircraft so Sergeant Reeves climbed down the static line although the friction burnt through his gloves and blistered his hands. On finding the main parachute could not be freed he gave orders to cut the static line, then went into free-fall still holding the other man. When it was safe to do so he released the learner's parachute but stayed with him to be sure he did not entangle with the sixteen feet of drifting static line, and that the man was in control. Then when he deemed it safe to do so he released his own parachute at what was described as 'a height a little lower than is considered usual for normal parachute deployment' – in other words when the ground was becoming extremely close. He was awarded a George Medal.

Major Muir Walker, MC, nicknamed 'Red Rory' from the colour of his hair, was Assistant Military Attaché in Jakarta, Indonesia, in 1963. When the Federation of Malaysia was proclaimed the Indonesians decided to express their feelings by attacking the British Embassy. A crowd estimated at 5,000 surrounded it and soon began hurling stones at the plate-glass windows. Walker, wearing the SAS beret and uniform, then began walking up and down amid the hail of stones, playing the bagpipes. Indonesian police tried to grab him and pull him out of danger but he shook himself free and continued the entertainment.

In 1959 Walker had been the first man to beat the hour in the *Daily Mail* Air Race, travelling from Marble Arch, London, to the Arc de Triomphe, Paris; he used motor-cycles, a helicopter and a plane. Walker's speed of movement and presence of mind had proved of military use on more than one occasion; in 1957 he had led a team into the Malayan jungle to rescue the crew of a crashed helicopter and had accomplished the task in $1\frac{1}{2}$ hours.

But it is not only the regulars or 'old hands' who impress. A former troop commander in 21 SAS mentioned that in his troop he had one not very robust member who was a stationery salesman in civilian life. On an exercise in which the troop was going to parachute into Denmark it was obvious that he was not fit to jump for he had developed severe gastric flu; he had therefore been tucked away in a corner of the aircraft preparatory to being put straight into hospital on landing. But when the moment to jump came he dragged himself into line – he could hardly walk – and jumped.

In the local paper recently a letter described the SAS as 'tough but gentle'. It was a description of which they would approve. However, the citizens of Hereford might be surprised to learn how varied are the activities of their fellow citizens (as the SAS are proud to feel themselves). They might not be surprised to hear that four of them, including a doctor, had walked across the North Pole, but they would be, perhaps, to learn that Brigadier M.S.K. Maunsell, the Inspector-General of Prisons, had borrowed a team from the SAS to test the new prison fences from the inside; the SAS had made short work of them.

A reputation for being daring and unorthodox can however have its drawbacks. When on 8th August 1963, £2½ million in used banknotes was stolen from a Glasgow to London express the 'train-robbers' dressed themselves in Army uniform adorned with SAS badges. It seems that if interrupted by the police they were planning to pretend it was a Territorial exercise, and all just jolly good fun. The kit left behind at Leatherslade Farm was subsequently auctioned off to a public which paid considerably more than cost price for the items concerned – including SAS badges.

Patience and understanding are usually less associated with military life than their opposites but in the SAS man they are vital qualities. During the Malayan campaign the Commander-in-Chief, Far East, sent the following message to the SAS:

Since your formation in 1951 you have had the task of deep jungle reconnaissance and of fighting Communist Terrorists in areas inaccessible to other forces. You have accounted for 124 Communist Terrorists, which is indeed a fine performance, but as important as these victories has been your achievement in winning over aboriginal tribes to our cause, and this will have a lasting effect long after the jungle war has been forgotten. You have shown by your operations in the deep and unknown jungle over a period of three months and more at a stretch that the British soldier can adapt himself to the most difficult conditions and can defeat the most cunning enemy on his own ground.

Winning over aborigines did not consist merely of talking to them, treating their varous ills, which included malaria and TB, but called for imaginative understanding of what was important to them. For example, they believed earnestly in dreams and trackers would be reluctant to move off in the morning until they had carefully discussed and analysed any unusual dreams of the night before. To a patrol itching to get on the trail this could be somewhat irksome but in the circumstances the best solution was not to show impatience but to join in the discussion and try to help it to a satisfactory conclusion.

SAS philosophy was summarized by Colonel W.M.

Wingate-Grey when he concluded his five years service with the regiment:

I believe that service is the best description of our philosophy, service without regard to class, fear, favour, or race. From this stems our capacity to do anything, go anywhere, to be flexible and efficient. Our vaunted toughness is only a means to the end of getting the job done, and the head must always rule the body in our affairs.

The ability to act intelligently however frustrated, weary and unhappy a man may be, is the quality sought for in endurance tests, however remote their setting may be from the one in which he might have to operate. The Australian SAS regiment has a 'Recondo' (Reconnaissance/Commando) course in which those chosen to take part endure hunger, thirst, exhaustion and occasional physical danger, for three weeks, with an average of only three or four hours of sleep a night. At one point in the course you may reach the coast in time to receive sea transport but if you do not make it you have the mortification of seeing the transport out at sea while you have to face further gruelling journeys because you missed it. A feature of the course is to ensure that everyone on it is doing something useful all the time for it is now believed that in quite brisk battles half those present are contributing absolutely nothing while the remainder do all the work whatever the place, time or reason.

The Belgians have a roughly similar course with the added refinement that they are accompanied by one man who has a servant and ample supplies. While they lie half-starved in the open their companion reclines in his comfortable tent awaiting the evening meal which they can smell cooking and whose delicious aromas will soon be succeeded by the smell of cigar-smoke, and the clink of the wine-bottle which their sensitized hearing could not miss.

It is a surprise to most people to learn that such a highly individualistic and versatile regiment as the SAS can be committed to NATO, but this is so. It is, in fact, the only Special Force so committed. It is not difficult to visualize the sort of targets they could attack, nodal points, power stations and the like. Exercises tend to be of the 'escape and evasion' type in which a party of SAS is given the task of slipping through a cordon of troops who are searching for them. But SAS troops do not talk about training or exercises. If anyone ever does wish to comment on his experiences with the regiment it may be assumed that he is a person of whom they had a poor opinion and probably discarded. This is not necessarily a harsh criticism. It is fair and reasonable for soldiers to reminisce over their experiences and fight battles again in retrospect. It is not however appropriate for Special Forces to think like that. The Battle of Waterloo may have been won on the playing fields of Eton but wars of the future will be prevented by knowing the way minds work when playing chess in Moscow or Mah-Jong in Peking.

The question which naturally enough comes up at this point is whether there is any special characteristic which might be said to be typical of the SAS man. It would obviously be absurd to say that it is dedication to his profession because that is found in many regiments and in many places outside the Army. Possibly the only word which fits is 'loyalty'. Without this everything would fall apart. It appears in widely differing careers and circumstances. John Cooper was probably the first man David Stirling recruited to the SAS. He was in the desert, Sicily, Italy, France, Belgium, Holland, Germany and Norway. When it was dissolved he went to the Green Howards but when it was recreated he was soon back and in Malaya, where he led a jungle endurance team as well as pioneering parachuting into trees. Inevitably he was in the Oman.

To many, Dare Newell is the quintessential SAS man. During World War II he was SOE and did not come into the SAS until the 1950s. In Malaya he was noted for his ruthlessness in selection; after Malaya he went to Group HQ; possibly there are others who have contributed more intelligent thought and application to furthering the cause of the SAS, but if there are no one seems able to identify them.

In a recent exercise in Denmark there was a frozen lake to

be crossed. Unfortunately it was not frozen very hard and if it cracked there was a fair chance that the patrol would disappear until their bodies were found the following spring. It began to creak. They could have turned back. After all it was only a TA exercise.

Their leader – a young millionaire incidentally – had decided that if you were doing an exercise you should take it with all its implications; they went on.

But you do not have to be a millionaire, or a peer, or an Etonian, or a superb athlete, to make it with the SAS; you just have to have your priorities right.

For the SAS soldier this is the finest life in the world. Trained to a high peak of physical fitness, surrounded by hand-picked men whom he can trust with his life, and often does, he can be a free-fall parachutist, a canoeist, a sub-aqua diver, a mountaineer, a skier, an explorer – the possibilities are virtually unlimited. He will learn to drive every make and type of vehicle, become a crack shot, learn two or three languages, and be nearer the centre of important matters than most people, however influential. He will also have ample opportunity at more conventional sports. The world will be his oyster. In the regimental lines at Hereford you will see the more serious papers being read, *The Times*, *Telegraph*, *Economist*. The SAS soldier wants the facts. He is by no means averse to a bit of cheesecake but he will not accept it as a substitute for news, only as an addition. But SAS men do not appear over-dedicated or even intense; quite the reverse. They make excellent part-time medics. They are trained to kill, but so is every soldier. An SAS man will not like killing any more than anyone else although he may be quicker and more efficient at it. One, for example, refuses to fish or shoot for sport, as he does not believe you should kill animals or fish for sport. But, on an assignment that man will be so swift and ruthless that he will appear to be like a machine.

Nor are they, in spite of all, exclusively interested in things military. Many are married – to rather long-suffering wives.*

* The Regimental magazine *Mars and Minerva* has a wives' section entitled 'Ma's and Minerva'.

They don't even look tough, most of them. Undoubtedly they are, but their life is not necessarily everyone's choice. Fortunately for the country it is theirs, and if they ever need a second motto to add to their present one it would be: *Si vis pacem, pare bellum* – If you wish for peace, prepare for war.

# CHAPTER XII

# Poacher turned Gamekeeper

(An unofficial chapter)

The story of the SAS from 1941 to 1971 was that of an enterprising, unorthodox, inventive regiment. It had performed extremely well against obvious enemies: in their turn these had been Italians, Germans, Chinese Communists and Indonesian soldiers. However, in the 1960s it became clear that a new threat was appearing: the enemy who was waging war when officially everyone else was at peace. That enemy (he or she) might be an isolated fanatic, prepared to destroy innocent people in order to gratify some half-crazed wish, or might be one of a highly-organised, well-financed, terrorist group. He might easily be one of a team which aimed to damage this country by sabotage, assassination or disruption. Whatever category this new type of enemy came into, he would be a very difficult opponent. His methods of operation would be not unlike those which the regiment had developed in the past. It was appropriate that it should now prepare itself to counter them.

At the same time it would never be overlooked that the SAS is a regiment in the Order of Battle of the British Army and is committed to NATO. Anti-terrorism would be only one of its functions.

The majority of the public still remained unaware of the skills of the SAS, or even of its existence. Having had an official history written to cover the first forty years, the regiment decided that that was enough for the moment. However, during the 1970s there was much curiosity among journalists about the regiment's employment. Was it still in the Oman? The SAS neither confirmed nor denied rumours about its activities. It was attracting enough of the right sort of recruit and had neither wish nor need for publicity. Attempts by television and film companies to make documentaries were politely but firmly rebuffed. As the official historian I was frequently approached for assistance but my information was of the past not the present. Obtaining that had been difficult enough, for the Government's 30-year rule concerning official documents had straddled the whole period. Fortunately many former members of the regiment were able to co-operate, as the book was the official regimental history.

The period after 1970 offered a totally different scenario from what had preceded it. The SAS, which preferred to move silently and secretly, soon found itself caught in a blaze of publicity. The first sign of coming events occurred in May 1972. As the QE2 was almost midway on an Atlantic crossing, a telephone call to Cunard (the owners) announced that unless the comparatively modest sum of just over £100,000 was paid over, bombs which had already been planted on board would go off, thus sinking the ship with its 1,500 passengers and crew. A mixed team of SAS and Royal Marine Special Boat Service was hastily assembled, and parachuted into the Atlantic near the ship. Once on board, the team made a thorough search but found nothing. It was a false alarm but good practice.

The need for special thought and preparation against terrorist attacks was underlined later the same year when a 'Black September' squad killed two and kidnapped nine Israeli athletes at the Munich Olympics. 'Black September' was an Arab terrorist group which had already assassinated the Prime Minister of Jordan. Unfortunately for the hostages, the German police tried to kill the terrorists as they were putting their hostages on board an aeroplane; in consequence all the hostages and five terrorists were killed. Three terrorists were taken prisoner but were released later as the ransom for a hijacked German airliner. The Germans realised all too clearly that this was not the way to tackle the terrorist/

hostage/hijack problem, and took the decision to create a special anti-terrorist unit.

The Munich disaster combined with several other hijackings in Europe to draw attention to the continuing need for a military unit skilled in anti-terrorist operations. So far, terrorist operations had been on a fairly small scale; if they increased rapidly in size or numbers considerable force would be needed to cope with the situation. Specialized equipment was clearly necessary and one of the devices now developed – which would receive much publicity later – was the 'stun' grenade. The stun grenade would not kill but if used correctly would provide sufficient time for terrorists to be overwhelmed. In addition to the appropriate training a number of exercises were carried out in suitable areas. This was the classic army internal security/counter-terrorist rôle – the army being called in to assist the civil power. Some members of the public became alarmed when soldiers, suspected of being SAS, were seen at London Airport. It was surmised that either there was a crisis or that dirty work politically was about to occur.

In 1976 the British public woke up to see newspaper headlines proclaiming that the SAS had been sent to Northern Ireland. This was under the instructions of the Cabinet presided over by Mr Harold Wilson. The sudden decision caught everyone by surprise, not least the regiment which, with training and other activities, had its members scattered far and wide; barely a troop was immediately available. The cause of this over-publicized move was the Cabinet's fear that Northern Ireland was lurching towards the brink of civil war and that this must be prevented. The SAS can scarcely have welcomed this assignment but in the army you go where you are sent. And they were there, like the rest of the army, in support of the civil power.

At least it put an end to the rumours. Since 1969 there had been persistent reports that the SAS was already in Northern Ireland. Known SAS men were said to have been sighted. It was highly likely that former SAS men would have been in Ireland for, as we have seen, many men join the SAS for a period then return to their own regiments. When those regiments went to Ireland – and most of them did – the former SAS men would of course be with them.

The decision had one particularly interesting aspect. All highly-trained, expert, secret units are darkly suspected of being prepared for a coup d'état of the Right or Left. Certain sections of the Press had long nursed the view that the SAS was only waiting in the wings for a national emergency which would presumably be exploited by the Right. The fact that a moderate Socialist Cabinet committed the SAS to an assignment aiding the civil power settled the suspicions of all but the lunatic fringe. Over and over again the fact had been emphasised that the SAS was the instrument of the democratically elected government of the day. Now it was seen to be so.

Growing up alongside this realisation that the SAS is nobody's private army had been the recognition that anyone might be very glad of its protection, hostile media men included. If a television station, public building, newspaper office, ministry, or even private house, were suddenly to be seized by terrorists who threatened to kill everyone there unless absurd demands were met there could be few who would not hope that the SAS had been alerted and was at that moment putting into operation plans to secure the immediate release of the hostages.

This had been dramatically proved by what became known as the Balcombe Street siege in December 1975. Following a series of terrorist incidents in London, Guildford and Birmingham during 1974–5, the police gradually closed in on suspects. After a car chase, a four-man team from the Provisional IRA took refuge in a flat in Marylebone. The occupants were a man and his wife, who were promptly made hostages. The area was soon surrounded by police marksmen, not to mention Press and TV representatives. The turning point came when a BBC announcement that the SAS had now arrived on the scene was heard on a radio inside the flat. The terrorists, who had thought they might have held off the police long enough to strike a bargain or make their escape,

269

promptly surrendered; the SAS was a different proposition.

The fact that some of the SAS rescues have been dramatically spectacular has inevitably led to a spate of books and films, often fictional and bizarre, purporting to describe activities in which the SAS has taken part. In other European countries the improbable adventures of imaginary SAS men provide a whole series of books in which the heroes operate from China to Angola and Thailand to Spain. *Voilà le mystique.*

The one feature these fantasies have in common is that they totally misrepresent the SAS philosophy. The SAS man is not a spy, gunman, acrobat or detective; he is a soldier with well-developed skills.*

The year 1977 brought two different types of terrorist attack, in one of which the SAS was used as advisers and in the other was actively involved, though only on a small scale.

The first was when a party of young 'Moluccans' seized a train and a school at Assen and Bovensmilde in Holland. The Moluccas are a group of islands between Borneo and New Guinea, which form an outlying part of Indonesia. The 'Moluccans' who were natives of Holland by birth and upbringing, were demanding an independent state of Molucca. This seemed a fair example of the lunatic fringe but, as 105 children were held prisoner in the school, was no laughing matter. After three weeks of fruitless negotiation, the Dutch decided to resolve the crisis. They stormed the train, killing six terrorists and capturing seven; unfortunately two passengers were killed.

October 1977 saw the end of a nightmare hijack at Mogadishu in Somalia. The terrorists on this occasion were Palestinian supporters of the notorious Baader-Meinhof gang, most of whom were imprisoned in Germany after a series of terrorist offences. The Baader-Meinhof gang was drawn from middle-class intellectuals and its aims, apart from spreading death and destruction, were difficult to

* An excellent photographic documentary, *This is the SAS*, by Tony Geraghty, makes this point very clear.

identify. The saga began in October 1977 when a Lufthansa Boeing took off from Majorca with 83 passengers on board. Unknown to the rest, the complement included four Palestinians, two men and two women, who had brought a number of weapons in their baggage. Obviously, in those days, aircraft security measures were minimal.

The hi-jackers then made their demands known. The Baader-Meinhof terrorists must be released, a ransom of £9 million be paid for the aircraft, and the terrorists granted legal immunity. The West German government refused the demands and the Boeing began a five-day journey round the world, receiving fresh consignments of fuel but being refused any other concessions. Eventually it was announced that the aircraft was to land at Dubai. The German anti-terrorist unit (named GSG-9) flew to Dubai and so, at the request of the German Chancellor after consultation with the British Prime Minister, did a small SAS unit. Before anything practical could be achieved the aircraft took off to Aden, where the terrorists killed the pilot after accusing him of using his radio for messages, and then on to Mogadishu in Somalia. Here the end came when two SAS men smashed through the side of the aircraft using stun and flash grenades. This let through fourteen of the German GSG-9 who fought it out with the terrorists, killing three. The passengers were below the line of fire but, aware that their luck was running out, the terrorists had thrown aviation spirit around the inside of the aircraft, prepared to burn everything and everyone. Fortunately, the grenades they used to facilitate this did not go off. An unexpected effect of the failure of this hijack was that three of the Baader-Meinhof gang imprisoned in Germany committed suicide in their cells as soon as they learnt the news.

But the event which really brought the SAS to the eyes of the British public was the Iranian Embassy siege of May 1980.

The Iranian Embassy is (or was) an attractive building in the quiet south-west London district of Princes Gate. Here at 11 a.m. on 30th April 1980 a group of six previously unknown Iranian terrorists took over the building making prisoners of most, but not quite all, the occupants. This made a total of twenty-six, of which seventeen were embassy staff, eight were visitors, and one was a metropolitan policeman who would distinguish himself for his calm and courage in the next few days.

When the terrorists' requests became known it was obvious that this siege could scarcely end in compromise or peaceful negotiation. Their demand was for autonomy for the province of Khuzistan in Southern Iran, which would be re-christened Arabistan, and for the release of political prisoners. For several years there had been a campaign, often violent, for autonomy in this area, but it had been ruthlessly suppressed first by the Shah and later by the Ayatollah Khomeini. As the days passed it was obvious that the terrorists knew little English and had no strong backing, but were totally unpredictable. The best that can be hoped for in such circumstances is that the terrorists will feel sorry for their captives, even develop a friendship with them, and give themselves up. This possibility appeared to be shattered when the terrorist leader quarrelled with the embassy Press attaché and shot him. The body was then dumped outside and an announcement made that one hostage would now be shot at intervals unless their demands were granted.

It was now May 5th. At 7.20 p.m. that evening ITN watchers suddenly saw one of the most dramatic live incidents ever to be shown on a television screen. It lasted eleven minutes.

For days Press and TV had been keeping watchful eyes on the Embassy, speculating on what was going on inside and what was being said in Downing Street. A TV camera had been smuggled to the window of a flat inside the police cordon which overlooked the Embassy. This could, of course, have jeopardised the entire operation and lost many lives. Cameramen never seem to lack courage: commonsense and discretion seem to be less readily available.

What happened next astonished the audience of millions and gave the SAS publicity which it probably did not welcome. Armed men, dressed in combat gear and wearing

Balaclava helmets and respirators, suddenly appeared on the roof and the balconies. They were seen to abseil down from the roof, blow in windows, and create clouds of smoke and flashes. Fire broke out and swept through the building but the only deaths were of the two men who had been killed by the terrorists and five terrorists killed by the SAS; the latter had tried to fight back from the shelter of the hostages but their attempts had not been successful. The Balaclava helmets were not worn to dramatize or create fear but for protection against fire. The names of those who took part have never been disclosed. It was just another job.

But the SAS had not become merely a super anti-terrorist unit. It had been in an ordinary war between 1970 and 1976 and would be involved in another one in 1982.

The first was in the Oman. Much water had flowed under the bridge since the 1958 operations described earlier in this book. From the early 1960s there had been signs that destabilizing factors were at work in the area. The Oman controls the Straits of Hormuz, through which half the West's supply of crude oil passes on its way from the Gulf wells to Western refineries. The Oman was not a colony or protectorate but a close ally. The Sultan had a navy, army and air force, all of which maintained close links with Britain.

In 1970 the ruler, Sultan Said bin Taimur, an ageing despot, was deposed by his son Qaboos. The new Sultan had progressive and realistic ideas, was firmly pro-Western, and had been educated at Sandhurst. He promptly invited the SAS to come and look at the problems posed by the rebel-held areas in his country. The SAS commitment rarely extended beyond one squadron but its influence was considerable.

The war began with a 'leaflet' raid by the Sultan's Air Force, and this achieved the notable success of winning back a guerrilla leader who had joined the rebels through disillusionment with the policies of the deposed Sultan. He proved a valuable asset. As other rebels changed sides they were organised into small anti-guerrilla units known as 'firqas'. The SAS rôle was to assist in training and advising the

Sultan's own forces as well as to assist in what has become known as 'hearts and minds' – providing medical care and help with everyday needs such as well-boring, road-making or even agriculture. The SAS party was known as the British Army Training Team; many of them spoke fluent Arabic.

However on July 19th 1972 the small SAS training group at Mirbat found themselves in an entirely different form of activity. Occasional shells and mortars from the nearby hills had indicated the presence of rebels, but with the constant heavy rain of the wet season it seemed unlikely that a major attack would occur. In addition to the SAS – who numbered only eight – there were 30 poorly-armed Askaris, a better-armed firqa numbering 40, and 25 members of the Gendarmerie.

An attack was launched at 5.30 a.m. by 250 well-armed rebels who had been planning this assault for months. Determined though their assault was, it was met with equal ferocity as the garrison fought back. Although the battle did not last long it made up for its shortness by its intensity. Some relief was given to the beleaguered garrison by air strikes on rebel positions but the issue was really settled by close-quarter fighting. At the end of it the SAS had had two men killed and two wounded. The rebels left thirty dead but it was reported that many were dragged away to die later. The inspiration of this battle was Captain M.J.A. Kealey who was awarded a DSO for the action. Sadly, he died of hypothermia on the Brecon Beacons five years later. He had put himself on a re-training course after a period away from operational work. The weather was exceptionally bitter, but he had survived such ordeals before. Everything does not always go right, even for the experienced SAS man.

Mirbat, although four years before the end of the war, effectively sealed it by proving to the guerrillas that their best efforts would fail. But there was still a long, hard way to go. By the end of it, the number of SAS killed had mounted to twelve but peace had been restored and the country vastly improved economically. And the threat to the Western oil supplies vital to our defences had been removed. The full story of the campaign is told in *SAS Operation Oman* by Colonel Tony Jeapes (published by Kimber).

Inevitably the SAS was in the Falklands War of 1982. The Argentines first occupied South Georgia in March, then invaded the Falklands on April 2nd. The SAS moved into the area in the same sequence. The first reconnaissance unit, which landed on South Georgia from helicopters on April 21st, was abortive, for the party was caught in a 100 m.p.h. gale on a glacier. It was taken out again at a cost of two helicopters. The second party of fifteen, which went in in Geminis was almost defeated by the appalling weather, but nine men landed and took up posts to observe the enemy. The remainder were eventually rescued by helicopter. However an SAS group was to the fore in securing the surrender of the Argentine garrison at Grytviken.

By now the SAS had reconnaissance teams in the Falklands and when our landings took place on May 1st they were able to report enemy strength, targets and movement, all of which were vital to successful naval bombardment. Lying up undetected, exposed to extremes of weather, tested SAS training to the limits. As the campaign progressed the regiment was able to take a more active part. On the night of 14th May they destroyed eleven Pucaras, one of the more deadly Argentine aircraft, and nearby fuel and ammunition dumps. (It could have been the desert in 1942, apart from the weather!) This was followed by a policy of deception, giving the Argentines a totally incorrect impression of the numbers they were up against and the direction of the attack, and the occupation of the vital strategic point of Mount Kent by helicopter-borne SAS troops.

But not everything went right. Just prior to the final assault a Sea King helicopter exploded and crashed into the sea, drowning eighteen SAS men. It was their biggest single loss since 1945. There was no enemy action at the time and it seemed that the cause must have been sea birds sucked into the engine inlets.

At the end of the Falklands campaign when the awards were published the SAS broke with tradition in disclosing the names of serving members of the regiment. Perhaps the outstanding achievement was that of Captain G.J. Hamilton, awarded a posthumous Military Cross, who after two helicopter crashes fought with such determination and courage that the Argentinians described him as the bravest man they had ever seen.

In forty years the SAS had come a long way but in many respects is still the regiment that David Stirling created in the desert. It certainly has the same standards and the same attitudes. It will always be thinking ahead. The SAS man must always aim for the highest standards militarily, physically, intellectually, culturally. But with it all he must always remain a modest, unassuming, ordinary person.

It seems to work.

# APPENDICES

## APPENDIX I
*The Long Range Desert Group*

Lieutenant Colonel (now Major General) David Lloyd-Owen, DSO, OBE, MC, who commanded the LRDG wrote about it as follows in *The Desert My Dwelling Place:*

In the years between the wars there was a small number of enthusiastic explorers who spent their leaves and any spare money they could raise in travelling over the Libyan Desert. Among them were Ralph Bagnold who was in command when I joined, Guy Prendergast who took over from him, Bill Kennedy Shaw who was the Intelligence officer and who had previously been in the Palestine Civil Service, Pat Clayton who was in the Egyptian Survey Department before the war and Teddy Mitford, a regular officer in the Royal Tank Corps, whom I found as my Squadron Leader when I joined the Long Range Desert Group.

These were some of the small group of people who enjoyed the desert and were prepared to give up their spare time and money to traverse it in peacetime. They had little or no official backing, except perhaps an occasional grant from the Royal Geographical Society, which certainly gave them tremendous support and encouragement in other ways. All of those whom I have mentioned were experienced in desert travel and were to join Bagnold after he started the unit.

They had learned to live hard, carrying the minimum amount of food and water, and to navigate their small parties across miles of unforgiving and featureless sand, they had learned to extract their cars from the ever-shifting dunes and from the soft patches which were salt marshes, and to calculate the amount of petrol that would be needed to cover a given distance in various conditions of 'going'. They had also found the way to fix their position by the stars at night, and to conserve water from their radiators by fitting a condenser, how to read the tracks of other men, vehicles or camels so that they could estimate how many and in what direction others had passed before.

It was from these trips that the sun-compasses, the sand channels and the vehicle condensers were perfected that were used on all vehicles by men of the Eighth Army in their advances across Libya to Tunisia.

W.B. Kennedy-Shaw describes the water-condenser in his book *Long Range Desert Group:*

The water consumption of the cars was kept at a minimum by a simple condenser. From the top of the radiator, the overflow pipe of which was blocked up, a rubber tube led into a two-gallon can bolted to the running-board and half-filled with water. When the water in the radiator boiled the steam condensed in this can, and when it had ceased boiling the vacuum in the radiator would suck the water back and fill it up again. If all the joints were air-tight there would be no need to 'top up' the radiator for hundreds of miles.

Four days after Italy declared war on the Allies (June 10th 1940) Bagnold's proposals for deep reconnaissance and harassment of the Italians were adopted.

The first members were New Zealanders, and it could not have been a more fortunate choice. As Kennedy-Shaw says: 'No men could have fitted themselves more quickly, more efficiently and more whole-heartedly, and with such good humour into the rôle in which they were soon cast.' The first patrols (three in number) consisted of two officers and twenty-five soldiers. They used 30 cwt Chevrolet trucks. They ventured forth into what von Ravenstein – a German general – described as a tactician's paradise and a quarter-master's hell.

Not least of the LRDG's problems was communication. Initially they used the No. 11 set. As this has an official range of 20 miles and it was required to send and receive over distances of up to 1,000, the qualities required of the signaller may be imagined. He was required to pick up weak signals from a background of 'slush' – atmospherics and interference – but he also had to abandon the procedure he had been taught and use French commercial procedure. Operators soon become familiar with enemy procedure, and can often recognize individuals by the way they send; it was therefore essential not to give away the fact that our operators were all inside enemy territory: hence the French commercial procedure.

In 1931 the Italians had captured Kufra oasis from the Senussi. On March 1st 1941 a party of Free French under the command of Colonel the Vicomte de Hauteclocque – known for convenience as Colonel Leclerc – assisted by the LRDG recaptured it. Although it was lost again at intervals it proved a vital base for seven months in 1941 and again for seven months in 1942.

Kennedy-Shaw gives the routine of a typical reconnaissance day; breakfast – porridge, a sausage, biscuits, and a little tea – was at dawn.

The start could be leisurely for until the sun had risen twenty degrees or so above the horizon it would not throw a sharp shadow on the sun-compass dial. Moving on, in open, 'air' formation with an aircraft spotter up on the back of the truck the first hour would be cool and you drove coated and bare-headed, then towards nine or ten, hitting you on the ridge tops in waves of warm air, the heat began. In summer by eleven (sun time) it would be scorching and soon after with the sun almost vertical and its shadow too short to reach the graduations on the compass there was an excuse to stop. If the enemy was far off and there was no need for camouflage tarpaulins stretched between two cars gave good shade, and so you lay for the midday heat, not sweating for sweat dried as it reached skin surface, dozing or talking of the unfailing summer noontime topic – drink. Only the wireless operator had to stir himself, listening in case Group Headquarters had a message, and the navigator following the sun, falsely pale and cool through the smoked glass

279

screen of the theodolite, on its climb to the meridian. By one o'clock the sun-compass could be used again and the patrol moved on. This was the best part of the day, for after 3 pm it would at least be growing hourly cooler . . . Towards sunset you camped.

Needless to say not all days were as peaceful as this. On many occasions LRDG patrols lay for days on end right in the middle of enemy camps, observing as long as they remained undetected and then moving off swiftly in a blaze of gunfire.

Kennedy-Shaw explained navigation as follows:

Navigation in the desert has two parts – a 'dead reckoning' course by compass and speedometer, and an 'astro-fix' by observations of stars or sun to check the accuracy of the DR position. A magnetic compass is not much use in a car. The magnetism of shifting loads, changing gear levers and varying engine speeds makes such a compass almost impossible to compensate accurately; the only way to get a correct bearing is to stop and walk a few yards away from the car. In our long journeys this would have meant frequent delays so we used sun-compasses whenever the sun shone – and occasionally with the moon!

The sun compass was ideal for the job. The sun compass consists of a horizontal circle, divided into 360 degrees, with a central needle casting a shadow across the graduations. By rotating the circle, which is fixed to the dashboard of the car, throughout the day to correspond with the sun's movement through the sky, the shadow is made to indicate the true bearing on which the car is travelling. Without worrying about the induced magnetism of the car or the earth's magnetic field it gave directly the true bearing which had to be plotted on the map.

For the astro-fix observations we used theodolites. Before the war I had spent many desert nights sitting for hours cramped on an empty petrol tin before the car's headlights, working out the elaborate formula which ended – if all went well – in a latitude and longitude. But by 1940 things were easier, and this thanks to the progress of aviation. In an aircraft at night, when you are taking star shots with your bubble sextant it is no use if it takes you an hour to compute the results, for by that time travelling at 200 mph you may be over the next continent. So the airmen had produced books of tables which greatly reduced the former labour and would give you a 'fix' which was accurate to a mile or so.

There were, of course, occasions when the sums went wrong and a page of careful calculations showed us to be in Alaska or St. Paul's. Then the weary navigator must unpack his theodolite, find new stars and do his work over again.

And navigators were weary. They well earned the shilling a day which in 1942 the War Office approved to be paid to those who had passed the test for the new army trade – 'Land Navigator'.

Sitting all day beside the driver in the navigating car, with one eye on the sun-compass, the other on the speedometer and the third on his watch he would record the course and the distance run, seizing his chance between the joltings of the truck to write down each bearing and mileage. At halts, crawling under the car for shade, or crouching with his back to the winter wind, he must plot his course up to date in order to be able at any moment to show the patrol commander the position. And, at night, when the rest of the patrol were (more or less) comfortably in bed, sharing with the tired wireless operator the light of a hooded inspection lamp, he must chase Arcturus or Aldebaran through the flapping pages of the Astronomical Navigation Tables, Volume G.

In time, goaded by Bagnold, the Army came to realize that there must be something in this navigation business after all, but not before one formation, ordered to march on a given bearing, disappeared from the battle along the grid line of the same value, which is not at all the same thing.


It should not be thought that the LRDG spent their time peacefully mapping the desert or even silently observing enemy convoys from roadside hiding places. There were occasions when the LRDG found themselves in some very rough situations indeed. Everyone had a share but an extract from *G Patrol* (Michael Crichton-Stuart, MC) gives a fair account of what any LRDG unit might find itself engaged in. The occasion was the Barce raid in 1942:


Running to a low wall circling the barracks we began hurling bombs through the windows ... When we attempted to scale the wall, shots from troops who had managed to get out of the barracks into some slit trenches sent us back. We retaliated with Mills bombs, and by the time our supply of grenades was exhausted all was quiet again.

The lull seemed to indicate that his purpose had been achieved, so Sergeant Dennis decided to move on to the railway station. But as he led the Patrol out of the barracks on to the road he saw two tanks trundle into position at the corner of the barracks blocking the patrol's only exit. Reckoning that his best chance was to lure them into the barracks among the buildings and then dodge out, Dennis turned back and drove behind a row of buildings with his lights on. As the tanks opened fire he smartly blacked out.

Hearing the tanks start up and move forward as he had hoped, he doubled round the block and into the road again, only to find a tank right in the middle. He had been misled himself, as only one tank had moved. He swerved violently, tearing the wing of the jeep against the tank's tracks as it fired over their heads, and led the Patrol back again among the buildings. After parting from G Patrol at the fork roads, T Patrol had made straight for the main entrance of the aerodrome, where Witcher opened the gate and led the way in. Some Italians who came running were shot and the Patrol drove on to the airfield throwing grenades into buildings on the way and by good luck setting fire to a tanker which lit up the whole scene.

In the glare they drove in file round the aircraft parked about the ground, firing incendiary bullets into them, and placing time-bombs in any which did not blaze. They destroyed or seriously damaged thirty-two aircraft, while the Italian ground defences went into chaotic action without causing a single casualty in the Patrol.

Needless to say LRDG units were not always as lucky, and rarely escaped unscathed.

Of R.B. Mayne and David Stirling, Lieutenant Colonel David Lloyd Owen, from the LRDG, had this to say:

Paddy – an Irish Rugger International and a barrister – was an enormous man with tremendous physical strength and an attractive Irish brogue. He was a most gentle and kind person who possessed all the qualities of leadership, which made him so successful. He had an aggressive and ingenious brain, which was always seeking new ways to harry the enemy and he was the type of man who would never ask anyone to do anything that he had not done himself.

Yet his gentle appearance and nature were sometimes deceptive and I would have hated to have found myself on the wrong side of Paddy Mayne. It took little to upset him and then it was very difficult to control him. As a fighter he was unsurpassed for his very

282

presence in the full flood of his wrath was enough to unnerve the strongest of human beings ...

I need say no more of his courage than that he had won four DSOs by the end of the war and I have no doubt that he would have won more if he had not been so modest and if some of his more remarkable feats had not been in single combat.

His was a truly lovable personality and one day the story of his exploits will make wonderful reading ...

Paddy Mayne was the perfect instrument in the hands of David Stirling's genius. David had many of Paddy's characteristics – his aggressive outlook, his courage, his quite remarkable powers of leadership. I would say that he was probably more balanced but they both possessed the same disregard and contempt for authority, unless it was the kind of authority that was likely to help them further their aims.

David Stirling must have dreamed of ways in which to confuse and embarrass the enemy for he produced more ideas in a week than would be expected of fifteen normal men in a campaign. Some were undoubtedly quite unsound for they took little heed of the administrative problems connected with them. But others were the ideas of genius and I have no doubt that David Stirling was a genius in the field of guerilla warfare.

But not only did David produce these ideas but he had burning faith in his ability to carry them out and a quite tireless energy in seeing that they were. Of course, he also picked splendid subordinates to assist him but that, in itself, is only further evidence of his greatness.

He also had a power over men which I had never seen before. I believe that if David had asked his men to jump into the midst of an enemy Armoured Division in broad daylight they would have gone with him without question and in the knowledge that David would find a way to subdue the tanks and bring his men out unscathed and the overwhelming victors.

Where that power lay is hard to define. I came under its spell because I was carried away by his enthusiasm, by his energy, by his oratory – for he would convince any man that black was white! – by his sheer determination, courage and endurance.

I know full well that David knew what fear was. He could recognize the symptoms and he did not like them. But he could control that fear, which was very real in him, and that is the measure of true courage and supreme self-confidence.

David had both. I knew of no other man who did more to deserve a

Victoria Cross and who was so inadequately decorated for his exploits.

The moment I met David in the early light of dawn on 20th November 1941 I was captivated by his charm and self-assurance. Even then he had been through quite a lot. He had suffered the torture of failure – failure of an idea which had cost him much to promote – he had walked a long way in foul conditions of wind and weather and it was the hour when the morale of ordinary mortals is seldom high.

# APPENDIX II
*Operation Chestnut*

During the Sicily invasion an attempt was made to disrupt German communications. This was partly successful but also had a number of setbacks. The operation was cryptically described by Corporal Summers but it is unfortunately not possible to give this report here. Summers jumped with a pigeon tied on his chest and although landing among rocks was not hurt. Unfortunately the party was separated and also lost its containers. Summers' detachment moved around looking for information to send and installations to demolish, not to mention food to eat and ammunition and weapons to acquire. The going was very difficult especially on the slopes of Mount Etna where the scenery resembled slag heaps and where the lava cut their boots to pieces. Demolitions consisted mainly of telephone wires, which were also booby-trapped. The local people were pleased to see them and somewhat prematurely welcomed them as liberators. In one village they were subjected to Allied bombing and had to reassure the inhabitants that no harm was meant as the bombs were aimed at German military targets only. In order to reinforce this view they stood in the open when the bombs fell but did not enjoy the experience as some of the bombs came very close.

Summers' report was interesting because it brought out the difficulty of finding targets once you had landed behind enemy lines. It was by no means easy to know exactly where you were, and very often you might get lost by having to take hasty evasive action from a substantial contingent of enemy.

In Sicily key targets were usually surrounded by large numbers of alert soldiers, and unless you had surprise, and sufficient numbers and mobility to exploit it, progress was difficult.

# APPENDIX III
*The Corps*

Regiments are raised under a 'Corps Warrant'. In the desert period there was no authority for the SAS to exist as a separate regiment as there had been no authority under a Corps Warrant. Subsequently it was temporarily regarded as part of the Army Air Corps in company with the Glider Regiment and Parachute Regiment. When the 21 SAS (Artists) became a Corps it was with the authority to raise – if necessary – other regiments for SAS type work. A Joint Staffs Memorandum laid down the proviso that if any special force was required for the future it would be provided from the SAS. This commonsense provision meant that there would no longer be the extraordinary situation which had prevailed in World War II of an individual being able to collect a little private army and employ it more or less when and where he saw fit.

A Corps normally numbers about 10,000 and includes three brigades. The smallest Corps in the Army is the Royal Military Academy Sandhurst Bands Corps – numbering 30!

## APPENDIX IV
*Weapons*

The SAS used every weapon they could lay their hands on – British, American, German and Italian – if it suited their purpose. The following gives some information about weapons mentioned in the text.

### The .50 Browning:

This was a heavy calibre air-cooled machine-gun, weighing 84 pounds. It fired 400–500 rounds a minute and had a range of 7,200 yards.

### The 2-inch Mortar:

Range up to 500 yards. Could fire $2\frac{1}{4}$ pounds of high explosive or 2 pounds of smoke. It weighed 19 pounds.

### The 3-inch Mortar:

Range up to 2,800 yards, fired 10-pound bombs (smoke, HE or illuminating) but weighed 44 pounds, plus a base plate of 37 pounds and a mounting of 45 pounds.

### The 4.2-inch Mortar:

Range 4,100 yards, but weighed minimum of 257 pounds.

*81 mm Mortar:*

Range up to 3,000 yards; Weight 136 pounds.
*(Mortars had a minimum range of approximately 100 yards.)*

*Grenades:*

The most popular was the 36 Grenade which weighed 1½ pounds and had a four-second fuse. It was thrown by hand but could not, for obvious reasons, be used among trees. It was not very effective on soft ground, but devastating on a hard surface.

*The Bren Gun:*

A gun of Czech design originally produced by Skoda. It weighed 20 pounds but could be, and often was, fired from the hip. It had a range of up to 2,000 yards but was usually fired at about 600. Gas-operated, reliable, but would overheat unless the barrel was changed after every ten magazines. Originally .303 but later converted to 7.62. The .303 Brens were the first light machine-guns in the world.

*7.62 Rifle SLR (Self Loading Rifle) Gas-operated:*

20-round magazine, can fire automatic or single shot. Muzzle has flash eliminator and a lug which can be used either for a bayonet or for the Energa anti-tank grenade. Total weight with full magazine 11 pounds. Range up to 600 yards. Reliable and easy to maintain. Belgian design.

*(The calibre of a rifle – and thus the size of the bullet – is worked out to give the best stopping power and range. A slim bullet may go a long way and pass through a man but may not stop him. A man shot with such a bullet may kill you before he himself dies. Hence the optimum size – 7.62.)*

*75 Howitzer:*

This is classed as Light Artillery although those responsible for transporting it might not have agreed. The total weight of howitzer, recoil mechanism, and carriage, was 1,479 pounds. It could fire six rounds a minute to a range of 9,760 yards. A round weighed just over 17 pounds.

*Anti-tank weapons:*

55 Boys Anti-tank rifle – an unpopular weapon used in 1939 and 1940 with a kick which some of its users complain they can still feel. Alleged to be effective at 500 yards.

*PIAT:*

The Projector, Infantry, Anti-Tank – could be fired from the shoulder and project-armour-piercing, smoke, and anti-personnel bombs up to about 600 yards. Weighed 32 pounds. Popular.

*Bazookas:*

The correct title was Rocket launchers, Anti-tank, but it is unlikely that anyone ever used it. They were entirely different from guns, being tubes open at each end which were used for launching a 31-pound rocket which propelled 5 pounds of high explosive. Range to 700 yards and very effective against tanks. Originally 2.36 calibre but later 3.5.

*The 20 mm cannon:*

An aircraft weapon weighing 112 pounds which could fire 650 shots a minute from a 60-round magazine. Fully automatic.

*(Weapons designed for one Service were often used by a different Service in a way never contemplated by the designer.)*

*Sub-machine guns:*

The Thompson sub-machine gun, better known as the 'Tommy gun', was a .45 weapon of American manufacture which fired either 20-round clips or 50-round drums. With a drum it was awkward and heavy. It could fire on single rounds or automatic and was credited with a range of 300 yards. As it fired at 725 rounds per minute it used up a lot of ammunition; it was too cumbersome to be very popular but was an excellent weapon for short-range fighting.

*The Sten:*

A light but unreliable weapon. All unnecessary weight was stripped off, e.g. the stock was a skeleton outline .9 mm calibre, it carried a 32-round magazine and was effective at about 175 yards, firing 500 to the minute. Cheap but unstable.

*The Patchett or Sterling:*

Replaced the Sten. 9 mm and similar to Sten though shorter range. Stable and ideal for street or jungle fighting.

*Machine-guns:*

The most satisfactory water-cooled machine-gun was the Vickers MMG. This was fed on the belt system and would fire at 500 rpm. Range was 3,000 yards. A belt held 250 rounds. The Vickers weighed approximately 42 pounds and had an overall length of nearly four feet.

The American .30 Browning was roughly equivalent.

*German weapons:*

The most popular and best known German infantry weapons –
as far as souvenir-hunting British troops were concerned –
were Lugers, Walthers and Machine-pistols.

The Luger (9 mm self-loading 08) pistol: this was originally
designed by an American called Borchardt but was developed
by a German called Lueger. There is no explanation why the 'e'
was dropped.

The Luger can fire 8 rounds to a maximum range of 1,200
yards but is accurate up to 75 yards only. With an overall length
of 8¾ inches . . . and a weight of 30 oz it had obvious advantages
but was superseded by the 9 mm Walther 'P.38', which had
approximately the same size, weight, and characteristics but
was slightly more efficient.

(These names – and a few others – are much beloved by the
writers of thrillers, possibly because they sound more romantic
than the British stand-bys – the 9 mm, the .38, and the .45.)

The Schmeisser Machine-pistol: the early versions of this
weapon were built outside Germany to outwit the provisions of
the Versailles Treaty, and thus occur in other armies too. With
a calibre of 9 mm it had a 32-cartridge magazine and could fire
500 rpm effectively to 150 yards.

German ammunition became progressively less efficient
owing to shortage of metals but managed to kill large numbers
of people nonetheless. In 1944 the SAS encountered snipers
with wooden bullets which had a range of 100 yards. The
Germans were said to have experimented with some very
unpleasant ammunition such as cyanide-holding pistol
bullets, explosive bullets, and bullets which behaved like
Dum-Dums without actually being such.

*Vehicles*

Ferrets are light armoured-cars which are used for liaison and
light reconnaissance work. Mark I, with an open top, is used for
command and liaison; Mark 2 has a turret which can be closed

down when on reconnaissance work but lacks the range of vision of Mark I. The Ferret can climb 1 in 2 gradients, cross rivers with the engine submerged, and cover very rough or soft ground. It has a speed of up to 60 mph, a range of 180 miles, and carries enough light arms and ammunition to be disagreeable to challengers.

Jeeps: the virtue of this ubiquitous vehicle has already been mentioned in the text. Its proper title is: truck ¼ ton, $4 \times 4$. It was modified in many ways unenvisaged by the designer.

Basically it was planned for a crew of two, one .30 machine-gun, and a total load – plus the driver and his assistant – of 800 pounds. (At times it carried eight men, plus ammunition, guns, and spare petrol.) It was 11 feet long, 5.2 feet wide, and measured 4.4 feet to the top of the steering-wheel. Ground clearance was 8¾ inches, and weight 3,253 pounds. Maximum speed was given as 65 mph, and the range of the four-cylinder engine, with a 15-gallon fuel tank, was quoted as 300 miles.

An enterprising American soldier, serving overseas, posted home the parts of a jeep, planning to assemble it after his demobilisation. However, the postal authorities found some of the latter consignments a little too bulky. The Land Rover, which is in widespread use, is too well known to need description here. The short wheelbase Land Rover was specially built for the SAS and with its GPMGs (General Purpose Machine Guns) and .30 Browning looked like an elder brother to the wartime jeep.

# APPENDIX V
*Aircraft*

*Vickers Valentias:* usually mis-spelt Valencia, they had been in service since 1934 but very few were still flying in 1941. They were good reliable troop-carrying aircraft (22 troops), biplanes, with a top speed of 130 mph at 5,000 feet. They had a range of 800 miles. They were powered by two 650 horsepower Bristol Pegasus engines. Unlike their predecessors, the Victorias, which had a tail skid, the Valentias had a tail wheel. The fuselage was a combination of metal and wood, the wings were metal covered with fabric.

*Gloster Gauntlets:* Open-cockpit, fighter biplanes which were the mainstay of the RAF 1935–1939, but were soon after replaced by Hurricanes and Spitfires. They were single-seaters, powered by one 645 horsepower Bristol Mercury engine, all metal in construction, covered in fabric. Top speed of 230 mph and range of 460 miles.

*Gloster Gladiator:* similar to the Gauntlets but a little faster and more manoeuvrable. Performed exceptionally well in several theatres other than the desert. Originally had two Vickers and two Lewis guns but these were later replaced by Brownings. The Vickers from obsolete Gloster aircraft gave the SAS its enormous concentrated firepower.

*Vickers Valettas:* they were produced between 1947 and 1952 but some were still in service in 1966. Called the 'flying pig' from their appearance in the air. A most versatile aircraft which carried VIPs, troops (34), parachutists (20), freight or casualties. Some were equipped to tow gliders. Crew of four.

Twin-engined (Bristol Hercules) maximum speed 294 mph; cruising speed 172 mph. Extreme range 1,400 miles, but paratrooping range 530. Could climb to 10,000 feet in 8 minutes.

*Blackburn Beverleys:* these had a distinguished record of service from 1955 to 1967. Maximum speed was 238 mph and cruising speed 173 mph. Maximum range was 1,300 miles but normal loaded range 230. They could carry 94 troops, 70 parachutists, or 45,000 pounds of freight, but their enormous advantage was that they could carry heavy bulky equipment and drop it by parachutes from the rear; thus helicopters could be delivered. They could also operate from very small airfields. Powered by four Bristol Centaurus engines.

*Bristol Bombays:* first flew in 1935, but did not come into service till 1939. Used as a transport (24 troops and a crew of 3) but also as a night-bomber. Powered by two Bristol Pegasus engines (each 1,010 horse power) it had a maximum speed of 192 mph but cruised at 160 mph at 10,000 feet. Its maximum range was 2,230 miles (with extra tanks) but normal range was 880 miles. It was armed with two Vickers K guns, at nose and tail.

# INDEX

The index does not include every reference in the text but only the more important ones.

# A selection of bestsellers from SPHERE

## FICTION

| | | |
|---|---|---|
| THE STONE FLOWER | Alan Scholefield | £1.95 ☐ |
| TWIN CONNECTIONS | Justine Valenti | £1.75 ☐ |
| YOUR LOVING MOTHER | Deanna Maclaren | £1.50 ☐ |
| REMEMBRANCE | Danielle Steel | £1.95 ☐ |
| BY THE GREEN OF THE SPRING | John Masters | £2.50 ☐ |

## FILM & TV TIE-INS

| | | |
|---|---|---|
| THE PROFESSIONALS 14 & 15 | Ken Blake | £1.25 ☐ each |
| E.T. THE EXTRA-TERRESTRIAL | William Kotzwinkle | £1.50 ☐ |
| E.T. THE EXTRA-TERRESTRIAL STORYBOOK | William Kotzwinkle | £1.95 ☐ |
| THE IRISH R.M. | E. E. Somerville & M. Ross | £1.95 ☐ |

## NON-FICTION

| | | |
|---|---|---|
| THE HEALTH & FITNESS HANDBOOK | Ed. Miriam Polunin | £5.95 ☐ |
| ONE CHILD | Torey L. Hayden | £1.75 ☐ |
| GARBO | A. Walker | £5.95 ☐ |
| BEFORE I FORGET | James Mason | £2.25 ☐ |

*All Sphere books are available at your local bookshop or newsagent, or can be ordered direct from the publisher. Just tick the titles you want and fill in the form below.*

Name _____

Address _____

_____

Write to Sphere Books, Cash Sales Department, P.O. Box 11, Falmouth, Cornwall TR10 9EN

Please enclose a cheque or postal order to the value of the cover price plus:

UK: 45p for the first book, 20p for the second book and 14p for each additional book ordered to a maximum charge of £1.63.

OVERSEAS: 75p for the first book plus 21p per copy for each additional book.

BFPO & EIRE: 45p for the first book, 20p for the second book plus 14p per copy for the next 7 books, thereafter 8p per book.

*Sphere Books reserve the right to show new retail prices on covers which may differ from those previously advertised in the text or elsewhere, and to increase postal rates in accordance with the PO.*